SUNY Series, The Social Context of Education
Christine E. Sleeter, Editor

THE OTHER STRUGGLE FOR EQUAL SCHOOLS

*Mexican Americans during
the Civil Rights Era*

Rubén Donato

STATE UNIVERSITY OF NEW YORK PRESS

Published by
State University of New York

©1997 State University of New York

For information, address the State University of New York Press, State University Plaza, Albany, NY 12246

Marketing by Hanna J. Hazen
Production by Bernadine Dawes

Library of Congress Cataloging-in-Publication Data

Donato, Rubén, 1955–
   The other struggle for equal schools : Mexican Americans during
the Civil Rights Era / Rubén Donato.
      p. cm. — (SUNY series, social context of education)
   Includes bibliographical references (p.) and index.
   ISBN 0-7914-3519-9 (hc : alk. paper). — ISBN 0-7914-3520-2 (pbk.
: alk. paper)
     1. Mexican Americans—Education—History—20th century.
2. Children of migrant laborers—Education—United States–
–History—20th century. 3. School integration—United States–
–History—20th century. I. Title. II. Series.
LC2683.D66 1997
371.829'6872'07309046—dc21   97-13021
                                                                             CIP

1 2 3 4 5 6 7 8 9 10

For my parents,
Maria and Juan Donato
and
David Tyack,
mentor and friend

Contents

Acknowledgments

I wish to express my gratitude to several individuals who assisted and encouraged me in the preparation of this book. My oldest debt, however, extends further back in time. As my advisor and mentor in graduate school, David Tyack guided me through some wonderful years at Stanford. Words alone can never adequately express my gratitude for the way he nourished my curiosity about American educational history and encouraged me to pursue this work. In addition, the input and criticism from Albert Camarillo, Arturo Pacheco, and Beatriz Arias were invaluable during this period.

At the University of Wisconsin at Madison, Carl Kaestle, Herbert Kleibard, and Francis Shrag provided me with a constant source of intellectual stimulation and constructive criticism. I was also fortunate to have two outstanding research assistants, Lew Zippin and Jack Dougherty, who listened to me puzzle out many of my ideas.

I am also indebted to my colleagues and doctoral students at the University of Colorado at Boulder: Kenneth Howe, Ernest House, Leonard Baca, Paul Michalec, and Angela Johnson. Special thanks to Ken Howe for our conversations related to educational equality and social justice. Toward the end of this project, several friends from outside of Boulder kindly offered constructive comments: Herman Garcia, Jose Salvador Hernandez, and Rudolfo Chavez Chavez were all shrewd critics.

I am grateful to the National Academy of Education, Spencer Post-Doctoral Fellowship. Spencer allowed me to dedicate one full year to this project. Also, the University of Colorado IMPART grant provided the means to revise different parts of the book. I want to recognize Philip Distefano, former Dean of the School of Education at Boulder, for providing me with an environment that allowed me to continue and complete this project. The University of Colorado Norlin Interlibrary Loan Department, especially Reggie Ahram, deserve special praise. She and her colleagues were extremely helpful in locating even the most obscure documents, as they generously responded to my constant stream of requests. Special thanks go to Sage publications for permission to use a revised article published in this book: "The Irony of Year-Round Schools: Mexican Migrant Resistance in a California Community," *Educational Administration Quarterly* 32: 181–208.

Finally, special thanks to the individuals from Brownfield who shared their experiences with me. Without them this book would not have been possible.

Introduction

In the 1960s, American education entered a time of enormous change and turbulence. A proliferation of scholarly studies poured from the presses with ample documentation that public schools were failing to serve poor and minority children. Proposals for reform, plans for interventions, and legal mandates followed one another with fervent acceleration. School integration, compensatory education, decentralization, and community control of schools became familiar topics of discussion across the nation. But as American education was being challenged by new participants, the jolting mix of clashing forces, values, and legal pressures, in retrospect, gave the impression that school reform was exclusively an African American issue. That is, while many scholars were examining the effects of race, class, and ethnicity on the schooling experience, their inquiry evoked dominant themes in the literature that focused on the African American community. This important trend is reflected in the school desegregation literature, the pursuit for community control of schools, and the appeal for curricular and pedagogical reforms. The plight of the African American has received so much attention since the civil rights era that it dominates historical memory and often serves as a frame of reference for current discussions on educational reforms.[1]

Other minority groups were actively challenging their schools, but their efforts were not as visible. The rapid growth and pronounced regional concentration of the Mexican American population, for example, caught the attention of federal, state, and local educational policymakers. Although Mexican Americans had become the second largest minority group in the United States, very little is known about their schooling experiences. This book is about the Mexican American struggle for equal education during the civil rights era of the 1960s and 1970s in a California school system and community I call Brownfield.[2] The task here is to

1

examine how a predominantly white educational system and its surrounding community responded to the growing number of Mexican Americans in schools during that era, how Mexican American parents challenged the relative tranquility of school governance, and what the mix of federal, state, and local politics was that produced educational reform.

For decades, conventional wisdom has tended to view Mexican Americans as passive victims accepting their educational fates.[3] The notion that they were complacent about their schooling conditions became an entrenched myth, surviving over several decades, probably because very little was researched and written about their resistance to unequal education. As Armando Gutierrez and Herbert Hirsch point out, the Mexican American has been "treated as a docile, 'sleepy,' minority." In truth, continue Gutierrez and Hirsch, there "has in fact been a history of political turbulence and political oppression."[4] Evidence shows that Mexican American communities have been actively protesting discriminatory educational practices throughout the Southwest since the early twentieth century. Mexican American parents in *Independent School District v. Salvatierra* (1930) in Texas, for example, proved that the school district had illegally segregated their children on the basis of race. A year later in California, Mexican parents successfully overturned school segregation through *Alvarez v. Lemon Grove*, where the court ruled in favor of the Mexican community on the grounds that separate facilities for Mexican American students were not conducive to Americanization and that they retarded the English language development of Spanish-speaking children. Very few Americans realize that *Lemon Grove* was the first successful desegregation case in the United States.[5]

In 1946, a higher court ended *de jure* segregation in California when Judge McCormick, in *Mendez v. Westminster*, found that school board members had segregated Mexican American children on the basis of their "Latinized" appearance and had gerrymandered district boundaries in order to ensure that Mexican Americans attended separate schools. Concluding that there was no statute or congressional mandate that permitted school boards to segregate Mexican American students, McCormick stated that the Fourteenth Amendment and the ratification of the Treaty of Guadalupe Hidalgo had guaranteed Mexican Americans equal rights in the United States.[6] Despite these court cases, Mexican Americans continued to experience school segregation, inferior school facilities, and other forms of educational inequalities. It was not until the 1960s and early 1970s that federal and state policies attempted to provide Mexican American children more equitable schooling opportunities.[7]

Educational historians have recently shed more light on Mexican American struggles for equal schools.[8] But there still remains a large void in the literature. Much more needs to be known about how federal and state policies affected these struggles during the civil rights era and how Mexican American parents negotiated their fates with white educational power structures. One way of gaining insight into how Mexican Americans interacted with their schools is to examine specific settings. Michael Katz made a similar point in the early 1970s about Progressive education. He noted how educational historians had paid little attention to educational reforms at the local level, and how "almost no case studies . . . trace attitudes and developments in particular communities and try to find out exactly what sorts of change happened in schools."[9] The same criticism can be made about Mexican American educational historiography.

Brownfield appealed to me for several reasons. First, it is a school system that has experienced rapid demographic changes. Mexican American enrollments, for example, grew from less than 5 percent in 1940 to 44.3 percent in 1979.[10] Second, Brownfield is a medium-sized town with an unusual blend of rural and small-city conditions, avoiding the added complexity of an urban case. As Henry Trueba et al. observe, urban schools systems are "so massive and complex, that the changes cannot easily be observed and analyzed."[11] Third, unlike most studies portraying minority groups led by intellectuals, national organizations, or trained activists, this study illustrates that reform efforts began with working-class Mexican American parents. The notion that Mexican Americans reacted blindly to uncontrollable forces discounts the creativity and courage they often displayed. Finally, although the events in Brownfield may not be exactly duplicated elsewhere, the Mexican American experience there provides an important example of the kind of resistance that came to characterize many communities across the Southwest by the 1970s.

After graduating from college, I taught school in a small district in Northern California. I also met a Mexican American teacher from the classroom next door who sparked my interest in initiating this study. In our conversations, she mentioned something about being part of a movement during the late 1960s and early 1970s that had challenged the Brownfield school system. The group, along with other local Mexican American organizations, had pressed for school reform; they had pressured the predominantly white educational power structure on four issues: to establish one of the first bilingual-bicultural schools in the region, to provide Spanish-speaking paraprofessionals in classrooms, to reexamine policies that placed Mexican Americans wrongly in special education classes, and to utilize federally allocated Title I funds in ways that indeed benefited their children. I listened to her stories and found them interesting, but several years passed before I gave much thought to what she had shared with me.

Several years later, I was studying American educational history at Stanford University. I became interested in consolidating my intellectual interests: history, education, and the Mexican American people. But I was disappointed in how little had been written on the schooling experiences of Mexican Americans. A conversation with my father, however, became the inspiration for this study. He remarked how "Mexicanos" were challenging the educational status quo over in Brownfield. This prompted me to rethink the conversations I had had with my colleague when I was teaching public school.

Upon informing my graduate school adviser that I was interested in the Brownfield schools, I conducted a preliminary study to determine how much information was available. I contacted the superintendent of schools, told him what I was interested in, and he gave me permission to access school district records and other information that was related to the history of the school system. I also contacted the teacher I had worked with, shared my thoughts with her, and asked for more detailed accounts of the school and community events during the late 1960s and early 1970s. To our meeting, she brought several colleagues who had been actively involved in the movement, to help her recall the events. They brought local newspaper clippings, letters, a copy of the organization's constitution, proposals for projects, issues of a local alternative bilingual newspaper, and other information. As I listened to them, they spoke with pride that they had been part of a movement that had made a difference in the lives of the Mexican American community and its children. The discussion also prompted disturbing memories and anguish when they recalled the resistance their reform agendas had generated in the community.

Data for this study were collected between 1984 and 1992. I utilized traditional historical sources such as local newspapers, yearbooks, school board minutes, unpublished district manuscripts, documents submitted to the Office for Civil Rights, racial/ethnic surveys, California State Department of Education records, U. S. government documents, and other written sources. I also interviewed some individuals who were school board members, administrators, teachers, students, and community activists during that period. These conversations were especially useful, for they not only helped me to develop a richer understanding of what had occurred during this time period but also enabled me to elucidate viewpoints that were only hinted at in written documents. I also discovered a doctoral dissertation written in 1965 about a small school and community in Northern California. In what might be described as a "complacency shocker,"[12] Theodore Parsons documented how a school in this community kept Mexican Americans firmly subordinate to whites. In a particularly chilling example, Parsons asked a teacher why "Johnny" (a white boy) was leading five Mexicans in an orderly fashion out of a classroom. The teacher replied that "[his] father owns one of the big farms in the area and . . . one day he will have to know how to handle the Mexicans."[13]

But the Brownfield school situation in the late 1960s and early 1970s was not a simple case of white domination of Mexican Americans. As I became more immersed in the history of the school system, events became more complex, stories were tangled with contradictions, and ironies of local school reform appeared everywhere. For example, I wondered why affluent white residents from the northern part of the district voted in favor of school district consolidation during the early 1960s when many knew it meant merging with a community that was experiencing dramatic Mexican American enrollment growth. I was confused as to why Mexican American leaders challenged Brownfield's year-round school proposal when the reform, allegedly, provided more flexibility for Mexican migrant families and improved the attendance record of their children. Finally, I was puzzled as to why school administrators aggressively pursued California's bilingual education mandate in the late 1970s, yet stubbornly resisted desegregation between the northern and southern parts of the district. Eventually, I decided to concentrate on these issues during the period 1964 to 1979. In the process, I also attempted to distinguish the events that were unique to the Brownfield schools and community from those that corresponded with Mexican American efforts for equal schools at the national level.

The body of research on Mexican American education has grown substantially since I began my research. Although during the first half of the twentieth century George I. Sanchez and Herschel T. Manuel were documenting unequal conditions for Mexican American youth in U. S. public schools,[14] it was Thomas Carter and the U. S. Commission on Civil Rights series on *Mexican American Education* that brought their plight into the educational limelight.[15] Serving as the authoritative work on the subject during the early 1970s, the studies by Carter and the U.S. Commission reported that large numbers of Mexican American students attended ethnically segregated schools, achieved at the lowest quartiles in all academic subjects, were tracked in low ability courses, faced biased teachers, dropped out at exceedingly high rates, and that their parents were marginalized from their schools.

Before the writings of Carter and the U. S. Commission, schools consistently maintained an assimilationist perspective: that the academic success of the Mexican American, according to Carter, depended "on the degree to which his home has been oriented to Anglo middle-class culture."[16] Carter, however, began a discussion about how dominant educational power structures suppressed Mexican American aspirations for equal schools, how public schools equipped Mexican American children only with the skills and knowledge appropriate for low status, and how they inculcated the "values necessary to a law-abiding, although nonparticipating and essentially disenfranchised, citizen."[17] Particularly noteworthy about Carter's work was that he deviated from oft-cited deficit models of education, which historically ascribed Mexican American student failure to social, cultural, linguistic, and economic differences. He also began to raise questions about unequal power relations between Mexican American and white communities.

The tempo of research picked up after 1987. "As late as 1985," noted educational historian Guadalupe San Miguel, "not one single book providing an interpretation of [Mexican American] experiences in schools had been published."[18] After this period, researchers began to move from a mechanistic, deterministic conceptualization of the relationship between school and society and placed more importance on human experience in analyzing complex relations between Mexican American communities and their schools. Guadalupe San Miguel, for example, looked at the Mexican American struggle for equal schools in Texas.[19] He argued that the racist attitudes of Anglo educational leadership played a major role in influencing their decisions to establish and expand school segregation during the early twentieth century. A major theme in his study was that school segregation aided in the reproduction of the existing castelike system of dominant-subordinate relationships between Mexican and white communities in Texas.

A few years later, Gilbert Gonzalez examined schooling experiences in the Southwest.[20] Although he intentionally excluded the state of New Mexico and focused on Southern California, he also, like San Miguel, looked at the expanding segregation of Mexican American children during the first half of the twentieth century. Gonzalez, however, looked at the nature and impact of several educational reforms on Mexican American children during the early twentieth century. He found that through the use of IQ testing, curricular differentiation and vocational education became entrenched schooling practices for years to come. Both San Miguel and Gonzalez found that school segregation limited the opportunities for Mexican Americans in U.S. society.

Douglas Foley studied the decolonization of a Texas community (Northtown) and how Mexican Americans became political actors in the struggle for equal schools during the late 1960s and early 1970s.[21] He looked at how a school became a place where inequality was staged, echoing popular cultural practices. He analyzed how a major sociocultural transformation had taken place in the town. Specifically, he looked at how old restrictive rules of being "seen but not heard" were challenged by Mexican Americans, how "Mexicano people had shattered the social territories that Anglos assigned them," and how Mexican Americans "had created their own social, expressive space." In short, he described how Mexican Americans rose to a political consciousness and how they came to share power with people that had historically dominated them.

Trueba, Rodriguez, Zou, and Cintron brought together historical and contemporary data to show how Mexican Americans in Woodland, California, were able to succeed in creating educational experiences that reduced the alienation of their children, how the schools promoted the worth of their language and culture, and the process by which school reform was connected to social action by the Mexican American community. As Michael Apple noted, what was portrayed in Woodland, California, was "but one instance of an attempt by a community—acting in its political, economic, and cultural institutions—to protect its youth and culture." It was not a national movement, but an account of how disenfranchised people realized they were not entirely powerless and how "change from below [was] indeed possible."[22]

Although, in my view, the African American struggle for equal schools dominates the literature on school and community relations, I benefited from several insightful studies that applied to the Mexican American. The work of Don Davies, Paul Peterson, Mario Fantini and Marilyn Gittell, Richard Saxe, Frederick Wirt and Michael Kirst, Donald McCarty and Charles Ramsey, and others, for example, examined the persisting dilemma of community control of schools, the meanings of educational equality, and the interplay of federal and state politics at the local level. These studies did not specifically look at the Mexican American experience, but they provided me with a theoretical tool on school-community relations to inform my work.[23]

My analysis has also been influenced by educational historical revisionist interpretations.[24] Indeed, during the early twentieth century, public schools were bent on socializing Mexican American children as a source of cheap labor within the larger political economy. Gilbert Gonzalez maintained that the educational isolation of the Mexican American child corresponded with the economic interests of local white communities throughout the Southwest and "became a means of domination and control, the antitheses of equality and freedom; and it was intrinsically racist both in that it was based on racial social theories, and in that it led to educational practices that reinforced a pattern of social inequality based on nationality and race."[25] Although Gonzalez accurately interprets the pre–civil rights era, I do not think that we know enough about Mexican American education after 1965 to fully account for their schooling experiences in terms of theories of social and economic control.

The civil rights era of the 1960s and 1970s brought dramatic reforms to American schools and society. Social policymakers and school reformers attempted to provide more equitable schooling opportunities for children of color, including Mexican Americans. From this perspective, my research led me to ask questions with regard to how school officials in Brownfield viewed the problems Mexican Americans faced, why they chose specific remedies, and how their perceptions of federal and state educational policies corresponded with the desires of the Mexican American community.

Finally, this book attempts to provide a better understanding of the relationships formed between Mexican Americans and the schools that served them. It aims to describe a dialogue of ideologies and educational reform proposals from the mid-1960s to the late 1970s, but without implying that there were universal solutions. It is an account of the political emergence of the Mexican American community, the educational reforms they sought, and how the school system and white community responded.

Chapter 1 provides a historical overview of Mexican American schooling experiences from the 1920s to 1954. It covers the Southwest in general and California in particular: how social, political, and economic trends helped shape the schooling experiences of Mexican American youth, how school segregation evolved, and how ideologies of language, ethnicity, and culture were used to disenfranchise them.

Chapter 2 provides the background of the Brownfield community and the evolution of its schools, beginning with the politics of school district consolidation. More than twenty small school systems served the area during the early 1940s. Influenced by the school consolidation movement that swept the nation during the first half of the twentieth century, a majority vote unified the Brownfield schools into one large school system in 1964. Whether unification was considered successful depended on whether one spoke of long- or short-term consequences. For many white middle-class residents in the northern part of the district, the long-run results became problematic. Unification later generated a controversial discussion about school integration. But for Mexican Americans, school unification inadvertently produced serious questions about desegregation and equal educational opportunity.

After the Brownfield Unified School District was formed, the plight of the Mexican Americans began to emerge. People began to comment on the Mexican Americans' low educational achievement and high dropout rate, and how virtually none were going on to college. As the number of Mexican Americans increased, class differentiation became obvious. Privilege characterized the white student experience, while most Mexican American students led a "third-class" existence.

Chapter 3 describes the mobilization of the Mexican American community and the challenges it mounted against the local educational power structure. Seeking a voice in school policy decisions and wanting to affirm a positive cultural and linguistic identity, Mexican Americans began to demand changes in the educational system. They understood that participation was a central part of the democratic formula, that it was a means to hold local educational institutions accountable, and that it was, perhaps, a means to penetrate and integrate the Mexican American community into the educational policymaking body. The struggle to reform the schools, however, did not come without conflict, struggle, and power politics within the schools and community.

As Mexican American enrollments continued to soar in the district, overcrowding became another serious issue. Chapter 4 examines the controversy over year-round education and its effect on the Mexican migrant community. Year-round education offered Mexican migrant children a more flexible schedule and provided them more days of school. Yet the program conflicted with the seasonal work schedule of the migrant family and posed a dilemma for their economic survival. More important, the year-round program was produced through a decision making apparatus that excluded the input from the Mexican American community. Since the call for year-round schooling had not arisen among, or been associated with, Mexican American resistance, but had been an elaborate plan of a professional elite within the U. S. educational power structure, Mexican Americans in Brownfield became instinctively distrustful. Mexican American leaders looked to see how the program that the power structure had offered would adversely affect their interests.

The constant flood of Mexican immigrants entering Brownfield in the 1970s resulted in a significant increase in the number of students with limited English proficiency in the district. Chapter 5 examines school and community reactions to mandated bilingual education. Between 1968 and 1972, Mexican American leaders struggled for curricular reforms that would recognize their children's language. By the mid-1970s, however, landmark court cases were transforming the demands placed on public schools regarding language minority students. Although *Lau v. Nichols* did not mandate bilingual education, the decision paved the way for California Assembly Bill 1329 in 1976, which required bilingual education (under certain conditions) in public schools. Bilingual education became mandatory in the state, but in Brownfield, white interest groups aggressively challenged its implementation.

Unlike the debates about African American segregation that dominated most urban school systems during the 1960s and 1970s, the isolation of Mexican Americans was largely ignored by scholars, educational policymakers, and the news media in the United States. Chapter 6 investigates the politics of school desegregation: how white parents from Atherton (the district's affluent northern community) opposed two-way busing, due originally to the district's geographic formation, and how, allied with policymakers, they resisted integrating white students from the Atherton area with low-income Mexican American children from the Brownfield schools.

The book illustrates some of the enigmatic, contradictory, and sometimes stubborn issues related to the schooling of Mexican Americans. It depicts circumstances where the Brownfield schools came under attack for their failure to recognize the needs of Mexican American students. The concern for respecting and preserving the cultural identity of Mexican Americans found itself at odds with the traditional values of the Brownfield school system and the larger white community. This contradiction, however, went deeper than just conflict over the preservation of ethnic heritage, because the civil rights era of the 1960s and 1970s called for major educational reforms. Despite the claim that Mexican children were being processed by a neutral school system, public schools across the Southwest were rife with ethnic, linguistic, and class biases. If one of the prime values of the Brownfield schools was uniformity, then there was an inherent conflict between the organization of schools and the desires of the Mexican American community.

ONE

*Schooling in the Pre-*Brown *Era*

The first half of the twentieth century has been one of the most popular periods of research for educational historians. It is not surprising that many have written on the Progressive era, that fascinating period that extended from the 1890s to the late 1930s. Articulated by John Dewey and other scholars during that time, the Progressive movement gave birth to a radically new educational philosophy. It rejected the rigid pedagogy that typified public schools, the uniformity of curriculum, the stress on passivity, and teachers' reliance on rote memorization. Shifting to a "child-centered" curriculum and instruction, Progressive education called for learning experiences that fostered social, cultural, and intellectual meaning.[1] Researchers, however, have consistently pointed out that the Progressive movement was based more on a generalized faith. That is, it lacked grassroots support, it avoided systematic critique of the economic order, and it almost entirely ignored issues of race and ethnicity. Progressivism evolved in a period when bureaucratization, tracking, testing, Americanization, and vocational education became entrenched schooling conditions in American public schools.[2] Progressivism, in short, seemed to strive in vain for a humanistic and egalitarian educational system.

Progressivism sought to enlist schools to build a better society, so a central theme of the movement was to lend a human hand to the lives of poverty-stricken immigrants.[3] Hence, one of the tasks of public schools was to assimilate immigrant children into full-fledged Americans. Even though some scholars have recently moved away from characterizing the immigrant experience in a monolithic way, the research trend has nevertheless focused on European immigrants. Within this context, very little has been written on the schooling experiences of Mexican Americans during this period.[4] In this chapter, I examine the history of Mexican American education during the first half of the twentieth century. The purpose here is not to offer a full treatment of all the questions that might be asked about the schooling experiences of Mexican Americans. The issues I treat are limited, but comprehensive enough to provide an understanding of the role public schools have played in the lives of Mexican American children. I concur with Gilbert Gonzalez that the schooling of Mexican Americans during the first half of the twentieth century in the Southwest functioned as a means of social control, an attempt to socialize them into loyal and disciplined workers, and the instrument by which social relations between Mexican and white communities were reproduced. To address these issues, I analyze how the theoretical and practical constructions of school segregation, Americanization, migrant education, intelligence testing, and vocational education affected the Mexican American child. The goal of this chapter is to provide a brief history in order to better understand the Mexican American struggle for equal education during the 1960s and 1970s.

SEGREGATION

Architects of the common school believed in forming national unity, in a place where public education was free, where a common curriculum was provided for all children, and where children from diverse backgrounds were able to learn under the same roof.[5] But although public schools assimilated more than thirty-five million immigrants during the late nineteenth and early twentieth centuries, they failed to integrate a significant portion of the U.S. population. Educational historians have established that people of color, especially African Americans, were marginalized in schools.[6] *Plessy v. Ferguson* (1896) and *Brown v. Board of Education* (1954) had an enormous impact in the United States. These court cases also created a national consciousness that viewed school and social segregation as an African American problem.

Americans have either forgotten or never realized that most Mexican American children were segregated into "Mexican classrooms" or into entirely separate "Mexican schools." Whenever Mexican American enrollments grew, school boards across the nation developed strategies to keep Mexican children apart from their white counterparts. But unlike the segregation of African Americans, which was straightforwardly based on race, the isolation of Mexican children was more complex because it was tangled with issues of language and culture.[7] During the 1930s, for example, the Texas Department of Education reported that segregating Mexican children on educational grounds in the early grades was permissible because, according to one report, "it is wise to segregate, if it is done on educational grounds, and results in district efforts to provide the non-

English-speaking pupils with specially trained teachers and the necessary special training resources." State officials reasoned that Mexican children needed to correct cultural and linguistic deficiencies before mixing with their "American" peers. Although Texas officials supported the segregation of Mexican youths, they also recognized that many educators were interested in isolating them in order to give "Mexican children a shorter school year, inferior buildings and equipment, and poorly paid teachers."[8] Annie Reynolds, Associate Specialist in School Supervision for the Office of Education during the 1930s, claimed that segregating Mexican children was based on the fact that "American parents [were] against sending their children to schools attended by Mexican children."[9]

To the extent that the segregation of Mexican American children differed from that of African Americans, a closer examination of local educational policies revealed that cultural and linguistic differences were used as a pretext to keep them apart from white children. In other words, the ethnic background of Mexican children was often the reason for their segregation. University of Texas professor Herschel T. Manuel, in fact, wrote about how curricular and pedagogical rationales were being used to provide Mexican children "schools distinctly inferior to those provided for other White children in the same community."[10] Similar to Manuel, Pauline Kibbe, Executive Secretary to the Good Neighbor Commission of Texas, found that many school boards were segregating Mexican children because of their ethnicity. According to Kibbe, white parents were pressing school administrators and school boards to enact policies to keep Mexican children in separate facilities. Educational professionals, however, did not need to be convinced that segregation was best, because they shared the values of their white communities. In one community, for example, a superintendent said Mexican children needed at least "five or six years of Americanization before being placed with American children." He refused to mix the groups because the Mexican "standard of living is too low."[11] In California, Annie Reynolds found a similar trend: politicians in Los Angeles were being pressured by white parents to gerrymander school boundaries in order to ensure that specific schools absorbed "the majority of the Mexican pupils in the district."[12] Throughout the Southwest, school boards established segregationist policies as soon as Mexican enrollments became noticeable.

By 1930, eighty-five percent of Mexican children in the Southwest were attending either separate classrooms or entirely separate schools.[13] In Southern California, for example, a significant number of public school districts had schools with between ninety and one hundred percent Mexican American enrollments. The following facts demonstrate the extent of their segregation: San Bernadino had sixteen Mexican schools; Orange County, fourteen; Los Angeles School District, ten; Imperial, eight; Ventura, four; Santa Barbara, two; and Riverside, two.[14] Many school districts in the state had designated classrooms where Mexican children were "required to attend."[15] During the 1940s, the Brawley School District (in the Imperial Valley) continued to have designated schools to which "all Latins must go if they cannot pass the English-language examination."[16] Unlike the African American experience, where segregation was permanent, educational professionals frequently pledged that as soon as Mexican children learned English and became Americanized (during their first few years of school), they would instantly be integrated with white children. Evidence shows, however, that integration almost never occurred, because many English-speaking Mexican American children were found in segregated schools.[17]

The segregation of Mexican children became a hot topic during the 1920s and 1930s. Scholars and students of education were writing at length about the limits and possibilities of school segregation for Mexican children. Milo Hogan, for example, became interested in finding out how schools in the Imperial Valley were serving Mexican youth. He claimed that most schools were ill equipped to serve Mexican students in general and those who had limited English proficiency in particular. Searching for a remedy to solve the problems Mexicans were encountering in public schools, he recommended that "whenever possible, separate classes be made for those children who come from homes where a foreign language is used." Hogan declared that segregation was best for both groups because, he said, "Mexicans may . . . have the drill in English that is necessary and will not have to waste time in a class that is working on a different level." In addition, he urged school officials to segregate Mexican children because they were not as "independent" as their white peers. Hogan's point was that classroom integration had the potential to hinder the academic progress of white children.[18]

Hogan's ideas were accepted by many educators in California. Even the more liberal educators expressed concerns about Mexican children being expected to "compete in English with Anglos." They feared that Mexican contact with bright white children had damaging effects on the Mexican children's psychological well-being. One teacher described the social and academic climate of segregated classrooms: When Mexican children were placed in classrooms with their own kind, their "faces radiated joy," they "[threw] off their repression that held them down when they were in the schools with other children," and there "was no one to laugh at any peculiarity they might possess."[19] As true believers, liberal teachers were convinced that ethnic integration created negative classroom environments and that it discouraged Mexican youth from staying in school. Whether Mexican children were being segregated for curricular and pedagogical reasons or to protect them from negative psychological effects, many educators believed they "must not be expected to compete except within their own group."[20]

Some social policymakers and educational professionals, however, were not as covert about segregating the Mexican American child. From their perspective, Mexican children were culturally and linguistically distinct and were seen as an entirely different racial group. In California, for example, the government had classified Mexicans as Caucasian. In order to legally segregate them, government officials needed to reclassify their racial/ethnic background. In 1930, Attorney General Webb attempted to categorize them as Indians. He claimed that "the greater portion of the population of Mexico are Indians." And because many of them migrated to the United States, "they are subject to laws applicable generally to other Indians." In 1935, the California legislature tried to pass a law to officially segregate Mexican students on the basis that they were Indian. Without mentioning the term *Mexican*, the school code prescribed that the "governing board of the school district shall have power to establish separate schools for Indian children, excepting children of Indians who are the wards of the U. S. government and children of all other Indians who are the descendants of the original American Indians of the U. S., and for children of Chinese, Japanese, or Mongolian parentage."[21] This code could have been interpreted as a way to segregate Mexican children, given that they were descended from Indians in Mexico. As Donato, Mechaca, and Valencia noted, "Mexican children became the principal target of the discriminatory school code without being identified, and American Indians, though named directly, were released from legally mandated segregation."[22]

Proposals to legally segregate Mexican children at the state level never passed into law, but segregation did become local custom. In many ways, the schooling experiences of Mexican children reflected those of African Americans because they were in fact separated from white children and were never expected to assimilate into the American mainstream. As the school segregation discourse continued, researchers incorporated questions of Mexican morality, temperament, hygiene, and virtues. Americans take for granted, said Charles Carpenter, that among other things Mexicans are "dirty," "stupid," "lawless," "disease spreaders," and "lazy." Interested in whether this characterization was accurate, Carpenter set out to study Mexican children in the Azusa, California, city schools.[23] He also became interested in the social conditions of the "average" Mexican home, their mode of "behavior," their physical problems, and other social aberrations. Carpenter claimed that Mexicans had different "ideals of honesty, morality, justice, and cleanliness . . . from those of the average American family."[24] Given the "Mexican temperament, the high percentage of juvenile arrests among Mexicans, and the nature of offenses committed, and their low moral standards," said Carpenter, "it would be advisable to segregate the Mexican and American children in school."[25]

In this vein, numerous studies supported the segregation of Mexican children because they were deemed to be dishonest, immoral, and violent. Katherine Meguire contended that Americans who were "familiar with the Mexican people list such traits as irresponsibility, imitativeness, thriftless-ness, sex-consciousness, individualism, and procrastination as being among the ones which hold them on the low plane at which most of them in the United States exist."[26] Like Carpenter, Meguire also supported segre-gation and proclaimed that it was inherently wrong to mix Mexican and white students. Although educational professionals frequently maintained that Mexican children were being integrated with white students as soon as they became Americanized and learned English, it almost never oc-curred, because by the time they reached their junior high school years most had already dropped out. Even though the American high school was becoming a mass institution during the early twentieth century—as the graduation rate of all seventeen-year-olds rose from 3.5 percent in 1890 to 28.8 percent in 1930—Mexican youth almost never attended.[27] This trend in various parts of the country is shown by high Mexican enrollments at the elementary level and very low rates at the high school level. One example was school attendance in Orange County, California: 4,037 Mexican children were enrolled in 30 elementary schools, but in the county's 10 high schools, there were only 165 Mexican students enrolled.[28] In California's Santa Ana school district, there were 1,031 Mexican elemen-tary students attending school; at the high school level only 53.[29] Paul Taylor found a similar trend in San Antonio, Texas: 11,000 Mexican American students attending elementary schools, only 250 at the high school level.[30]

But the most extreme example was found in Sugar Land, Texas (near Houston), during the mid-1930s. In this case, Mexican children repre-sented 56.6 percent of the elementary school population in the district but constituted only one percent of the eighth-grade class. Several years later, enrollments increased to 59.5 percent at the elementary level, but only 1.9 percent were enrolled in the eighth grade.[31] The point here is that while high school enrollments were increasing at the national level, Mexican youth were barely able to receive a junior high school education.

Historian Meyer Weinberg claimed that school systems were struc-tured in a way that deliberately denied Mexican children secondary school-ing. "[F]armers sat on school boards," said Weinberg, "where they could put their educational philosophy into effect. As an instrument of exploi-tation, the schools often seemed to be hardly more than an extension of the cotton field or the fruit-packing shed."[32] On the surface, educators maintained that segregation at the elementary level was best for Mexican American children in order to serve them properly when in fact the goal was to keep them apart from white children and, ostensibly, to maintain a supply of cheap labor in their communities.

AMERICANIZATION

For many Anglo Americans, the influx of immigrants from Southern and Eastern Europe to inner cities was straining the social fabric of the United States. This demographic shift posed enormous problems in public schools. In 1908, the United States Senate Immigration Commission conducted a study in thirty-seven major cities and found that "58 percent of all students had fathers who were born abroad."[33] One of the puzzles of this period was that although these new immigrants were seen as a culturally backward mass, social reformers were indeed working to assimilate them into American life. Thus, public schools assumed the role of introducing these children—who spoke numerous languages, hung on to traditional folkways, and possessed multiple loyalties to their mother countries—into the mainstream of U. S. life.[34] Assimilating some European immigrants, however, was a complex task.[35] Stanford University professor Ellwood P. Cubberley wrote in 1909 that Southern and Eastern Europeans were "illiterate, docile, lacking in self-reliance and initiative," and lacked "the Anglo-Saxon conceptions of law, order, and government." He warned social policymakers and school reformers that these new immigrants would "dilute tremendously our national stock, and corrupt our national life."[36] But despite Cubberly's views, many social and educational reformers worked at integrating Southern and Eastern Europeans into the U. S. mainstream.

In dealing with this new wave of immigrants, educational reformers were forced to define "American" values more self-consciously. To become an American meant learning the English language, lessons of American culture, and new modes of behavior. If immigrant children were unhygienic, non–English-speaking, and politically corrupt, said Sara O'Brien, it was the responsibility of the school to bathe them, teach them English, and inculcate a new set of political values.[37] Teachers across the country made it their business to take over the duties regularly performed by immigrant parents. Hopes ran high among educators that public schools could assimilate the newcomers and cure the nation's social ills. Assimilation, however, also meant that immigrant children needed to reject their own language, culture, identity, and, in essence, their parents. Many immigrant parents feared losing their children through Americanization; others saw it as the doorway to social mobility and new opportunities.[38]

Unlike European immigrants, Mexicans were looked upon as outsiders who would never blend into the mainstream. Merton Hill, a prominent Americanization specialist in California, for example, cautioned social policymakers and educational reformers that one "of the most momentous problems confronting the great American Southwest is the assimilation of the Spanish-speaking peoples that are coming in ever increasing numbers."[39] From Hill's perspective, it was a grave mistake to assume that Mexicans could ever assimilate into the U. S. culture. Like many educators, Americanizers characterized the Mexican people as violent, unambitious, and barbarous. Conducting a study on the schooling experiences of Mexican children in Orange County, California, Simon Ludwig Treff wrote about the culture of Mexican adults, how they congregated "in poolrooms and restaurants and drank and played cards until a late hour," how fights were frequent, and how their "favorite weapon was the knife."[40] But the most acerb critique of the Mexican people came from Hazel Bishop, noting that Mexicans failed to "look upon lying and stealing as grievous crimes." In her study she claimed Mexicans were "deceitful," and their "emotional phases [were] largely animal-like."[41] Within this context, many Americans believed nothing was wrong with residential and school segregation.

Very few scholars were criticizing social and educational discrimination against the Mexican people during this period.[42] Historian and social critic Cary McWilliams, however, wrote that Americanization specialists were socializing Mexican children for subordinate social and economic positions: "Instead of assisting a process of gradual acculturation," said McWilliams, "we have abandoned the [Mexican] people to chance and circumstance. And thereby we have permitted the extension to them, as a group, of a caste-system which had its origins in a semi-feudal slave economy and which has never been obliterated in the United States."[43] Most scholars continued to defend U. S. public education, claiming that the Mexican's station in American life was attributed to poor medical care and low wages. It was a sad state of affairs, said Edward McDonaugh, that economic reality forced them, "including their children, to work in order to survive."[44]

Some white scholars professed superiority over the Mexican people because white Americans somehow placed more value on formal education. McDonaugh believed that Mexicans were at a considerable disadvantage because, in his words, their

[c]ulture has been geared to an agricultural tempo, and the conflict between rural and urban values is part of the problem. A number of studies are available that point out the fact that the educational status of the Mexican is low because of poor school

attendance, limited average grade completion, and frequent school failures. Some of this low educational status may be explained in terms of high mobility necessitated as transient workers, difficulties centering upon bilingualism, and perhaps a culture that values "living: rather than schooling."[45]

This view was held by many educational professionals in the United States. The belief that Mexicans were indifferent about education was used as a pretext for educators to absolve themselves from responsibility for the Mexican child. Educators blamed school failure on poor school attendance, high transience, bilingualism, and a culture that was unresponsive to school.

Americanization specialists struggled to integrate European immigrant groups into U. S. life. They were virtually unsuccessful with the Mexican people. Because Mexicans were segregated in their schools and communities, reformers believed that public schools needed to give them the skills necessary for their station in American life.[46] The theory that Mexican children needed to be segregated until they became Americanized became an idea accepted by the educational profession in most parts of the Southwest.

VOCATIONAL EDUCATION

Educational historians have written extensively on the evolution of the American high school, how it was transformed from a selective institution to one that opened its doors to a more diverse student clientele. They explored, in particular, how high schools at first were serving a small portion of the U. S. student population, how they experienced curricular and pedagogical reforms, and how working-class and immigrant children began to attend them. Within the high school literature, an enormous amount of attention was also given to vocational education. That is, how vocational education became an important element in the development of comprehensive high school, how schools were organized to develop human capital through training, and how students were matched to educational programs to meet labor market needs.[47] Throughout this literature, evidence shows that vocational education programs attempted to train "working-class, immigrant, and black children into manual jobs." More specifically, it demonstrates that the vocational education movement became a "response to the specific job training needs of the rapidly expanding corporate sector than an accommodation of a previously elite educational institution—the high school—to the changing needs of reproducing the class structure."[48]

In examining the history of vocational education in California from the late nineteenth to the early twentieth centuries, Harvey Kantor maintained that vocational education never fully succeeded in training workers for industrial occupations. What the movement did accomplish, according to Kantor, was to make preparation for jobs the major function of the American high school. Moreover, it made educators and social policymakers think of education as the cure for the nation's economic ills.[49] To the extent that the classic high school was serving a small percentage of the nation's youth, the Commission on National Aid to Vocational Education claimed in 1914 that vocational education was the way to equalize schooling because it recognized different abilities.[50] The commission was convinced that vocational education would provide better opportunities for all youth at the secondary level; its report resulted in the passage of the Smith-Hughes Act in 1917, which provided federal funds to expand vocational education programs in U.S. public schools. The Smith-Hughes Act, however, had far-reaching effects, as it resulted in "strengthening and legitimizing the evolving dual system of education."[51] According to educational historian Edward Krug, the act contributed "to a widespread bias against the so-called academic side of school work, particular for the alleged 'masses.' This bias," continued Krug, "flowed from the attempt to promote industrial education by disparaging the work of what were referred to as the 'literary' schools."[52] By establishing a system of education that separated youths into academic or vocational tracks, the movement created a class-based education. It also assumed that poor and minority children would be best served by vocational education programs.

The vocational education debate highlights one of the most complex issues concerning the relationship between schooling and democracy. For example, it was argued that providing an education that met individual needs and interests was democratic because it placed youth at the center of educational decisions. But it was also undemocratic because it provided youth with educational opportunities that stratified them into social classes.[53] A dual system of education, in this case, meant that working-class and minority youth were given the skills necessary for the lower echelons of the labor market while middle-class youth received an academic education that coincided with the social and cultural hegemony they already possessed. During this period, the high school became a mixture of planned social and academic activities with a variety of curricula that attempted to prepare a new generation for a society that was based on large organizations and occupational specialization.[54] Within this context, very few educational historians commented on how vocational education affected Mexican American youth.

Mexican children were tracked in vocational education programs because educators believed they possessed a natural capacity for the manual arts. Gilbert Gonzalez notes that school districts in Los Angeles conducted surveys "of students' interests to see whether labor needs and student interests corresponded." An important mission of schools in this area, reported Gonzalez, "involved bending, if necessary, the students' interests to meet the available occupational opportunities."[55] Public schools acquainted Mexican students with vocational education programs and counselors matched them to specific curriculum tracks. By sorting students to either vocational or academic placements, some youth were prepared for white collar jobs while others were trained for local labor markets in low-paying vocations.[56]

Many students were sorted into vocational education tracks based on ostensibly "scientific methods." Among a variety of tests to ascertain occupational abilities, the earliest instrument was developed by Harvard University psychologist Hugo Munsterberg, who pioneered a vocational-aptitude test. Munsterberg's goal was to bring together scientific management and vocational guidance. In the same way that scientific management studied industrial organizations, Munsterberg examined the job performance and aptitudes of individual workers.[57] Although "specific tests" were used to guide youth into vocational tracks, teacher judgment, student grades, student behavior, and student social and ethnic background were also used as sorting devices. Educational historian Herbert Kliebard notes that school reformers instituted "a process of scientific measurement leading to a prediction as to one's future role in life. That prediction," he said, "would then become the basis of a differentiated curriculum."[58]

In examining the vocational education movement and its effects on Mexican American youth, Merton Hill claimed that because Mexican children demonstrated a "considerable aptitude for hand work . . . courses should be developed that will aid them in becoming skilled workers with their hands."[59] Hill advocated programs to train Mexican boys to become skilled laborers and Mexican "[g]irls . . . to become neat and efficient house servants."[60] While the expressed goal was to train Mexican youth for skilled vocations, there was an emphasis on matching them with low-level curricula. And because most Mexican youth were unable to reach the high school level, some reformers waged a campaign to introduce manual training during the elementary school years. William Ward claimed that public schools needed to give Mexican children less academic preparation and "more handwork and practical arts." It was necessary, he said, to introduce "[m]anual training and domestic science, hygiene, home-making and repair . . . in the fourth and fifth grade."[61] In Colorado, Philip Pratt also advocated the introduction of the "manual arts, home-making, music, and art . . . earlier in the curriculum." According to Pratt, these were "the subjects that the Mexican can grasp and which will be of practical use to him later in life."[62] But unlike other advocates wanting to introduce vocational education during the elementary school years, Pratt added that such training was better than the agricultural labor most Mexican youth performed. From his perspective, vocational education "might spur some of them on to greater achievement."[63]

To the extent that Mexican American women were usually restricted to domestic services, there was a desire to teach Mexican girls the virtues of thrift, responsibility, and morality. Katherine Meguire, for example, urged public school teachers to give Mexican girls skills in "manual arts and home-making" during the upper elementary grades so they may one day learn "how to live wholesomely."[64] Meguire urged public schools to teach Mexican girls "something about cleaning, table-setting, and serving."[65] Similarly, Inez Whitewell became interested in educating Mexican girls in Arizona who were unable to attend high school. Whitewell campaigned for a curriculum and pedagogy that prepared "Mexican girls to . . . fulfill the requirement of people of the community who might desire to hire them to help in the care of children."[66] There was a general consensus among vocational educational reformers that a Mexican girl needed the kind of training necessary to "become proficient in the home and in the community of which she is a part."[67]

Mexican children were frequently channeled into vocational education programs. Separate industrial secondary schools were also constructed especially for them. At the Andrew Jackson Industrial Arts High School in Los Angeles, for example, William McGorry said "the curriculum is industrial in nature, providing vocational training and skills which will make possible occupational orientation and employment. This type of curriculum," wrote McGorry, "has proven valuable to the school's Mexican boys because of their unusual manual ability and concrete intelligence."[68] In the Chaffey School District in Southern California, however, Merton Hill pushed vocational education for Mexican children because "Mexican children are actually making only 42% as satisfactory progress through the schools." He was adamant about "building and equipping an industrial high school for Mexican adolescents . . . in order to provide a partial solution of the problem of educating" them.[69]

Although the vocational education movement opened up some opportunities to poor and minority youth, it also paved the way for a dual system of education in the United States. After creating a structure that guided all youth into academic or vocational tracks, the reform was seen as the natural course of study for Mexican American youth. In the end, the reform established closer relations between schools and local political economies, and vocational education became a part of the schooling experience for Mexican American youth for years to come.

PSYCHOMETRICS

The manner in which Mexican American youth were being sorted began to raise serious questions among progressives about the openness and fairness of the social class structure. Educational professionals, however, needed to construct a method to sort students in an objective and scientific way. Curriculum differentiation and segregation were strengthened by the use of the "objective intelligence test." Particularly after World War I, the capitulation of schools to business values and concepts of efficiency led to the increased use of intelligence testing as an ostensibly unbiased means of measuring the product of schooling and classifying students. However, if the rhetoric of educational reform during the early twentieth century was "Progressive," much of its content was supplied by the new science of evolutionary genetics. As educational historian Clarence Karier noted, "nativism, racism, elitism and social class bias were so much a part of the testing and Eugenics Movement in America."[70]

Intelligence testing captured the interest of educational reformers in the United States. Between 1921 and 1936, more than 4,000 articles on testing were published; by 1939, approximately 4,279 mental tests were being circulated.[71] To the extent that the psychometric movement was based on notions of human excellence and genetic endowment, other differences such as moral character, social worth, and race and ethnicity became part of this work. Within this context, many studies professed Anglo American intellectual superiority. Professor Henry Goddard, for example, found that 83 percent of Jews, 80 percent of Hungarians, 79 percent of Italians, and 87 percent of Russians were feebleminded, based on "culture-free" tests.[72] In the testing literature, educational historians have documented the uses and misuses of intelligence testing on various immigrant and minority groups. Very little has been written about Mexican American children.

The study of intelligence has always been controversial. The field, in fact, developed into a heated discussion between "hereditarians" and "environmentalists," better known as the "nature versus nurture" debate. Alfred Binet and Thomas Simon became the authoritative figures on the subject during the late nineteenth and early twentieth centuries. In constructing the first "scale of intelligence," the original idea behind their work was to study the "feebleminded." By 1908, Binet had become interested in studying the concept of normal intelligence among children. The purpose was to "measure the intellectual capacity of a child . . . in order to know whether he is normal or retarded." Binet's work had important implications for schooling. He believed some children were unable to profit from regular instruction, that schools were unable to serve their special needs, and that teachers needed to be mindful about the future capabilities of these pupils. Binet also became interested in the ability to judge, comprehend, and reason. These capacities, according to him, were the "essential activities of intelligence." Reporting a correlation between intelligence and academic achievement, Binet concluded that IQ was a strong predictor of academic success.[73]

Binet received international acclaim for his scale of intelligence, and educators became interested in using the instrument to sort students and to control problems of "retardation." Stanford University professor Lewis Terman, in fact, saw the social significance of intelligence testing as a way to select and sort the "feebleminded." Convinced that intelligence testing would bring "ten of thousands of these high grade defectives under the surveillance and protection of society," Terman also believed that it would decrease the "reproduction of feeble-mindedness and [would aid] in the elimination of an enormous amount of crime, pauperism, and industrial inefficiency."[74] In addition, Terman saw intelligence testing as a way to identify high-ability children. Because poverty and neglect concealed the raw talents of many children, he said, locating those who were gifted was extremely important because a nation depends on its geniuses.[75]

The construction of intelligence tests took a major leap forward during World War I. Psychometricians collected data from testing more than 1.7 million U. S. Army recruits, the nation's largest testing effort. Although several types of examinations were used, results came primarily from the Army *Alpha* and *Beta* tests. The Alpha exam was designed for literate English-speaking recruits. Attempting to find general attributes of intelligence, the test included items such as the ability to follow oral directions, solve mathematical problems, demonstrate common sense, recognize synonyms and antonyms, unscramble fragmented sentences, complete number series, and identify analogies. The Beta exam was designed for illiterate recruits or those who were non-English speaking. Relying on visuals and manipulatives, these recruits were asked to demonstrate the ability to trace a path through a maze, count the number of cubes in a picture, complete a series of letters according to a pattern, match or substitute digits from one to nine, determine whether pairs of numbers matched, complete a picture by adding missing parts, or assemble pieces of a puzzle to form a square. Psychometricians analyzed the data and found that African American and immigrant recruits scored lower than white "natives." In terms of the average (median) Alpha scores, white Army recruits of native birth ranked first, foreign-born whites second, northern blacks third, and southern blacks fourth. Although the Beta score median difference was generally smaller and more favorable for black recruits, the rank order of the racial/ethnic groups remained unchanged.[76]

In 1918, Robert Yerkes, head of the United States Army psychology team, proclaimed that the results of the testing program exceeded original expectations. In addition to sorting out the feebleminded, he noted that its results were also capable of identifying those with superior intelligence. Like Terman, Yerkes envisioned intelligence testing as a vehicle to scientifically identify bright children and classify them at an early age.[77] Other psychologists, such as Carl Brigham, used the Army test results to illustrate racial and ethnic superiority. He tried to confirm the belief that the "Nordic Type" was intellectually superior to African Americans and Southern and Eastern Europeans.[78] Brigham strengthened the hereditarian position, his ideas became firmly entrenched in academic circles, and it became interpreted as scientific proof that there were differences in racial intelligence.

As the testing movement continued, some psychologists became interested in Mexican children.[79] Lewis Terman, Thomas Garth, William Sheldon, Kimball Young, O. K. Garretson, and B. F. Haught, to name a few, attempted to verify that Mexican children were innately inferior to their white peers. Sheldon, for example, compared 100 Mexican and 100 white first-grade children in Roswell, New Mexico, in 1923. Using the Cole-Vincent test on a group of fluent English-speaking Mexican and white students, Sheldon found that "whites were decidedly superior in tests involving (all degrees), judgment, and the higher associative processes, especially where attention and accurate observation were necessary." In contrast, the "average Mexican child was found to be fourteen months below the normal mental development for White children of the same age and school environment." Sheldon's main finding was that "Mexicans as a group possessed about 85 per cent of the intelligence of a similar group of White children."[80]

During the same time period, University of Denver professor Thomas Garth compared the intelligence of Mexican, biracial Native American (that is, white and Indian), "full-blood" Plains, Pueblo, Navajo and Apache Indian children. Using the National Intelligence Test (NIT), Garth found that biracial Native Americans scored highest, Mexicans second, Plains third, Pueblo fourth, and Navajo and Apache fifth. Although Garth was a staunch hereditarian, he gave some credit to the environment position. He used the perspective of a superintendent from an Indian School in Oklahoma to explain why biracial children were performing better than full-blooded Indians. The superintendent believed that higher test scores were attributed to Indian exposure to white environments. In the words of the superintendent:

I think there is no question but that the presence of a child in
the home where one parent is white will influence the child to
behave more as a white man behaves. It is simply a question of
the influence of environment. In the full-blood home the atmosphere of the home is more backward and less influenced by the
white civilization.[81]

Although Garth believed that whites were genetically superior, he also
admitted that his comparative study of "mixed" and "full-blood" Native
Americans disproved "innate racial differences in intelligence . . . [but
that] . . . differences in opportunity and in mental attitude toward the white
man's way of thinking and living are made apparent."[82]

In subsequent years Garth focused on Mexican children. He tested
1,004 Mexican children from Texas, New Mexico, and Colorado in the
third to the eighth grades. Using the National Intelligence Test, he claimed
that Mexican children, as a group, had an IQ of 78.1. His results were
significantly lower than those found in the previous studies. The average
IQ test score for white children was 100, but one study showed 79.0 for
a group of Mexican children of sugar-beet workers in Colorado; Young
found 87.5 in California; 83.0 from Garth's previous study in San Antonio;
and 89.0 from Sheldon in New Mexico.[83] One of the more important
findings Garth wanted to convey to school reformers was that the retardation level of Mexican children was thwarting the quality of public
education in the Southwest. He maintained that 80.5 percent of Mexican
children tested were retarded.[84]

University of Texas professor O. K. Garretson spoke more directly to
questions of Mexican American retardation. In a study of factors that led to
academic retardation, Garretson tested 117 Mexican children in a small
Arizona school district. In addition to his claim that Mexican children were
genetically inferior, he also said that irregular school attendance, transient
residence patterns, and linguistic differences exacerbated the level of their
school retardation.[85] Most psychometricians, especially Garretson and Garth,
lacked insight about what contributed to the problems Mexican children
were facing in school. They failed to raise questions of power, low wages,
ethnic discrimination, and power differentials between Mexican and white
communities. Whether or not social scientists were considering these issues
at the time, Garretson blamed Mexican academic failure on the environment
and inferior natural capacities. His theory about Mexican intellectual inferiority, however, became accepted as conventional wisdom by most
pyschometricians, social policymakers and educational professionals.[86]

At the same time psychometricians were purporting that Mexican
children were innately inferior to their white counterparts, environmental-

ists were challenging this claim because a significant number of non-English speaking children were being tested. The point critics made was that IQ tests were mismeasuring the intelligence of Mexican children. Garretson responded that his results were accurate because his sample included Mexican children from the third to eighth grades and that most Mexican children were given the opportunity to learn English before they were tested in the third grade. Garretson, however, failed to acknowledge that many non-English-speaking Mexican children were entering school at different grade levels, that is, not all non-English-speaking children coming to the United States were beginning school at the kindergarten level.

Some psychometricians attempted to discount the language issue by constructing a test that was supposedly "completely independent of language."[87] As a case in point, Franklin Paschal and Louis Sullivan designed "a test or scale that can be applied by an American to the Mexican child or adult and despite his limited use of English obtain results as free from personal error as the theory of mental tests demands."[88] (As an example of how this test functioned, children were given oral directions in English or in Anglicized Spanish.) University of New Mexico professor B. F. Haught pushed the language-free intelligence test issue a bit further. He became interested in finding "objective evidence that such a language difficulty does or does not exist."[89] To the extent that Mexican children were scoring below the "standards obtained by those of Anglo descent," Haught, like Paschal and Sullivan, disputed the idea that low performance was a result of "a language difficulty encountered in taking tests."[90] According to Haught, the intelligence of Mexican children failed to increase with age and "older children are handicapped as much as the younger, [so there seems] to be no justification for assigning the difficulty to inability to use or understand English." He claimed that intelligence declined when Mexican children reached the age of ten. With this in mind, he said that the Mexican child's "intelligence quotient is 79 compared with 100 for the average Anglo child."[91]

Florence Goodenough, a psychologist at the University of Minnesota, also became interested in constructing a language-free intelligence test. Devising a nonverbal exam and administering it to 2,457 children in the United States, Goodenough also included 367 Mexican children from Los Angeles. Not only did she claim that her verbal test was "completely independent of language," but that her results corresponded with the "rank order of the various nationality groups . . . found by means of other intelligence tests."[92] She claimed that whether Mexican children took the standardized IQ exam or one that was "independent of language," they were intellectually inferior to their white peers.

Emulating the research trend of prominent psychometricians, students of education reached similar conclusions. Rollen Drake, for example, tested 144 Mexican and 173 white seventh and eighth graders in a Tucson, Arizona, school. Using the Pinter nonlanguage test, the National Intelligence Test, and the Stanford Achievement Test, he concluded that there was "a racial difference in mentality between Mexican and white children." Like Haught, Goodenough, and Pascal and Sullivan, Drake concluded that the "language handicap is of but small importance by the time the Mexican child has completed the sixth grade." From Drake's perspective, the "racial problem which exists when Mexican children are present in the upper elementary grades of the public schools is not due, to any great extent, to the fact that the Mexican children speak a foreign language, but probably due to the fact that they are definitely lower mentally than white children."[93]

In another study, Philip Pratt compared a group of Mexican and white students from Colorado. He contrasted the academic achievement of 95 Mexican and 146 white children in reading and math from the third to the eighth grade. Pratt's conclusions, based on the Stanford Grade Equivalents, was that with "two exceptions, that of total arithmetic in the sixth and seventh grades, the Mexican mean in every instance was lower than the mean of the whites." He found that the mean intelligence quotient for Mexican children was 79.5, and 89.8 for their white peers.[94] Unlike other studies that merely compared Mexican and white children, Pratt's study made various recommendations to improve their schooling conditions: a curriculum that was suitable for the Mexicans' station in life, and schools that emphasized the manual arts, music, and hygiene in segregated environments up to the fourth grade. He also acknowledged the importance of having access to books and magazines in the home, parent participation, social living and citizenship courses, and the enforcement of compulsory school attendance laws for Mexican children.[95]

Wilbur Cobb studied the children of Mexican migratory workers in Ventura, California. Cobb became interested in finding out the extent to which Mexican migrant children were retarded, and its economic impact on the community.[96] After testing 1,909 Mexican migratory children with the Stanford Achievement Test, Cobb found that 87.6 percent were retarded, 11 percent were performing at grade level, and 1.2 percent were accelerated. He also asserted that most Mexican children were two years and six months behind in reading, one year and eight months in math, three years and two months in history, three years in language, three years in literature, two years and seven months in physiology and hygiene, and two years and three months in geography and spelling. Cobb bypassed the economic burden of retardation on the community, but he did point out that during the harvest season Mexican migratory school children outnumbered white students two to one. From his perspective, the Mexican presence posed "a hardship on the local community." Cobb recommended state intervention in order to reduce the "financial burden of educating the migratory children . . . [in] . . . particular school districts."[97]

As the testing movement continued, University of Texas professor George Sanchez began to challenge psychometricians. From his perspective, there was a mismatch between IQ tests and the Mexican child's language, culture, and socioeconomic background: The IQ test merely measured environmental effects and the Mexican's range of ability differed very little from any other group's. Sanchez made it clear he did not intend to discredit the field of testing. It "would be shortsighted to propose the abandonment of mental tests in the bilingual problem," he said, "and nothing herein should so be interpreted." His point was that psychometricians needed to be more cautious about testing children in a language and culture the subjects did not understand and, more important, using results to marginalize them.[98] Despite Sanchez' critique, intelligence testing became an accepted educational practice across the nation, it became an important part of the Mexicans' school experience, and it became a method to classify and sort them into different courses of study.

CHILDREN OF THE HARVEST

Chicano historians have pointed out that, contrary to conventional wisdom, Mexican Americans were "strongly represented in most of the Southwest's cities."[99] Ricardo Romo found that the percentage of the Mexican population in urban centers in the Southwest was distributed in the following way: 18.6 percent in New Mexico, 36.0 in Arizona, 46.6 in Texas, and 66.3 in California.[100] Although a significant portion of the Mexican population was urban, many others were living in rural areas and tied to the nation's agricultural economy. Some were following the harvest season throughout the United States. Unlike the Mexican urban worker who was able to earn a very modest living with one income, Mexican agricultural workers depended on the labor of the entire family, including women and children. As a result, Mexican migrant children and their families faced different problems than their urban counterparts.

The agricultural economy of the American Southwest had always relied heavily on Mexican labor. The region's mild climate, fertile soils, and early-twentieth-century technological innovations led to an economic dependence on Mexican labor.[101] In the 1940s, Cary McWilliams described the agricultural economy in the Southwest as "factories in the fields," an exploitative system that was relentless and inhumane.[102] American growers sought the Mexican family because, noted Cary McWilliams, they "stick together; they work and camp and move as a unit. This, in turn, helps to organize the labor market and it also gives the contractor a closely knit working organization."[103]

The economic worth of the Mexican migrant family to U.S. agriculturists had considerable consequences for public schools. In some school systems, for example, local growers and educational professionals worked in tandem, separating migratory children into different schools, shortening their school days, and, in many communities, refusing to admit them to school.[104] The decision to limit or deny schooling opportunities to Mexican children was rooted in an educational philosophy that disregarded them as part of the nation's public school clientele. As Charles Gibbons and Howard Bell wrote in 1925:

> [L]ocal school districts [in Colorado] in which these families are living while working the beets are assuming no responsibility for the schooling of the Mexican children; they simply do not want them in their schools. Ostensibly their reason for not wanting them is that as soon as beets are over the family will move, and therefore to force them in would disorganize the school. This argument has some merits but its validity is weakened by a knowledge that the children are not wanted on the grounds that they are Mexican.[105]

Mexican migrant children in the Southwest were not being served equally to whites because of indifference, because local economies depended on their labor, and because they were ethnically distinct. In 1933, Annie Reynolds found that the employment of Mexican migrant children had serious consequences on their school attendance. The U.S. Bureau of the Census, for example, compared the attendance record of Mexican and white children from ages six to fifteen in various counties in the Southwest. The bureau found that Mexican attendance was disproportionately low. For example, while the percentage of white attendance ranged from 71 to 96 percent, that of Mexican children varied from 39 percent to 89 percent.[106] In Colorado, Paul Taylor found that "during the seasons of beet work in spring and fall, Mexican children of school age are generally in the beet fields, and not in school."[107] A report from the Colorado White House Conference on Child Health and Protection also attested that the school attendance of Mexican children was extremely low. They found that in the sugar beet industry, public schools were evading the "Colorado compulsory school laws and child-labor laws by claiming that the children are employed by their parents who need the help of the child to support the family."[108]

These reports suggested that low attendance was attributed to the economic survival of the Mexican migrant family. Gibbons and Bell, however, went a bit further and spoke more directly to the problem of school discrimination. From their perspective, local communities were refusing to educate Mexican migrant children because of their ethnic background. They argued:

> Since most of the contract families are of Mexican descent, the question may properly be raised as to what their place is in the community. A barrier exists between them and the others in the community. . . . The root of the trouble lies much deeper than the Mexican's shortcomings; it is the fact that he is a Mexican. . . . The situation was well put by one man who said "The Mexican is a necessary nuisance," meaning that he was necessary because the culture of beets demanded him, a nuisance because he was a Mexican. . . . He is wanted because of his work, and that only. The local people feel practically no responsibility towards him; they see only his ability to work.[109]

Like Colorado, most communities in Texas regarded the Mexican migrant worker in the same manner—a necessary evil, according to Pauline Kibbe. Mexican migrant workers were nothing more than a necessary part of the harvest season, and "[j]udging by the treatment that has been accorded him in that section [west Texas] of the State," wrote Kibbe, "one might assume that he is not a human being at all, but a species of farm implement that comes mysteriously and spontaneously into being."[110]

The 1920s and 1930s was indeed an era when school systems and communities were refusing to take responsibility for the Mexican migrant child. School superintendents, principals, and teachers, however, continued to attribute the problem of irregular school attendance to poverty, indifference to education, lack of suitable clothing, poor health, and local discrimination. Herschel T. Manuel challenged local professionals and claimed that irregular school attendance was also attributed to the fact that very few cared whether Mexican children attended. It was understandable why so few actually went to school, given their inferior school facilities and the "shabby treatment often received from other children in school." Manuel also noted that it was not always a question of inferior facilities but also the "lack of sympathy on the part of their teachers."[111] In all, the Mexican migrant average daily attendance was approximately thirty-three percent whereas the corresponding figure for white children was seventy-five percent.[112]

The relationship between school and the local agricultural economies was indeed stronger in some locations than others. In the nut groves of Southern California, for example, the "La Hambra Mexican school" accommodated local farmers during the harvest season. The school began and dismissed school early in order to supply local growers with child labor. Despite the structure of many Mexican migrant schools, educators frequently rationalized that indifference to education was the root problem of low school attendance. Jessie Hayden explained that poor health kept many migrant children out of school and that "the loss of interest in school tasks through lack of proper motivation is doubtless the most important factor to be considered." Aside from the meager earning Mexican migrant families survived on, Hayden claimed that the "desire of the family to obtain larger family earnings is the cause for non-attendance."[113] He believed that the Mexican migrant family was more interested in making money than educating its children. Hayden avoided other issues, however, such as how the local school board and the La Hambra Citrus Association worked together to ensure that enough Mexican migrant labor was available during the harvest season.

Manuel discussed the number of ways schools and local growers were contributing to the low Mexican migrant school attendance. Unlike other researchers, he discussed problems of school and community discrimination. But there were other reasons why Mexican migrant attendance was so low in some communities. One Texas superintendent, in fact, openly admitted that many white citizens coerced Mexican families to keep their children out of school. "Whites scare them out of it," said the superintendent. "They tell them if they send their children to school, they will be out of a job." Fearful of losing their jobs, many Mexican families kept their children home.[114] Many white communities, in addition, felt it was in their best interest not to educate the Mexicans because, as one superintendent said, "white people claim that when a Mexican gets a little education he becomes bigoted, wants to become a contractor, etc. This," he concluded, "is very likely true."[115] Keeping Mexican children out of school, the superintendent continued, was not "a problem at all. . . . The larger number of Mexicans care nothing about going to school, and practically all the White people care not whether they go. This makes it easy. Where we have some 350 Mexicans in the community, only about 50 ever enter school."[116]

The Mexican migrant family became an important part of the nation's agricultural economy. Agribusiness purchased, sold, and transported them from one region to another. The priority was not to educate the Mexican children but to exploit their labor. As a result, educational professionals made it their business to supply farmers with child labor during the harvest season. In short, compulsory education laws did not apply to Mexican migrant children, school authorities frowned on their presence, white communities did not want to serve them, and Mexican migrant parents feared sending their children to school. This arrangement created a third-class existence, it intensified class divisions, and it defined ethnic relations between Mexican and white communities for years to come.

CONCLUSION

The educational sphere during the first half of the twentieth century was, among other things, an ideological medium through which scholars, social policymakers, and educational professionals dealt with fundamental questions of integration, language, culture, class, intelligence, and ethnicity. Mexicans were immigrating to the United States at a time when educational professionals were becoming empowered to classify children according to what they thought was best for their client, when the results of IQ tests were being accepted as proof of native ability, when those in control of schools generally agreed that their function was to sort and train students to fit into the existing economic structure, and when much writing in education and social science tended to portray Mexicans as a detriment to U.S. society. Educators and the lay public viewed Mexicans as lazy, dirty, stupid, deviant, disease ridden, and amoral. It was not surprising, then, that educators made concerted efforts to keep Mexican youth apart from their white peers. Many educators claimed that segregating Mexican children during the elementary grades—to remedy their cultural and linguistic deficiencies—was best for all children. Whether Mexican children were limited or fluent English speakers, they were placed in separate classrooms or in entirely separate schools.

In addition, well-known educational reformers wrote copiously about the need to assimilate European immigrants, they remained silent about Mexican children. The problem was that the inferior and low castelike status was seen as a fixed condition that public schools were unable to change. Whether Mexican children attended urban, suburban, or rural schools, they were tracked in disproportionate numbers into classes or schools that emphasized the manual arts or where low literacy skills were taught. Throughout the Southwest, Mexican youth were enrolled in separate vocational classes or in completely separate industrial schools, where boys were being socialized to take on unskilled occupations and where girls were still prepared to become domestic servants. As late as the early 1950s, most educators still believed Mexican youth were best suited for manual labor, where their intelligence and "temperament" matched specific curricular and pedagogical practices. These schooling practices, in turn, strengthened biased educational policies and codified the sociopolitical and economic relations between Mexican and white communities.

TWO

Evolution of a Community and the Making of a School District

One of the paradoxes of U.S. educational history is how little is known about the schooling experiences of Mexican Americans. As we saw, the roots of Mexican American school segregation were established during the Progressive era. Whether Mexican children attended urban or rural schools, segregation became a way of life. According to conventional wisdom, segregation was best because Mexican children needed to learn English and about the American culture before mixing with their white peers. A more accurate representation shows that Mexican children were placed in separate facilities because they were viewed as amoral, unhygienic, disease ridden, and retarded. Educational reformers also believed that Mexican children needed a practical education in order to give them the skills necessary for their station in American life. In many ways, argues Gilbert Gonzalez, the desired effect of public schools was to socialize the Mexican community in order to maintain "social and economic relations existing between Anglos and Mexicans."[1] This chapter examines the evolution of Brownfield and the forces that shaped its public schools. It looks at its schools and community before Mexican Americans became a significant minority. The history of the community and its schools must be seen in relation to one another if we are to understand the Mexican American pursuit for equal education during the 1960s and 1970s.

MEXICAN LOSS OF THE AMERICAN SOUTHWEST

Unlike most European immigrants coming to the United States, Mexicans who had colonized the Southwest along with Anglos were incorporated through military conquest. At the end of the United States–Mexican war

(1848), Mexico lost almost half of its territory. Arizona, California, Colorado, New Mexico, Texas, Nevada, Utah, and portions of other nearby states were carved out of Mexico's far northern frontier. After the war, the Treaty of Guadalupe Hidalgo settled the question of sovereignty, a new border was drawn, and the status of Mexicans in the United States was resolved. According to the treaty, approximately 6,000 Mexicans had to either move to Mexico or become U. S. citizens. Some moved and others remained in the United States, but there were those who resisted American hegemony. Most Mexicans became American citizens and accepted U. S. rule.[2] But for those who remained in the United States, life became difficult. As the American government began to take up issues of property and civil rights, Mexicans were displaced. Their displacement, however, varied widely according to geography, history, and politics. Of "all the territorial conquests in the American Southwest," wrote Rodolfo Acuña, "the colonization of California was, perhaps, the most tragic." Its mild climate, rich soils, natural resources, and location (convenient seaports) became crucial for the nation's economic prosperity. California became America's greatest prize.[3]

As Mexicans became "colonized" in the Southwest,[4] a group of wealthy "Hispanics" in California remained autonomous for several years after the United States–Mexican war.[5] They were known as "Californios." Historians L. H. Dann and Peter Duignan wrote that the American occupation in California "at first tried to maintain the old order. They accordingly enforced Mexican law, utilized Mexican administrative procedures, and appointed Californios to leading positions in the local government." The discovery of gold in 1850, however, crumbled the old order. An influx of white settlers reduced the Mexican/Californio population to a small minority.[6] As gold resources became depleted, miners turned to farming and squatting. "At first," wrote Leonard Pitt, "settlers would encroach only on the outskirts of an estate, often taking up uninhabited land in good faith and paying rent for it, even though they refused to buy it." But as each week passed in 1852, observed Pitt, "the number of settlers increased, and their field of battle grew wider."[7]

White settlers in the state quickly acquired political and economic control, noted Albert Camarillo, while "Mexicans suffered dramatic economic decline."[8] During the early 1850s, "every rancho within a day's march of San Francisco Bay had its contingent of uninhibited non-paying guests. . . . Sonoma, Napa, Solano, Contra Costa, Santa Clara, Santa Cruz and Monterey . . . experience[d] at least some of the typical settlers' agitation."[9] Mexican/Californios lost their land through physical violence, shady real estate deals, and high attorneys' fees.[10] Other factors also contributed to their downfall. Gann and Duignan argued that they "lacked the liquid capital that would have enabled them to tide themselves over bad times, to defend their rights in court in the endless legal battles that ensued upon the American conquest."[11]

The decline of the Mexican/Californio occurred on two fronts: First, squatters encroached on and physically harassed the rightful owners and, second, politicians challenged the authenticity of property titles through the Land Act of 1851. This Act not only called for documentation of land titles, but it also placed the burden of proof on Mexican/Californios. Many of them could not provide official titles because, in many cases, land ownership was established by tradition. Litigation dragged on, cases followed with appeals, and, as a consequence, the costs became destructively high.[12] Acuña pointed out that the "Mexican landowner was lynched, kicked off his land by armed squatters, taxed out of existence, or insidiously bled by the cost of litigation imposed by the Land Law of 1851."[13]

In an environment that was harsh, lawless, and violent, the U. S. government was not able to protect the rights of Mexican/Californios.[14] Pitt asserted that clashing views of land ownership also contributed to the problem. From the white settler's perspective, it was outrageous for anyone to own such large parcels of land. "In 1848," wrote Gann and Duignan, "an estimated two hundred Californio families were said to hold about fourteen million acres in parcels from one to eleven leagues (one league equals forty-five hundred acres)."[15] To the extent that these "magnates" were unable to defend their property, they became prey to Anglo American settlers. But in "all fairness to the more well-intentioned squatters," said Pitt, "it must be said that they probably did not mean to turn the Californios into the cold." They intended to "let the rancheros keep as much land as an ordinary farmer."[16]

In addition to politics and clashing views of property rights, California also suffered several natural disasters during this period. Although some Mexican/Californios managed to survive the droughts, rains, and floods, most were not able to adapt to new labor markets. California developed sheep, grain, citrus, and fruit industries and experienced an unplanned economic revolution.[17] By 1880, wrote McLemore and Romo, the Anglo American settler had gained "control of the machinery of politics and the economy. The traditional society of the Californio crumbled in the face of the industrial and agricultural developments that were ushering in the twentieth century"[18]

THE NORTHWARD TIDE

During the early twentieth century, increasing numbers of Mexicans were coming to the United States in search of a better life. While the United States was moving into international economic prominence stimulated by industrialization and improvements in agriculture, transportation, and manufacturing, Mexicans became the main source of labor.[19] Social historians, however, have disagreed on the number of Mexicans that immigrated to the United States prior to 1900 because official statistics were not kept at the time and because the United States–Mexican border was actually open during this period.[20] Table 2.1 demonstrates that the number of Mexicans entering this country was quite small during the late nineteenth century compared to the early twentieth century. Immigration scholars have questioned the pre-1900 figures, maintaining that their numbers were probably much greater than were reported.[21] A push-pull relationship evolved between Mexico and the United States during the early twentieth century. Mexico's feudal-like system of farming and ranching was forcing rural peasants to the cities, inflation was chipping away at the meager wages paid to the common worker, and the Mexican revolution of 1910 was pushing thousands of Mexicans to the United States. In addition, U. S. growth in agricultural production, the maintenance of the railroads, the construction industry, and manufacturing attracted scores of unskilled and semiskilled Mexican workers.[22]

Between 1910 and 1930, approximately ten percent of Mexico's total population immigrated to the United States.[23] Most were unskilled laborers. But there was also a group of upper-middle-class Mexicans (professionals, merchants, white-collar workers, skilled craftspeople, and petty bureaucrats) that were fleeing the revolution.[24] Most entered the United States through Texas but ended up settling in Arizona, Colorado, New Mexico, and California. Despite the social class of these newcomers, most were relegated to unskilled and semiskilled labor. Historians have consistently pointed out how California became the land of opportunity for many immigrant groups. Very little has been mentioned about how most Mexicans faced persisting economic divisions, social stratification, and various forms of racial/ethnic discrimination.[25]

Social and economic mobility was difficult to attain because of the way in which Mexicans were perceived by the dominant society.[26] During

Table 2.1. *Immigration to the United States from Mexico*

Decade	Number
1861–1870	2,191
1871–1880	5,162
1881–1900	Records incomplete
1901–1910	49,642
1911–1920	219,004
1921–1930	459,287

Source: Manuel, H. T. (1965), *Spanish-Speaking Children of the Southwest*, p. 18.

World War I, sociologist Emory Bogardus wrote extensively about the perils of the Mexican presence in the United States. He feared using Mexicans as a primary source of cheap labor because, after they were exposed to U. S. society, many were making America their home. Like other social scientists writing about the Mexican people, Bogardus characterized them as shiftless, individualistic, patient, and submissive. An interesting contradiction began to appear during this period. The American lay public despised the Mexican presence; U. S. employers were "interested only in the work which the Mexicans can do." American agencies were recruiting thousands of Mexican unskilled workers to labor in the railroads, factories, and the sugar beet fields across the Southwest.[27]

Despite this demand for cheap Mexican labor, the American public was becoming more hostile toward Mexican workers. By the late 1920s, California governor C. C. Young and his "Mexican Fact-Finding Committee" reported that "Mexican immigrants have gained a strong foothold in California industries, undoubtedly supplanting other immigrant races and native Americans."[28] The Mexican, continued Young, had become "a principle source of farm labor" and worked at "tasks white workers will not or cannot do."[29] On the eve of the Great Depression, the stock market crashed; many Americans became unemployed, and many experienced poverty, hunger, and hopelessness. The Depression, however, probably struck California harder than any other state because its thriving economy came to a sudden standstill. Thousands of unemployed white Americans from the plains states migrated to California to search for work and to flee harsh winter conditions. This migration pattern saturated the labor market, jobs became more competitive, and it exacerbated racial/ethnic tension between Mexican and white workers.[30]

Although many Americans were experiencing economic despair, it was an especially trying time for the Mexican American population. Mexicans were usually the most poorly paid, they were the first to be fired, and they were the ones who were being blamed for the nation's economic problems. From urban centers to agricultural regions, white Americans asserted louder than ever before that Mexicans were taking jobs away from U. S. citizens and that they were a serious burden to the economic well-being of the nation. As a result, the U. S. government repatriated more than 400,000 Mexican workers.[31] This occurrence stands out as one of the most deplorable governmental acts committed against the Mexican people.[32] The issue here was how little attention the government gave to distinguishing between Mexican Americans and those who were undocumented workers.[33]

The congressional resolution to repatriate Mexican workers was led by the U. S. Department of Labor and supported by President Herbert

Hoover, who also believed that Mexicans were draining the nation's economy and that they were taking jobs from U. S. citizens. Between 1931 and 1933, approximately 75,000 to 100,000 Mexicans were repatriated from California. State authorities focused their efforts in Southern California, making raids in areas where most Mexicans lived. "With such a purpose in mind," said historians McLemore and Romo, "thousands of people in various cities who looked 'Mexican' were rounded up and deported."[34] Though raids took place in several large cities throughout the Southwest, one "of the largest raids," wrote Camarillo, "took place in 1931 in Placita Park, the downtown Los Angeles plaza frequented by Mexican families for many generations. Immigration agents and Los Angeles police officers surrounded and questioned four hundred people in the old plaza area."[35]

Mexicans who had originally planned to return to Mexico but had inadvertently established roots in America feared losing what little they had accumulated over the years. The hostility by government officials and Anglo Americans during the Depression years forced some Mexican Americans to return to Mexico. Others returned voluntarily because life in their homeland could not be any worse than the conditions they were confronting in the United States.[36] An economic pattern developed between Mexico and the United States. In times of economic prosperity, the United States opened its doors, and during hard times, closed them. The border "was open to Mexican labor . . . during World War I," said Julian Samora, but "closed with the advent of the Great Depression."[37]

Table 2.2. *Number of Braceros* Imported into the United States, 1942–1964*

Year	Total Imported	Year	Total Imported
1942	4,203	1954	310,476
1943	52,098	1955	390,846
1944	62,170	1956	444,581
1945	49,454	1957	450,422
1946	32,043	1958	418,885
1947	19,632	1959	447,535
1948	33,288	1960	427,240
1949	143,455	1961	294,149
1950	76,519	1962	298,556
1951	211,098	1963	195,450
1952	187,894	1964	181,738
1953	198,424		

Source: Barerra, M., *Race and Class in the Southwest,* p. 117.
*Mexican laborers

As the U. S. economy began to recover and prosper during the early 1940s, Mexican workers were once again seen as an important commodity.[38] Faced with a serious labor shortage during the World War II, the American government devised an agreement with Mexico in 1942 for a supply of temporary contracted labor. Known as the "bracero" program, it allowed Mexican laborers temporary status in the United States. Table 2.2 shows the number of braceros imported into the United States over a twenty-two year period. During the war years (1942–1945),150,000 braceros labored in agriculture, the railroads, and in other urban industries. Although the bracero program was intended to be a temporary wartime measure, agribusiness and other industrialists lobbied for its continuance. Between 1946 and 1960 an average of 278,800 Mexican braceros were recruited into the United States each year.

The Mexican government favored the bracero program during the postwar years because it brought millions of dollars into the country. However, white American labor unions and Mexican American leaders joined forces with some Mexican officials and pressed Congress to discontinue the program. Although the program terminated in 1964, its legacy did not end without long-term consequences.[39] Some braceros went back to Mexico and never returned. Others married U. S. citizens and stayed. A significant number returned to Mexico but planned to return.[40] The bracero program, wrote Arthur Crowin, became the "great catalyst for Mexican migration, legal and illegal."[41] Moreover, as Wayne Cornelius noted, "the bracero program never really ended, it simply went underground."[42] Mexican immigration soared after the program was discontinued, and the influx of documented and undocumented workers never ended.

THE MAKING OF BROWNFIELD

California was annexed to the union in 1850, and Brownfield rapidly became a prosperous town, an important regional node to the nation's expanding agricultural economy. Located in Northern California, its population increased from 398 in 1860 to 1,799 in 1880, and on to 3,538 in 1900.[43] While the town seemed relatively small, the "valley" contained about 141 square miles. The census has never been able to report the accurate size of the area because several surrounding suburbs and unincorporated communities have not been included as part of the town. Virtually all portraits of the community begin with an irrefutable observation: It was settled by Anglo Americans—mostly English, German, and the Boston Irish. By the late nineteenth and early twentieth centuries, however, Italians, Portuguese, and Yugoslavians became an important element in the community.[44] Brownfield's racial minority was composed of Chinese, Japanese, and

Filipinos. Table 2.3 shows that the white population (that is, native-born whites, foreign-born whites, and foreign mixed people) constituted 97.2 percent of the town in 1900, 95.8 percent in 1910, 91.6 percent in 1920, 88.1 percent in 1930, and back up to 91 percent in 1940. Asians increased from 2.1 percent in 1900 to 9.0 percent in 1940. African Americans had always made up a small percentage of Brownfield and their numbers had actually declined over the decades, from 25 residents in 1900 to 6 in 1940.[45]

What distinguished Brownfield from other California communities was its Yugoslavian (Croatian and Serbian) population. More paradoxical was the extent to which the Slavs became major players in the community at a relatively early period. That is, while there was a national xenophobic climate predominating in the United States during the late nineteenth and early twentieth centuries, Slavic immigrants were able to integrate themselves successfully into the mainstream of Brownfield life and prospered economically. It was ironic because Stanford University professor Ellwood P. Cubberley was writing extensively about the threats of the Southern and Eastern European immigrants. Cubberley claimed that most were coming "from countries where popular education and popular government have as yet made little headway," and that Southern and Eastern Europeans lacked "initiative and self-reliance . . . [and the] . . . Anglo-Teutonic conception of government."[46] From Cubberley's perspective, only Anglo Americans were to be trusted and able to make significant contributions to American society.

But not all scholars were as negative toward Southern and Eastern Europeans. Sociologist Emory Bogardus, in fact, claimed that "Serbo-Croatians" were among the "best specimens of physical manhood that have come to the United States in the past fifty years." Bogardus explained that their "[r]ugged strength and crude morality [were their] outstanding characteristics."[47] Within this context, Slavs, in the eyes of many Anglo Americans in Brownfield, were perceived as hard-working people with promising futures and with strong possibilities to become assimilated into the town's mainstream. The Slavic contribution to Brownfield became one of the most remarkable success stories in the United States.[48]

Table 2.3. *Brownfield Population, 1900–1940*

Year	Total-Population	Native-White	Foreign-White	Foreign-Mix	Asian	Black
1900	3,528	. . .	. . .	. . .	74	25
1910	4,446	2,147	900	1,208	184	07
1920	5,013	2,289	883	1,416	414	11
1930	8,344	4,227	1,098	2,024	978	17
1940	8,937	8,088	1,074	. . .	806	06

Source: U. S. Bureau of the Census. See note[45] for details.

According to writer Jack London, Brownfield Slavs started out as common laborers in the fruit industry, they worked their way up to become owners of large apple orchards, and, by 1910, came to dominate the fruit industry in the area. This success was seen as one of the most impressive agricultural demonstrations in California. London wrote: "I'll show you what can be done with the soil and not by cow-college graduates, but by uneducated foreigners the high and mighty American has always sneered at." The Slavs labored in the fruit harvest and "began, in a small way, buying the apples on the trees. The more money they made the bigger became their deals." Within a short period of time, they started "renting the orchards on long leases, and now, they are beginning to buy the land." In 1913 London predicted that the Slavs would one day "own the whole valley" because, he said, many of them were "worth a quarter of a million already." It was more than incentive, London concluded: These "Adriatic Slavs are long-headed in business. Not only can they grow apples, but they can sell apples. No market? What does that matter? Make a market. That's their way."[49]

Slavic immigrants quickly carved out their niche in the town's economic structure. Unlike many places in the United States where Southern and Eastern Europeans were met with suspicion and mistrust, the Slavic immigrants were generally accepted by the larger Anglo community and admired for their work ethic and industry.[50] As early as 1914, Slavic business leaders were being commended for their economic contributions to the town. One Slavic leader, for example, was being honored by local Anglo businessmen for building one of the "most modern and up-to-date business blocks in the state." The commentary to the larger community was that Slavs were making serious investments in Brownfield, that their endeavors were resulting "in a building boom in the city," that their undertakings were stimulating "business and capital in the community," and, more important, that it was up to the "citizens of the valley [to] show their appreciation."[51]

Becoming part of the mainstream in Brownfield became an important goal for many Slavs. Slavic leaders made it their business to Americanize their compatriots as soon as they arrived. Holding its first meeting in February 1912, a local group of Slavic leaders planned to "educate the Croatian-Serbian people of the valley to acquire the true American spirit and also to elevate them in a moral as well as intellectual way." The group was commended for its Americanization efforts and the local newspaper "hoped that the new club will lead to [the] front."[52] The acceptance of Slavic immigrants by the Anglo American community, and by those who had already become important figures in the community, provided a smooth transition for other Slavic newcomers. In addition to the apple industry, they started small businesses, built hotels, and opened automobile dealerships. Moreover, they expanded the fruit industry in the areas of packing, canning, and, later, cold storage.[53]

Southern California was experiencing a large-scale influx of Mexican immigrants during the early twentieth century. During this period, however, their numbers were quite small in Brownfield. Table 2.4 shows that the Mexican American population in Brownfield grew from approximately 3.3 percent in 1900 to 8.4 percent in 1940.[54] Like other agricultural communities in the state which were becoming more dependent on cheap Mexican labor, Brownfield was also beginning to face a serious labor market problem: Local white farmers were challenging national policies that tried to restrict Mexican labor while other white residents were voicing serious concerns about the Mexican presence.[55] Some members of the white community seemed to tolerate Mexicans as long as they remained on the margins of community life. Others were not as generous, arguing that Mexicans were harmful to the local economy. Local attitudes had it that when Mexicans and whites worked side by side one of two things occurred: "either white labor has, therefore, to work for a wage which will not support a white man, to say nothing of a family, in even bare decency. Or else the Mexican laborer is getting a good wage—and carrying it all out of the country!" Critics were convinced that it was best to discourage Mexican immigrants from coming to Brownfield. From their perspective, they preferred to attract "wholesome peoples" from Europe who could successfully amalgamate with the community.[56]

But unlike the 1920s and 1930s, when public opinion in the state was openly hostile to Mexican workers, the impact of the labor shortage during the war years changed the local political climate. The labor shortage became so severe that many Brownfield farmers feared Mexican workers would leave before completing the harvest. The press drew parallels between Mexican workers and U. S. soldiers, communicating their view to the public that both groups were "away from home in a land

Table 2.4. *Whites, Mexican Americans, and Other Minorities in Brownfield; 1900–1940*

Year	Total Population	Percent White	Mex-Am	Percent Mex-Am	Percent Asian & Black
1900	3,528	93.9	118	3.3	2.8
1910	4,446	92.5	146	3.3	4.2
1920	5,013	...	...	...	8.4
1930	8,344	...	...	...	11.9
1940	8,937	82.6	757	8.4	9.0

Source: U. S. Bureau of the Census. See note[54] for details.

where language and customs differ from their own." What differentiated the groups, however, was that "men in the armed forces are not allowed to go home, where the Mexican can break his contract and go back to his native land." Business leaders recognized that a permanent supply of Mexican labor was necessary for the town's economic survival and future prosperity.[57] In the postwar years, Mexicans not only continued to come to Brownfield to work, but many began to establish permanent roots. This trend began to change the sociopolitical structure of the community and, later, its schools.

The expansion of public schools in the greater Brownfield community reflected the town's overall growth. Between 1859 and 1907, twenty-three schools were constructed in Brownfield and in its surrounding suburban and unincorporated communities. Although some schools closed during the later years of the nineteenth century, ten more were built between 1916 and 1946.[58] Enrollment data did not become available until the mid-1940s. County records indicate that the Brownfield area experienced dramatic enrollment growth. Figures show that between kindergarten and the twelfth grade, Brownfield public school enrollments grew from 3,291 in 1944 to 5,554 in 1954, and from 6,927 in 1960 to 10,307 in 1965.[59] It was noted in Chapter 1 that in many communities Mexican American school enrollments in elementary level schools were much higher than at the high school level, and that very few went beyond the upper elementary and junior high school. Within this context, it was very difficult to attain racial/ethnic data at the elementary level because such records were not kept at the time. A look at circumstantial evidence—high school yearbooks and the local newspaper—indicates that Mexican American enrollments were relatively small between 1940 and 1960. Table 2.5 shows that Mexican American high school enrollments (grades 9–12) grew from 1.9 percent in 1940 to 7.7 percent in 1960.[60] Similarly, Mexican American high school graduates rose from 1.4 percent (3) in 1940 to 5.0 percent (16) in 1960. At the junior high school level, their numbers were larger. In Brownfield's largest junior high school (grades 7–8), Mexican Americans made up 9.3 percent of the 149 students in the eighth grade graduating

Table 2.5. *Mexican American High School Percentages and Graduation numbers in Brownfield High, 1940–1960*

Year	Total High School Enrolmt	Percent Mex-Am	Total High School Grads	Total Mex-Am High School Grads
1940	858	1.9	295	3
1950	1438	6.5	309	4
1960	1676	7.7	316	16

Source: Various sources. See note[60] for details.

class in 1954. In another school (grades K–8), their eighth grade graduation percentage grew from 10.7 percent (out of 28 graduates) in 1940 to 26.5 percent (out of 49 graduates) in 1954.[61] It is important to note that in 1940 Mexican Americans represented 8.4 percent of the town's population, yet Mexican American students represented just 1.9 percent of total enrollments at the high school and only three had actually graduated.

THE POLITICS OF CONSOLIDATION

In addition to the curricular and pedagogical reforms that were taking place during the early twentieth century, the organization of American public schools also began to change. "Administrative progressives" wanted to remake loosely structured school systems into unified districts that were more efficient and cost effective. School districts throughout the nation were being encouraged to "consolidate" with their neighbors. The consolidation movement grew from conditions where many small rural school districts were unable to offer the full range of curricula in graded classes. Many rural children did not have the same educational opportunities as students in city schools. The idea behind the consolidation movement maintained that larger school districts would generate higher teacher salaries, bestow status on educators, yield administrative efficiency, and generate a tax base where minimum educational standards were met.[62] In the words of David Tyack, consolidators wanted to

> replace confused and erratic means of control with careful allocations of powers and functions within hierarchical organizations; to establish networks of communication that would convey information and directives and would provide data for planning for the future; to substitute impersonal rules for informal, individual adjudication of disputes; to regulate procedures so that they would apply uniformly to certain categories; and to set objective standards for admissions to and performance in each role, whether superintendent or third-grader.[63]

To accomplish this, geographic boundaries were broadened, educational administration was centralized, and smaller school districts were unified with larger school systems.[64] Table 2.6 shows the effect of the consolidation movement during the first half of the twentieth century.[65] The number of school districts was reduced from 128,000 in 1930 to 16,960 in 1972. One-room schools, moreover, decreased from 149,000 to 1,475 during the same time frame.

Some reformers viewed consolidation as progressive and equated it with modernization. Others expressed serious reservations because the

Table 2.6. *Number of School Districts and One-Teacher Schools in the United States, 1930–1972*

Year	School Districts	One-Teacher Schools
1930	128,000	149,000
1940	117,000	114,000
1950	84,000	60,000
1960	40,000	20,000
1970	18,000	2,000
1972	16,960	1,475

Source: Sher, J. P., and Tomkins, R. (1976), "The Myths of Rural School District Consolidation: Part 1," *Educational Forum* 4, p. 96.

reform meant forming larger school systems and unifying with neighboring districts.[66] This situation became problematic for some communities as they feared coming in "contact with objectionable moral conditions." Many communities struggled to maintain their identities, to preserve school life as it was, and they resisted the reform. But the consolidation movement as a whole triumphed nationally, and it altered the organization of the small school system.[67]

The desire to consolidate the Brownfield schools dates back to the 1920s and 1930s, when local progressives announced that some of their small rural school districts were not able to meet the demands of modern society.[68] It was foolish to have "fine modern homes and elaborate farm equipment," one resident said, but to continue to operate schools that were inadequate and too "small to do efficient work."[69] Local progressives complained that children left school before graduation, that many were being required to repeat a grade each year, that teacher turnover was high, and that some schools were in dire need of physical repair. Reformers publicly stated that they looked "forward to the time when rural school people will rise to the occasion of demanding better educational opportunities" for their children.[70]

But the consolidation discourse in Brownfield during the 1920s took place at a very superficial level. It was not until the 1930s and 1940s that state officials began to press local school districts to consolidate. The California State Superintendent of Schools, Vierling Kersey, ordered county school administrators across the state to conduct "unification studies." The purpose of these studies was to determine whether "districts favorably located, could come under the same administration to benefit all concerned."[71] As a result of forcing school systems to determine whether consolidation produced more efficiency and cost effectiveness, many school systems unified while others resisted. Those resisting mainly came from communities that were concerned about losing their voices in "the enlargement of unit supervision."[72]

Brownfield made a small step toward unification between 1940 and 1941. The Brownfield Elementary School District initiated a move to incorporate two small rural schools from the southern end of the district, in an adjacent county. Even though the schools were located outside the county line, board members from the elementary district maintained that the schools "logically belong" to the Brownfield Elementary School District.[73] Although the schools were consolidated with little initial controversy, more interest was aroused in ensuing years. A proposal to unify several small rural school districts, in fact, was held up in subsequent years by County Superintendent Edith Fink. Rallying around educational equity issues, county consolidators were adamant about providing small rural schools the same "advantages given pupils in the city schools." If people voted in favor of unification, county officials pledged to improve rural schools, including the curriculum, playgrounds, and transportation.[74] The decision to unify ten school districts into two larger systems came up for vote on January 18, 1946. Table 2.7 shows that the proposal was favored in Brownfield's Eastern Foothills by 91.6 percent of the voters. Support by the Northeastern part of the district was not as high, but it did pass with 68.7 percent of the vote.[75]

Table 2.7. *Unification Election in 1946: The Formation of the Eastern Foothills and Northern School Districts*

Eastern Foothills					
School District	Total	Yes	% Yes	No	% No
Number 1	35	33	94.2	2	5.8
Number 2	25	19	76.0	6	24.0
Number 3	9	7	77.7	2	22.3
Number 4	31	30	96.7	1	3.3
Number 5	31	31	100.0	0	00.0
Total	**131**	**120**	**91.6**	**11**	**8.4**
Northeast School District					
School District	Total	Yes	% Yes	No	% No
Number 6	49	45	91.8	4	8.2
Number 7	31	20	64.5	11	35.5
Number 8	21	5	23.8	16	76.2
Number 9	30	18	60.0	12	40.0
Number 10	93	66	70.9	26	29.1
Total	**224**	**154**	**68.7**	**69**	**31.3**

Source: The Brownfieldite, January 19, 1946.

County officials were pleased with the results of the consolidation proposal, but remained unsatisfied because too many small districts remained separate and autonomous. From their perspective, it was ludicrous to allow numerous school systems in the area to repeat the same administrative tasks. Under one large school system, they believed, the chain of command would become centralized, powers and functions would be organized hierarchically, and schools would become more efficient. Two years later, however, the desire to consolidate all the schools under one system drew fire and stirred a great deal of contention. Even though ethnic politics in schools was not an issue in the area, communities did vary in size, in socioeconomic status, and in the ratio of rural versus town folk. As such, each community started to question the consolidation reform in its own terms; they wanted more information to confirm that unification was best, and they wanted additional time to think about it. Unlike the 1946 consolidation election that passed without much debate, people from different communities in Brownfield were now forming "battle lines [against] the proposal to consolidate 10 elementary school districts under one five-member board administration."[76]

Consolidators stressed that the reform was best because a single tax rate would improve the quality of all schools. Children in poorer school districts would have the same access to a quality education as students in more affluent areas. Moreover, children were more likely to attend schools conveniently located. As for teachers, salary schedules and tenure processes would become standardized. School transfers would become simplified, and the reform allowed for the construction of a new junior high school. Critics from many sides, however, envisioned a number of problems. They anticipated higher administrative costs, an overly standardized curriculum, problems with busing (that is, children leaving for school earlier and returning home later), teacher transfers carried out at the board's will, school closures dictated by a powerful centralized school administration that would be unfamiliar with the culture of individual schools, and the risk that the academic standards of "better" schools would be "lowered to an overall average."[77]

Some people were concerned with issues of power and control. Others feared a dilution of academic quality and standards. In short, the question was how they were going to provide equitable schooling opportunities within a socioeconomically diverse community. Joe Chambers, a school board member from a small school district outside Brownfield, in fact pointed out that some "districts are more fortunate than others from a financial standpoint." Within the context of educational equity, Chambers asked if it was not better "for all children to enter high school with an equal chance?" He asked: Was it just for "a child born in a poorer

Table 2.8. *Unification Election in 1948*

District	Total	Yes	% Yes	No	% No
Brownfield Elementary (4 schools)	494	71	14.4	423	85.6
Eastern Foothills (5 schools)	242	25	10.4	217	89.6
Northeastern (6 schools)	144	19	13.2	125	86.8
Eagle	143	7	4.9	136	95.1
Pleasant Hill	47	4	12.3	43	87.7
Polo	260	11	4.3	249	95.7
Coral	156	10	6.5	146	93.5
Prairie	210	17	6.1	193	93.9
Stewart	118	17	14.5	101	85.5
Summerfield	36	4	11.2	32	88.8
Total	**1,850**	**185**	**11.8**	**1,665**	**88.2**

Source: The Brownfieldite, December 4, 1948.

district [to] suffer educational difficulties simply because he was born or has moved into a geographical location with a low assessment?"[78] Despite several well-planned attempts to promote consolidation, resistance persisted, people's qualms were too manifold and strong, and the move to unify failed on December 3, 1948. Table 2.8 shows 85.5 to 95.7 percent of the citizens opposed the unification. Local progressives were unable to convince the public that the consolidation of schools in Brownfield would be "large enough to be educationally adequate and economically efficient, yet small enough to retain popular interest and control to effectuate lay participation and lay leadership."[79]

Even though the school consolidation movement was taking its inexorable course in the United States, as the number of school districts declined from approximately 128,000 in 1930 to 40,000 in 1960, it came to a sudden standstill in Brownfield in 1948. Reform was met with effective resistance and became dormant for several years. State officials in California, however, continued to promote the reform because too many small school systems were failing to serve their children.

CONSOLIDATION IN THE 1960s

Educational historian and rural school specialist Jonathan Sher proclaimed that by 1960 consolidation had ceased to be a legitimate political issue for debate. Unification was no longer perceived as an educational reform "championed solely by the progressive elements of society" but had become an "accepted educational standard supported by the full range of the educational profession [and] by the mainstream of American society."[80] If unification became an accepted national educational standard, then the

Brownfield community was an anomaly, as the issue became even more controversial in the 1960s than in the 1940s. As we saw, the politics of consolidation in 1948 was based on a discourse centered on social class differences, power relations between rural and city folk, and uncertainty about administrative centralization. By the late 1950s, however, Brownfield was becoming more diverse. The Mexican American population, in fact, had grown from about 8.8 percent in 1950 (total population, 11,374) to 17.0 percent (total population, 13,293) in 1960.[81]

Even though ethnicity was not playing a significant role in Brownfield's consolidation debate, it was common folk conversation among local citizens. "In some small farming communities there were mostly white country kids," said local resident Phyllis Peninsular, "and then you come to [Brownfield] and you have completely different people. You have a lot of Mexicans."[82] Residents in surrounding communities, especially in the north, realized that Brownfield was changing. The level of concern, however, was low because they were located far enough from Brownfield to maintain a separate identity, yet near enough to take advantage of the town's tax base. Butch Tabasco, a middle school teacher, recalled that some communities "did not have the population base Brownfield had. They were suffering in terms of not having materials and buildings. By forming a unified school district," said Tabasco, "they found those accesses were now available. They could improve without going to a local tax base."[83]

Unification became more appealing to some people in the smaller suburbs and unincorporated communities because it was economically advantageous, that is, they would benefit from access to a larger tax base. Others refused to consolidate because it meant giving up autonomy to a larger school system. Losing power became such an issue that by the late 1950s organized resistance, led by prominent business leaders and members of small school boards emerged. Fred Bancoff, a school board member from the affluent Atherton community, and Harry Lynn, president of the Atherton Improvement Association, immediately challenged the plan to unify with Brownfield. Bancoff claimed that people in Atherton opposed unification and Lynn affirmed that residents in the community were "perfectly satisfied" with their schools.[84] Although Atherton was becoming an affluent resort community, it did not possess a strong commercial tax base. As residents began to discuss the limits and possibilities of reform, some looked to the economic advantages while others expressed serious reservations about merging with a school system that was becoming very different from their own. Bancoff and Lynn opposed the reform to the extent that they demanded that the county remove Atherton from the unification study. The county superintendent, Norman Leinberg, immediately responded to the business leaders. He said that no one in the area had the "privilege to withdraw [from the consolidation study] by stating so publicly."[85] He reiterated that he was simply ordered by the state to find ways to equalize the schools in the area, to coordinate the curriculum from the elementary grades to the high school, and to install a stronger philosophy of education.[86] But whatever the alleged benefits were, Bancoff and Lynn continued to demand exemption. County officials denied their appeal, claiming that they did not have the power to exempt themselves.[87]

Despite the anticonsolidation sentiment in the surrounding communities, some school board members from the Brownfield Elementary School District began to discuss other possibilities. Elementary school board members Mickels and Alexanderson claimed they were willing "to give favorable consideration to a survey relating to possible advantages of unification with" other schools in the area.[88] Although consolidation studies may have been mandated by the state, the decision to unify ultimately rested on local elections. The press, however, gave the impression that consolidation was mandated. Counties throughout the state were ordered to complete unification master plans by September 15, 1963. If communities refused to carry out the mandate, one local resident said, the state had "sufficient power in the legislature's control over school funds to see that unification is carried out."[89] With this in mind, many residents believed unification was policy. In one specific example, local resident Phyllis Peninsular said state officials told a group of local residents that unification was mandatory. "They told us we had to unify," said Peninsular, "that we could not have all these little schools around." State officials told residents that unification was the only way the schools in Brownfield were going to be equitable and cost efficient.[90]

Over time, many residents began to view the concept in a more favorable light. In addition to tax equity and cost efficiency arguments, consolidators maintained that the reform would enrich the district's curriculum and extend additional instructional services to students with special needs. In the Atherton area, however, a group of parents calling themselves the Small School Association (SSA) began to challenge county officials. The group said that under unification, a board of trustees "from outside your vanished school district will decide where the children go to school . . . what sort of school it is . . . what kind of teachers will teach them and how much taxes will be paid."[91] Though the SSA had raised historically familiar objections, newspaper reporters hinted that their resistance was also entangled with the fact that schools in Brownfield were becoming more diverse. Parents were nervous about unifying with schools where there were "substantial cultural and social differences."[92]

Some Atherton parents became so concerned that they petitioned for district boundary changes to avoid unifying with Brownfield. And as the pressure toward unification intensified, these parents requested consolidation with an adjacent school district farther to the north.[93] Since Atherton had an institutional history that linked them to the Brownfield schools, especially at the high school level, county officials said it was simpler and less expensive to consolidate Atherton with Brownfield. County Superintendent Leinberg spoke to approximately seventy white middle-class parents from surrounding communities before the consolidation election was held. He explained that unification had become a national strategy to equalize public schools. Parents replied that consolidation was fine for schools that needed to have their standards raised. But what about, they asked, the schools that "would be lowered to meet the uniform level." Leinberg replied that he could not understand "why students from a wealthier district should have a better free public education than ones from poorer districts."[94] He added that consolidation was not "communism," as one misinformed person in the community called it, but a way to provide everyone with a better "free" public education.[95]

As the unification election drew closer, residents pointed out that data revealed that unification was less cost-effective than county consolidators had hypothesized.[96] Many residents, however, came to realize that the reform would produce better schooling opportunities for their children.[97] Table 2.9 shows that unification won with 57 percent of the vote, and the Brownfield Unified School District was born. The results also show that communities were divided. Those voting against the proposal ranged from 41.3 to 58.4 percent; those supporting it ranged from 41.6 to 58.7 percent.[98]

Like most school systems in the state that had consolidated, Brownfield was expected to organize a new school system within a few months, by July 1965. The community had to elect a school board, hire a superintendent, and make numerous curricular and administrative adjustments. The Brownfield school system and the communities it served witnessed an enormous amount of competition for school board seats. Twenty-seven

Table 2.9. *Unification Voting Results in Brownfield, 1964*

District	Total	Yes	No	% Yes	% No
Northeastern	1,890	1,055	835	55.8	44.2
Coral	504	210	294	41.6	58.4
Eastern Foothills	850	424	426	49.8	50.2
Atherton	3,192	1,712	1,480	53.6	46.4
Brownfield (outside the city)	480	282	198	58.7	41.3
Brownfield (inside the city)	4,021	2,600	1,421	64.6	35.4
Total	**10,937**	**6,283**	**4,654**	**57.4**	**42.6**

Source: The Brownfieldite, November 4, 1964.

candidates competed for five seats. Of these numbers, twenty were white males, seven white females, and none were minorities. After the candidates competed, three males and two females won seats on the new school board. More important, the new school board membership consisted of a middle- and upper-middle-class group with strong ties to the town's social, political, and economic structures.[99]

As the new school district began to serve the larger community, the board was instantly confronted with several issues. The district was underfunded, enrollments were soaring, and the Mexican American student population was increasing at a disproportionate rate. More compelling was the number of schools where Mexican American children represented more than fifty percent.[100] As Mexican American children become increasingly visible in some schools, the local paper pointed out their problems, including poverty and academic failure, their inability to speak English, and that many were isolated from their white peers. Local educational professionals, the press noted, have "in limited ways . . . tried to meet the challenge." It was clear that school officials in Brownfield were not giving much attention to the academic needs of their growing Mexican American student clientele. But the local newspaper editor made reference to the fact that educational professionals were in a much better position to deal with the problem because the schools were now consolidated.[101]

CONCLUSION

At the time the Brownfield Unified School District was formed, the United States was experiencing dramatic change. Steering the Civil Rights Act through Congress and signing it into law on July 2, 1964, President Lyndon B. Johnson delivered his most idealistic promise: to grant all Americans their rights in employment, politics, and education. In his sweeping campaign for an all-out "War on Poverty," Johnson envisioned a "Great Society" in which all citizens had an equal chance to realize the American dream. Part of his plan was the allocation of federal funds under the Elementary and Secondary Education Act (ESEA) of 1965 to raise the achievement level of disadvantaged youth.[102] Calling for better schooling opportunities for Mexican American children in the Brownfield schools, the local press proclaimed that "all of our youngsters, of whatever race or background, deserve the same chance in school to acquire an education. If new [ESEA] funds make it possible for Mexican American children from non-English-speaking homes, who are every bit as bright as their school mates, to compete on an equal basis," the press continued, "then the entire community will stand to benefit."[103] But reforming the school district to meet the needs of Mexican American youth was not a pressing issue for local educational professionals and the new school board during this period. District administrators were more interested in devising a top-down approach to communication, a consolidated means of authority with careful allocations of powers and functions, and improved governance with clearly defined polices and practices.

Although many people in the greater Brownfield area were reluctant to create one large school system, in the end the quality of the school buildings was improved and a wider and more current curriculum was offered. Throughout the nation, wrote Tyack, the "new educational standards [under unification] reflected an increasingly cosmopolitan rather than local scale of values among schoolmen who sought to blur the differences between district and district, county and county, and even state and state."[104] One can argue that consolidation inadvertently came to offer better schooling opportunities for Mexican American children. Now that several small school districts had become part of Brownfield Unified School District, there was an institutional possibility (although it did not immediately occur) for Mexican American children to attend other schools in the district. The Mexican American community, moreover, now had a legitimate claim to schools they historically did not attend.[105] But providing Mexican Americans with better opportunities was hardly a goal in the consolidation movement. Unification had created other unintended consequences in Brownfield by paving the way for a serious discourse between Mexican Americans and school authorities about the distribution of districtwide educational equity, power, and control among Mexican Americans and affluent communities. In short, the consolidation movement, as a byproduct, had progressive consequences for the Mexican American community that were altogether apart from the typical claims of the reform.

THREE

Emergence of Grassroots Activism

Conflict is the best word to describe the civil rights era of the 1960s. Protest became a conventional method for social, political, and economic redress. People from different backgrounds were taking part in a cultural revolution that was changing American life. The Black Power movement, the Vietnam war, and the struggles of women and minority groups accelerated the unravelling of any sense of American consensus. In the midst of these social movements, Mexican Americans were becoming politically active throughout the Southwest. This period of enormous change inspired Mexican Americans to challenge the politics, assumptions, and principles of the established social order. "[P]olitical activists," noted historian Juan Gomez-Quiñones, "became increasingly concerned with understanding how economic and class exploitation and racism had shaped the Mexican American experience in the United States."[1] In addition, they looked to a cultural renaissance that fostered pride in their ethnic background, language, and history. Some Chicano intellectuals emerged during this period, as they found literary expression in their scholarly journals, political organizations, and academic meetings.[2] Others joined the effort of Cesar Chavez to organize and unionize Mexican farm workers. There were those who joined the Raza Unida Party, founded and led by Jose Angel Gutierrez in 1970, and those who joined Rodolfo "Corky" Gonzalez's Crusade for Justice in Denver, Colorado. Chicano youth were in the forefront of social change. Their political identity was charged with optimism that U.S. society could be reformed. For example, many Chicanos were drawn to the "Spiritual Plan of Aztlan," which claimed that the American Southwest was the home of their forefathers, that they did not recognize capricious boundaries formed by Anglo invaders, that the "Bronze Continent" belonged to the indigenous people who worked the land, and that the spiritual plan was "the only road to total liberation from oppression, exploitation, and racism."[3]

In a similar vein to the Plan of Aztlan, some Chicano youth were influenced by Armando Rendon's *Chicano Manifesto*. Rendon held that American society was but "a bastard issued from the promiscuous concubinage of several hundred of ethnic and racial people who have cast their cultural identities into the American melting pot." He portrayed North American culture as "callous, vindictive, arrogant, militaristic, self-deceiving, and greedy."[4] Chicano thought, however, was probably most clearly expressed in Rodolfo Gonzales's epic poem entitled *I Am Joaquin*. The poem was a social statement of the Chicano experience in the United States. In the words of Gonzales:

> I am Joaquin, lost in a world of confusion, caught up in the whirl of a gringo society, confused by the rules, scored by attitudes, suppressed by manipulation, and destroyed by modern society. My fathers have lost the economic battle and won the struggle of cultural survival. And now! I must choose between the paradox of the victory of the spirit, despite physical hunger, or to exist in the grasp of American social neurosis, sterilization of the soul and a full stomach.[5]

Gonzales despised technical civilization, abhorred capitalism, repudiated the technical and industrial giant called progress, and refused to be absorbed by a nation that rejected him. Though the poem represented only one of the many strands in early Chicano thought, his work was read by scholars, activists, and students alike.

Though Mexican Americans were concerned with larger issues of social justice, many focused their attention on the quality of their schools. They were convinced that social justice was linked to the extent to which their children were able to acquire a good education. Public schools, however, were oriented toward the white middle-class community. Moreover, Mexican American communities lacked sufficient political hegemony to be taken seriously by their schools. As Mario Fantini and Marilyn Gittell claimed, white middle-class communities were served well because "their values were shared" with educational professionals. In addition, public schools had distinctive problems sharing power with the poor, the working class, and racial and ethnic minorities.[6]

During this period, scholars such as Frederick Wirt and Michael Kirst began to provide different ways of understanding the political web of school and community.[7] From Wirt and Kirst's perspective, there seemed to be a blindness or indifference reinforced by conventional wisdom that "schools had somehow been sanitized against politics."[8] Within this context, school-community studies entered into the educational literature. One of the most important studies at the time was written by Donald McCarty and Charles Ramsey. They showed how power was wielded in different school systems and communities, specifically in their classification of community power structures, types of school boards, and the styles of superintendents. They further argued that the type of community power structure determined the nature of school board types and the administrative styles of superintendents.[9]

McCarty and Ramsey's work, however, was criticized. William Boyd, for example, claimed that instead of public schools being dominated by powerful community elites, educational policymaking was typically controlled by influential school administrators at the top.[10] Harmon Zeigler and Harvey Tucker documented how the American lay public was generally excluded from educational policymaking, finding that superintendents initiated nearly half of all discussions and that "educational professionals account for nearly 70 percent of the agenda; school board members control 24 percent of agendas, members of the public 7 percent, and representatives of other governments less than 1 percent."[11] Their main points were that educational policymaking was almost always restricted to those inside the school system. Joseph McGiveny and James Haught found that central administrations, mostly middle managers, resisted input from the public and tried to maintain control over most educational policies.[12] They found that the most important need of central administrators was to see themselves in control of situations.

Despite school administrators' actions to exclude the lay public across the nation, Fantini and Gittell described how some communities challenged traditional roles of lay participation, the mutually supportive roles of white middle-class associations with schools, and the political practices that denied poor and minority people access "to determine or influence policy decisions that affected them."[13] Public schools became entangled with ethnic politics because, in part, they had failed to achieve what was required by the civil rights legislation of 1964—namely to rid the schools of racial/ethnic discrimination and to provide equal educational opportunity. With increased participation by ethnic minorities came new issues, new challenges, and new forms of participation. But although the federal government instituted mechanisms to encourage parents who had been on the fringes of educational policymaking, the record of institutional participation through Title I Parent Advisory Councils, Follow-Through Councils, and Bilingual Parent Councils, for example, was yielding poor results.[14] While there is a large body of research on the issue of minority parent participation in educational policymaking, especially in large urban school systems, very little exists on the Mexican American experience.

To the extent that most Mexican American communities lacked political power within their school systems, very few scholars have documented the ways in which some were able to challenge local educational power structures during the civil rights era. Those few that have are important in that they have provided insights into how Mexican American communities gained the knowledge, the experience, and the resources necessary to be taken seriously in their attempt to shape local schools after their own vision. This chapter examines the mobilization of Mexican Americans, their quest for equal schools, and, with this context in mind, looks at how school officials and the white community responded to their demands and pressures. Moreover, it looks at how their efforts in Brownfield differed from those in other districts.

WAKING THE SLEEPING GIANT

Although Mexican Americans numbered more than five million in the Southwest during the late 1960s, they were, as Helen Rowan put it, "A minority nobody knows."[15] Their invisibility seemed ironic because most were living in "conditions that are worse in every respect than those of [other] nonwhites in America." Substandard housing, high unemployment, and low educational attainment characterized life for a large percentage of the Mexican American population in the United States. What was especially remarkable about this situation was not just that such conditions existed but how little was known about it. Rowan wrote that in "California Mexican Americans outnumber Negroes by almost two to one but probably not one Californian in ten thousand knows that simple fact." Despite their numbers and the social conditions of Mexican Americans, very few white Americans in the 1960s were discussing the issues that related to them. The news media gave little attention to their plight, politicians ignored their conditions and, reported Rowan, even "do-good organizations" focused their interests on other problems.[16]

Within this atmosphere of neglect, Mexican American communities began to organize, they started to demand better educational opportunities, and they even called for specific curricular and pedagogical reforms.[17] In East Los Angeles, the largest Mexican American community in the United States, parents formed a group in 1963 called the "Mexican American Education Committee." Before bilingual-bicultural education became a heated issue in American society, these parents were calling for specific reforms: for boards of education in the area to recognize their children's language and culture; for the teaching of Spanish at the elementary level; and for the inclusion of the history and literature of Mexico and other Latin American countries in the curriculum. Moreover, parents pressed school professionals to develop unbiased testing instruments that assessed their children. More important was their desire to "recruit, hire, and place bilingual teachers, counselors, and administrators [who understood] the Mexican-American child" in their schools.[18]

It was not until President Lyndon B. Johnson's administration that the federal government began to direct some attention to the plight of the Mexican American. Some Mexican American leaders wanted national visibility, "preferably through the lens of a White House Conference [that] focused on their many problems."[19] Demanding their fair share of the Great Society programs, they pushed for reforms that were "specifically designed for Mexican Americans."[20] Acknowledging that public schools were perhaps not serving Mexican American children as well as whites, the U. S. Office of Education created a Mexican-American Affairs Unit to find out how Mexican American children were faring in U. S. public schools. Directed by Armando Rodriguez, the unit was intended to coordinate and improve educational opportunities for Mexican American children in the Southwest. The task was to coordinate federal, state, and local officials to develop culturally and linguistically relevant curricula and pedagogy, special training for teachers, and various social services to meet the educational needs of Mexican American youth. Though the unit held only an advisory role, it was one of the few instances where the federal government dealt specifically with the schooling of Mexican American children.[21]

The Mexican American Affairs Unit viewed the plight of Mexican American youth with a sense of urgency. Although they already knew that Mexican American children were being underserved in many schools, they discovered that in Texas 80 percent fell two grades behind their Anglo class mates, most were leaving school in their junior high school years, and 89 percent were not completing high school. In California, 50 percent of Mexican American youth dropped out by the tenth and eleventh grades and, although they made up 14 percent of school enrollments in the state, they represented 40 percent of enrollments in "mentally handicapped" classes. In addition, Mexican American enrollments in the seven University of California campuses made up less than 0.5 percent.[22] As a response, California State Superintendent of Public Instruction Max Rafferty began to investigate the status of Mexican American education. State Assistant Superintendent Eugene Gonzalez was instructed by Rafferty to begin strategies to improve schooling opportunities for Mexican American youth, such as collaboration between schools and social services, curriculum and pedagogy, and ethnic relations. Among several projects focusing on curricular and instructional materials, Gonzalez pushed for research in technical assistance for specific school districts. While some members of Gonzalez's research team began serving certain school districts, they started to collect data to determine the extent of the problems Mexican American children were facing in schools.[23]

The Gonzalez research team surveyed 896 California school districts during 1966 and 1967. They found that 86 percent of the districts lacked programs for students with limited English proficiency, 68.5 percent failed to conduct regularly scheduled conferences between Mexican American parents and teachers, 80 percent had inadequate financial resources to serve migrant children, more than 50 percent of teachers were not qualified to work with these students, and 77 percent of district professionals did not participate in activities to help them prepare curricular materials for Mexican American children. Though school officials in these districts confessed that little was being done to serve Mexican American children, they absolved themselves of responsibility for this situation. They claimed that it was the students' poor home environment, nutritional deficiency, low aspirations, and unpredictable residency that contributed to their school failure.[24] The stereotype was that Mexican American parents were not interested in educating their children.[25]

In response to these inequalities, educational reformers in California began to organize special conferences to discuss the schooling of Mexican Americans. Eugene Gonzalez, John Plakos, and other members of the Mexican American Education Research Project held one conference in Lake Arrowhead in August 1966 and another in Anaheim in April 1967.[26] The purpose of the conferences was to promote the academic success of Mexican American youth and to explore strategies and programs to enlighten school boards about their educational needs. Conference organizers claimed that the educational standing of the Mexican American child was so poor that if something was not done immediately it was going to be a serious "loss to society as a whole." Some believed that mainstream curriculum and instruction were the major problems. Others claimed that real changes were not possible until teacher education programs were reformed. And there were those who felt that ethnic relations needed to improve before schools could be ameliorated.[27]

Educators at the Lakewood and Anaheim conferences were ideologically split about how to school Mexican American children. Some wanted to assimilate Mexican youth at all costs, convinced that it was wrong to keep "these children 'Mexican'" in the United States. They called for "total assimilation without reference to Mexican cultural traits, traditions, or values."[28] But there were those who felt it was essential to make "the Mexican cultural heritage known to its pupils as a form of educational enrichment." This perspective took the view that cultural and linguistic difference was an asset and that its elimination "would be a gross error and waste on the part of the United States." Mexican American educators supported the idea of taking "'Mexican' cultural traits and values into account when planning educational programs for these students." But the question became how white middle-class teachers were going to foster learning environments that allowed Mexican American children to "adapt successfully to a different culture without destroying their bilingual ability and without making them feel ashamed of the word 'Mexican.' "[29]

At about the same time the Lake Arrowhead and Anaheim conferences were held, a California State Advisory Committee to the U. S. Commission on Civil Rights was conducting meetings with minority communities. In East Los Angeles, state officials found enormous differences between Mexican and white student experiences. The number of school years completed for Spanish-surnamed persons, for example, was 8.6 while the figure for whites was 12.1. And although the East Los Angeles community was 76 percent Mexican American, 7 percent had no formal schooling and 9 percent had completed only one year of college. The dropout rate for both groups was especially striking. At Garfield and Roosevelt high schools (on the east side), the Mexican American dropout rate ranged from 47.5 to 53.8 percent while in Monroe and Palisides (the west side), the white student dropout rate ranged from 2.6 to 3.1 percent.[30]

Mexican American parents, educators, and activists alike were convinced that the culprit behind high dropout rates was negative teacher attitudes toward Mexican American children.[31] Parents had always believed that schools in the east side were used as a dumping ground for incompetent white teachers. "We feel that we are getting second-rate teachers," Mexican American parents said, "in all the Mexican American areas." Parents knew that many white teachers resented their teaching assignments in the barrio schools. But more important, the parents resented teachers' complaints about their children's lack of ability to learn.[32] Ben Gomez, a teacher in East Los Angeles, explained that Mexican American parents had a legitimate concern about white teachers expecting less from their children. "I have heard some remarks in the teachers' room," said Gomez, "like '[T]hese Mexican kids, why do they have to be here?' "[33]

Elnore Schmadel challenged the myth that Mexican American parents did not care about their children's education. She pointed out that Mexican American parents had always tried to participate in the East Los Angeles schools, but that most schools had made them feel unwelcome. Educators often conveyed messages to Mexican American parents that they did not know enough to participate.[34] One Mexican American parent in Los Angeles said she attempted to get involved in her child's education. She stopped trying because she was either ignored or told by teachers that "they don't want you there."[35] Other Mexican American parents stayed away from schools because it was difficult for them to forget their own negative "or even miserable school experiences."[36] But there as another dimension to the problem. Coming from a sociocultural background that held teachers in high esteem, many Mexican American parents, especially recent immigrants, believed it was not their place to challenge the schools. They regarded teachers as trained professionals serving all children. Some critics came to believe that it was this "unwarranted respect for the wisdom of teachers and principals" that created so many problems and "one reason why they have allowed their children to be pushed around for so long."[37]

Los Angeles teacher Frank Serrano characterized and challenged the stereotype of Mexican American parent indifference in the following way:

> We have heard many comments about the Mexican American parents, that they are not interested in the education of their children. We have heard that they are lazy, that we cannot communicate with them. But let me be as emphatic as I may— without taking my shoe off and pounding it on the table—that the Mexican American parents are very much concerned with the education of their children.[38]

A large segment of the Mexican American population recognized that white middle-class educators viewed them as uncooperative consumers of public education. This view became deeply embedded in the culture of schools as well as part of the defensive posture of educational practitio- ners. Without actually knowing Mexican American parents and without actually hearing their point of view, teachers and administrators developed negative stereotypes that justified their exclusion.[39]

Since the early 1960s, Mexican Americans in California had been complaining to state officials that schools were not meeting the needs of Mexican American children in general and the limited English proficient (LEP) in particular. The State Department of Education responded and created the Bilingual Task Force. Its aim was to develop special programs for Mexican American LEP children, in-service training for teachers, coun- selors, and administrators, technical assistance in program evaluation, improved school-community relations, and bilingual teacher training. The goal was to implement these reforms in districts "with the highest concen- tration of Spanish-speaking youngsters and the highest percentage of such students scoring in the first quartile on statewide reading tests."[40]

Similar to the pre-*Brown* era, very few scholars were challenging conventional wisdom about Mexican American school failure. Thomas Carter, however, presented three explanations for the problem. In the first, Carter maintained that mainstream educators saw Mexican Americans as culturally deficient because their parents did not possess the cultural currency to socialize their children to succeed in schools. From this per- spective, many educators believed it was the responsibility of the school to transform Mexican American children as much as possible into average white middle-class children. Carter rejected this perspective because it meant schools had to artificially provide Mexican Americans "with those experiences that the middle-class enjoys naturally." This approach was also biased because Mexican American children would be measured by the degree to which they became more like their middle-class peers.[41] Within this context, Carter claimed that there was "no clear evidence that the school can remake the ethnically distinct child into a facsimile of the standard American child."[42]

Carter's second explanation claimed that the academic structure of schools encouraged Mexican American children to fail. He arrived at this conclusion based on his findings that many schools in the Southwest were "sustained by such common conditions as cultural exclusion, fostering too rapid Americanization, rigid tracking, curricular rigidity, rote teaching, overly rigid behavioral standards, ethnic cleavage, de facto segregation, and biased and pessimistic staffs."[43] The major task, he believed, was to transform schools to better serve the Mexican American child. Even though many educators recognized that "standard middle-class schools have failed many Mexican Americans," very few were willing to institute "programs to substantially modify curriculums, teacher attitudes, school climates, home-school relations, or other crucial areas." Educational institutions were not "flexible enough to realistically adjust to local situations," observed Carter, "and a very limited number have objectively investigated negative school social climates." Carter believed that change did not necessarily begin with curricular and pedagogical reforms, but with the preparation of teachers. From his perspective, teachers needed to be trained at a very sophisticated level. They had to understand "and grapple with the often intangible, but multitudinous, aspects of their own and others' society, culture, language, learning styles, personality, and behavior." In short, teachers needed to possess a wider understanding of school and society as it related to the Mexican American experience.[44]

Carter's third explanation received little attention in the educational literature, perhaps because it was too controversial. Carter believed that the distinctive features of the agricultural economy and caste-like community structures of the American Southwest provided limited opportunities for Mexican Americans. Similar to Gilbert Gonzalez's view that schools processed Mexican American children as a source of cheap labor during the pre-*Brown* era, Carter maintained that education was organized around a conservative sociopolitical ideology that advocated the political disfranchisement and economic subordination of Mexican Americans. Moreover, academic perseverance and high school graduation, said Carter, did not necessarily guarantee Mexican American youth social status and economic rewards. Educational change was possible, he predicted, if local school boards and educators led "the way to change these community conditions and belief patterns." This change was unlikely, however, because "educational leaders [were] too intermeshed with conservative community power elements."[45]

As more Mexican American communities began challenging their schools, various state officials and the U. S. Commission on Civil Rights were forced to take a more active role in promoting the success of Mexican American youth.[46] One of the more notable efforts by the U. S. Commission was a booklet they produced to familiarize Spanish-speaking communities with services and recourses to achieve school reform. The publication provided a description of the Elementary and Secondary Education Act, the significance of Title VII, how programs functioned, how they were implemented, and a sample of successful programs.[47] This information had some impact on various Mexican American communities, especially those that were searching for ways to challenge their school districts. It served as a useful reference on federal, state, and local responsibilities to Mexican American children.

THE MOBILIZATION OF DISSENT

After 1965, Mexican American parents in Brownfield began arguing that their schools were failing to serve their children adequately. Their impression was that school officials were either unconscious of, or resistant to, curricular and pedagogical changes that would encourage the students' academic success, stimulate their cultural pride, and affirm their ethnic self-worth. It seemed that as long as schools were performing adequately for white middle-class children, almost nothing needed to change. Moreover, educators did not consider the Mexican American community as a serious threat because it lacked political power in the community and a collective voice to challenge the schools. Their silence, however, did not necessarily mean they were living harmoniously with their schools. It was more of an indication of the frustration and rejection parents felt because they were unable to communicate with their schools.

The idea that schools were inadequately serving Mexican American children only became an issue when the local press pointed out that the Brownfield schools were ignoring the problem. In the tradition of Oscar Lewis, local educators held a deficit perspective of Mexican children and felt that their home environment prevented many of them from attaining the necessary experiences to succeed in school.[48] But whether school failure was attributed to social, cultural, or economic differences, the local newspaper reported that it was difficult for Mexican Americans to earn a decent living, attain respect from the dominant society, or acquire positions of social status. From the local editor's perspective, Mexican Americans were unable to "take [their] rightful place in the community throughout their adult lives."[49]

Two years later, local newspaper reporter Bob Cohen wrote an article about Mexican American and white perceptions about education and ethnic discrimination. The groups differed dramatically on the issues, Cohen said. Whites looked "aghast at the suggestion that discrimination is practiced against Mexicans in town." Despite race or ethnicity, white residents felt everyone had an equal chance to succeed in school and local society. But after interviewing several Mexican Americans, they enumerated "case after case, many of them documented, of subtle, but definite discrimination." Housing discrimination was one example; many Mexican American families were living in substandard housing and paying above-market rents. In other cases, some property owners refused to rent to Mexican families.[50] But educational discrimination became the focal point of Cohen's article. Unlike the housing problem, unequal education was more difficult to document. One anonymous informant challenged the notion that everyone was receiving an equal education in the Brownfield schools. He asked why then were educators deciding "beforehand that [Mexican Americans] go to vocational programs, and that Anglos go to college." Teachers, he stated, "automatically expect that a kid's going to be a certain way because he's a Mexican."[51]

Although Mexican American parents and the local press had charged that the local schools had fallen short in serving the Mexican American child, it was the work of Nate Warran (a VISTA employee) that prompted school officials to discuss the issue more seriously. Warran specifically studied the problems Mexican American youth were facing at the local high school. He found that their dropout rate was forty-two percent in 1967, when Mexican Americans represented twenty-two percent of the school population.[52] Though teachers, counselors, and administrators looked at the dropout problem from different vantage points, most blamed the problem on social discrimination in general and the Mexican American family in particular. For example, one teacher believed that social discrimination, whether "real or imagined," certainly added to the dropout problem. As the Mexican American student population grew, it became marginalized by the structure of the school. The teacher also added that Mexican American youth were so pessimistic about their futures that regardless of their academic performance many believed they would "not have a chance in life." Mexican American youth were on the social periphery of the school; they rarely participated in clubs, academic organizations, or other extracurricular activities. Their isolation was so imbedded in the culture of the school that few could be found eating in the cafeteria. In a more revealing look at their social experiences up to the mid-1960s, Mexican Americans did not appear among the school's super-latives, the "wittiest," the "best looking," or the most "likely to succeed."[53] One teacher said that Mexican American students were so withdrawn from school that by the time they reached high school they were "almost unalterably alienated to school, adults, and even most of their peers."[54]

In Brownfield, as in other school systems experiencing racial and ethnic demographic shifts, Mexican Americans were unsuccessful at adapt-ing to a structure that traditionally served white, middle-class, mostly college preparatory students. They clashed with an assimilationist ideology that expected them to rise within the school's "meritocratic" academic order. Along the same line depicted in Gerald Grant's study of Hamilton High, Mexican Americans at Brownfield High were feeling "a widespread sense of failure." Grant partly attributed minority school failure to negative teacher attitudes: Most lacked interest in adjusting to a curriculum and a pedagogy that were culturally relevant for African American youth.[55]

Within this context, Warran informed school officials and other mem-bers of the community that Mexican American students were dropping out because the high school had so little to offer them. Its unfriendly social climate and negative teacher attitudes, he said, were pushing them out of school. A hostile response could have been expected from the central administration and school board, given that conventional wisdom had always blamed the Mexican American family. But contrary to that expec-tation, John Bowing, the head counselor for the high school, agreed with Warran's report. Bowing said the report was "fair in its assessment of the situation, particularly in regard to the attitude of rejection of Mexican American students." Though he admitted that the high school was perhaps less than a welcoming environment for Mexican American youth, he also said many saw "no value in [education]" and that most wanted "to get out" of schools as soon as they could.[56] Bowing's view reflected a general contradiction: Educational professionals admitted that public schools were inadequately serving Mexican American youth yet they were unwilling to make any changes because they believed many of these youth lacked interest in school.[57]

School officials downplayed the schools' unfriendly environment and ascribed the dropout problem to the Mexican American's low socioeco-nomic standing. Joey Windham, the district's director of child welfare and attendance, for example, found that a significant number of Mexican American youth who were leaving school during their freshman and sophomore years were living below the poverty line. Keeping these stu-dents in school was a difficult task, he said, because most of them were "concerned about money." On the one hand, Windham said, many of these students wanted dignity and respect. Instead of implementing a culturally relevant curriculum at the school, Windham envisioned "a wide work experience program that will get these students out earning the money they need."[58] He focused on a work-study program because he had "nothing to offer them in the way of a school program." Even if special programs were in place, he said, "most of them don't even want one." It was ironic that while compulsory education laws required all children to stay in school until the age of sixteen, Windham said he would "just have to look the other way and tell the father, through an interpreter, to please keep his children off the street."[59]

Instead of creating an educational experience that was responsive to the Mexican American language and culture, school officials were convinced that a structured work-study program would benefit the Mexican American LEP student. Despite the displeasure some Mexican American parents expressed over their children's receiving vocational education while many white children were being prepared for college, John Bowing insisted that a work-study program would help Mexican Americans see "more value, more reality, more relevance in . . . education." He introduced a program in which two hundred students would be enrolled in part-time work, which would succeed, he suggested, because the district was "getting a lot of cooperation from businessmen in the community."[60] Conventional wisdom continued to assume that reform was unnecessary because Mexican Americans were uninterested in school, and that they would be satisfied serving local labor market needs.

Work-study programs were becoming standard features in secondary schools serving non-college-bound students. Allowing these students the opportunity to earn money while attending school was the main objective. Although there were some successful programs, most tended to prepare Mexican American youth for minimum wage jobs within local labor markets.[61] Carter, for example, maintained that most work-study programs in the Southwest prepared Mexican American "girls to become domestic servants, restaurant helpers ('busboys'), garment workers, or perhaps waitresses." Mexican American boys were "introduced to shop skills, electricity, body and fender work, and mechanics." The expressed goal was to prepare Mexican Americans for skilled vocations, but most obtained menial jobs in their communities.[62]

Educational reformers looked at work-study programs from different vantage points but most concluded that it was the best approach to remedy their high dropout rate. Some Mexican American parents, a few white liberals, and the local press pointed out that work-study programs were unlikely to solve the problem. From their perspective, it was the curriculum, pedagogy, and negative attitudes that were pushing Mexican

American students out of school. Despite this challenge, school officials refused to make significant reforms.[63] Given the recalcitrant stance of most educational professionals, a number of Mexican American parents started to challenge the Brownfield schools more vigorously.

It was difficult to determine how much impact large inner-city school protests and college campus unrest had on the Brownfield Mexican American community at the time. One outgrowth was unequivocally clear: Mexican American pride began to grow, the years of self-doubt began to loosen, and they started to question the conventional educational order with an organized voice. Rejecting deficit models of education that explained why their children were failing in school, several parents complained that "too much talk has been going on lately," and they demanded concrete action from the schools.[64] Jim Torrez, president of the local Mexican American Political Association chapter, said parents were displeased with their schools and called for educational reform. They confronted the board by telling them that they would itemize a list of twenty problems and if the school board solved just one, the parents pledged to restore their faith in the system.[65]

Parents were especially concerned about teachers treating their children differently from their white peers. School board member Dr. Kim Barnes responded that in many cases Mexican American youth were creating problems for themselves. She described the rudeness her daughter was experiencing on the bus from Mexican American youth. Barnes implied that Mexican American parents needed to take more responsibility for their children.[66] In a subsequent board meeting, approximately thirty-five Mexican American parents attended. One parent, Manuel Rendon, told the board he wanted nothing more than his child to be recognized as being as good as a white student. One of the major problems in the district, said Rendon, was that "many students and even teachers regard Mexican Americans ... as third-class citizens." He said some teachers believed Mexican American children were "wasting their time in the classroom." Some teachers felt Mexican American students were better off working in the fields.[67]

One of the most important studies that partially dealt with negative teacher attitudes toward Mexican American children took place in a small rural school district in Northern California. Theodore Parsons described how white teachers in this school systematically ignored Mexican American children and consciously gave special attention to white children. Teachers explained that white students deserved extra attention because they were going to be future community leaders, and, more importantly, that Mexican American children might as well accept being led by Anglos.[68] Teachers stereotyped Mexican American children as "dumb" and inferior in capacity and performance. They also instilled in them the belief that whites were naturally superior to Mexicans. Ability grouping was practiced to such an extent that high-ability classes were almost entirely filled with white children. One teacher told Parsons that such classes were kept as "small as possible because we feel that brighter pupils deserve a chance to get as much as they can out of school without being held back by the kids who are dull or just lazy or don't care."[69]

Parson's analysis suggested that Mexican American schooling experiences within "colonial settings" were common phenomena in the Southwest. Douglas Foley described a similar situation in a South Texas high school, where he observed a teacher ignore Mexican American students and noted how he "mainly interacted with the Anglos." Similar to the Parson's study, the high school teacher in Texas told Mexican American students that they were "too slow to be in school" and that they were better off "in the fields doing something useful."[70]

School officials in Brownfield began to face inequalities that were increasingly hard to ignore, not because Mexican American parents were challenging them but because the local press was pointing out that Mexican American children were being "neglected, often exploited, sometimes repressed." No one was "more acutely aware of these facts," said local reporter Joe O'Neil, than officials from the Brownfield schools.[71] Though school officials acknowledged that Mexican American children were unlikely to perform well because schools were oriented toward "middle-class values in the community," the reforms that would substantially give access to a curriculum and pedagogy that would value their language and culture were discounted during this period. This attitude sparked the growth of a more militant movement by a small number of Mexican American parents.[72]

THE MEXICAN AMERICAN COMMUNITY STARTS TO RUMBLE

The exclusion of minority communities in school politics became a familiar topic of discussion in seminars, symposia, and conferences across the nation. Although researchers were consistently referring to the problems of African American communities, most remained silent when it came to Mexican American experiences.[73] Like African American activists, Mexican American educators pointed out that educational professionals were asking the wrong questions about how to improve schooling conditions. Professor Manuel Guerra remarked that educational professionals should ask what was wrong with the way they were teaching the Chicano child, rather than what was "wrong with the Chicano child." Guerra advocated a culturally relevant curriculum and pedagogy and in-service training for teachers. He underscored the importance of including Mexican American parents in "school board meetings and in other policy making bodies."[74]

Minority communities throughout the nation knew they were being marginalized by their schools, they knew their children were missing out on quality education, and they knew educational policymakers were failing to adequately use federal funds to serve their children. Carl Grant suggested that minority parents were being excluded from the knowledge needed to participate; no one "told [them] where they can find" the information and, in some cases, "guidelines of many federal programs [were] intentionally . . . withheld from minorities and the poor."[75] During the first years of Title I programs, for example, there were complaints of blatant misuse. In some locales, revealed Donald Reed and Douglas Mitchell, the money was being used "to supplant, rather than to supplement, regular state and local funds." In some districts, school officials were using Title I funds to "buy tuxedos for high school proms and band uniforms." Reed and Mitchell found that federal funds rarely found their "way to the poor," that school officials were "slow to establish the required new advisory councils," that they were slower to grant minority parents "considerable authority of Title I," and that they "did little to help citizens understand the program."[76]

The discourse on Mexican American education at the national level had some effects in the Brownfield community. The Mexican American pursuit for equal schools in Brownfield grew from individual complaints to the birth of an organized movement. Parents began to articulate basic questions about their exclusion. A small group of Mexican American parents came together in 1968 and formed the organization called Communidad Organizada Para Educación (COPE). Wanting to be included on decisions that affected their children, COPE sought curricular, pedagogical, and policy reforms.[77] Searching for ways to be included in the district's decision-making process, Mexican American parents discovered that the Brownfield schools had been receiving Title I funds but could not account for how these funds were being spent. COPE demanded clarification of the mechanisms that linked federal moneys to the Brownfield schools, how the district qualified, how funds were being spent, and what was being done to improve the education of "disadvantaged" youth in the district. Moreover, the group asked how school officials had created the Title I advisory committee, how it operated, and what kind of training was being planned for teachers and aides to serve disadvantaged children.[78] This challenge served to increase Mexican American activism in the community, and it became the impetus to question the educational power structure more vigorously.

COPE was able to acquire the support of other local Mexican American organizations. Pressing for educational reform, the Mexican American

Political Association, the United Minority Coalition, and the Dollar Club (a church organization) closed ranks (calling themselves the Educational Coalition) and presented a list of demands to the school board in a meeting. "[S]cores of people, many of whom could not speak English," one newspaper reporter wrote, crowded into Brownfield High School "to demonstrate their concern about what they considered the failure of the school system to provide their children with meaningful education." In their presentation to the board, Mexican American leaders said they were "forced to tolerate conditions that guarantee the perpetuation of continual poverty, bad housing, malnutrition, and ill health." In their challenge to the board, they said they would rally against an "education that has guaranteed that the majority of our children drop out of school without meaningful tools to break this cycle." Mexican American leaders were both critical and cordial but firm that their voices needed to be heard.[79]

Drawing school authorities into a heated discussion about local school reform, Mexican American leaders demanded the following changes: special training for Mexican American parents so they could evaluate Title 1 programs; accounting from school authorities on Title I expenditures (and dissemination of the information to all interested groups and the media); three bilingual aides to work with a district community liaison officer to serve as a link between the Mexican American community and the schools; support services for minority parents to encourage their participation; bilingual aides for minority schools; on-going training for all teachers in the methodology of English as a second language (ESL); aides for teachers working with Mexican American children; the inclusion of minorities in the curriculum; and free lunches served at low-income targeted schools.[80] The Brownfield school board agreed to hire between thirteen and fifteen teacher's aides but refused to implement the rest of the demands because, from their perspective, the district lacked the financial resources to make such reforms. Elias Orozco, a member of the United Minority Coalition, said Mexican American demands seemed reasonable to him since they had "been waiting 20 years for a satisfactory educational program." The superintendent told Mexican Americans that the district was making "sincere, honest attempts to meet the problems of Mexican American pupils."[81]

But Mexican American parents refused to believe that the professionals were serious about reforming the schools. Social and academic conditions were so inadequate at the high school level, for example, that three to four hundred students walked out in protest. Among their demands, Mexican American students insisted that teachers stop making "derogatory statements" about them, that school officials hire a female dean of girls, and that the school incorporate courses in the history and culture of U. S. minorities.[82] One major concern for protesting students was the lack of Mexican American educators in the high school. To give an example of their underrepresentation: In 1967, Mexican American students composed 27.5 percent of the student body in the district but only 3.7 percent (18 out of 477 teachers) of the education professionals had Spanish surnames.[83] This problem was evident in other communities outside Brownfield. It was a problem many school districts in the state were confronting. In 1968, for example, Mexican American students composed 21 percent of California's public school enrollments. Yet only 2.2 percent of teachers in the state were Mexican American.[84]

At Brownfield High, Mexican American enrollments had grown from less than 7 percent in 1960 to 22 percent in 1967. In spite of this increasing number, school officials refused to make reforms that would benefit the Mexican American population.[85] The school had a long-term commitment to educational excellence that manifested itself in an inflexible loyalty to a rigid academic tradition. In some ways the school mirrored certain issues that Gerald Grant described in his study of Hamilton High. Although Brownfield High (built in 1894) had a much longer history than Hamilton High (built in 1953), both schools were regarded as first-rate institutions when they were predominantly white.[86] But as minority student enrollments began to grow, demographic shifts began to strain the school's social, cultural, and academic structures. Recalcitrant teachers, administrators, and school board members were reluctant to adjust to the changing needs of their student clientele. The ideology in both schools was that minority students needed to change, adopt new values, and assimilate into the mainstream of school life. Although some individual teachers were willing to accommodate to the special needs of minority students, the basic structure of the high schools functioned to promote the success of white middle-class students. In Brownfield and in Hamilton, most minority students who remained in school were typically in low, average, or vocational courses. It was the exception rather than the rule for minority youth to be enrolled in advanced courses during the 1960s.[87]

One educator at a nearby community college, Rodolfo Orellano, remembered the walkout at Brownfield High. He said that the event was entangled with a silent politics of racism, power, and privilege. Among those students walking out of the school, said Orellano, "was a feeling that white students were privileged and Mexicans were second-class citizens." From Orellano's perspective, school authorities lacked the "sensitivity, the openness, and the attitude to open up the possibility to communicate with the Spanish-speaking community." After Mexican American students dropped out of Brownfield schools, some came to the community college. As a counselor, Orellano reports that Mexican Americans were excluded from advanced courses at Brownfield High. Some of these students "aspired to become doctors, lawyers, and engineers," said Orellano, "but the doors were slammed shut." Part of the problem was that many teachers believed "Mexican American students were not bright enough." Administrators, counselors, and teachers were so biased that even Mexican American students who "showed accomplishment were not given the encouragement and courses so they might be prepared for college." Orellano explained how some of them had enrolled in the local community college and then later transferred to four-year institutions and received their degrees. "There were not a lot of them," says Orellano, "but it makes the point." To the extent that the Brownfield district was undergoing dramatic social, cultural, and academic changes, Orellano noted that it "must have been so difficult to ask of those [white] folks, after being so successful with that [white] population, to change."[88]

The Mexican American student experience in Brownfield resonated throughout the Southwest. "Mexican American children who . . . aspired to careers other than those of their fathers," said Meyer Weinberg, "were often explicitly discouraged by school personnel."[89] Weinberg used the testimony of Texas Senator Joe Bernal in a state hearing during the late 1960s to demonstrate how Mexican American youth were being excluded in school. Looking back at his high school years, Bernal remembered telling his high school principal he wanted to transfer to a school in the northern part of San Antonio. The principal told him it was a bad idea because, in his words, there was "no use [of] your going to the North Side schools because you're not going to compete. If you stay over with your people," the principal said, "you may end up being a leader. If you go over there, they are going to minimize your potential and you are going to be competing with white students. Rather than have you mongrelize and water down the races," he advised Bernal, "stay [in] your part of town."[90]

These types of experiences triggered student protests or "blowouts" in high schools throughout the Southwest. "In Texas alone," noted Weinberg, "demonstrations occurred in Uvalde, Crystal City, Edcouch-Elsa, Kingsville, Alpine, San Antonio, Sierra Blanca, Lubbock, Abiline, and San Marcos."[91] But the largest and most publicized Mexican American student walkout took place in East Los Angeles. "Thousands of Chicano high school students [some 12,000] staged a dramatic walkout," noted Carlos Muñoz, "from five city schools located in the general East Side area of the Los Angeles metropolis." Among a list of thirty-six demands, Mexican American high school students wanted classes that were culturally relevant and the hiring of Mexican American teachers, counselors, and administrators.[92] What was particularly striking about the East Los Angeles protests was how Mexican American parents, in general, supported their children's demands. Some parents even called for the dismissal of "administrators and teachers that show forms of prejudice towards Mexican or Mexican American students."[93] The "student walkouts," observed Muñoz, "represented the first massive urban demonstration in the history of Chicano America and became the catalyst for Chicano political mobilization and protest against the schools." Moreover, this public school student unrest became one of the most important signs of "oppression and powerlessness [that] awakened many Chicanos to the need for political action against the educational power structure and generated a drive for community control of the schools."[94]

Data collected by the U. S. Commission on Civil Rights showed that Mexican American's academic achievement, holding rates, and participation in extracurricular activities all lagged behind those of their white counterparts.[95] Douglas Foley described the overrepresentation of Mexican American students in practical classes in North Town. Even after Mexican American parents had complained to the school board that their children were disproportionately placed in low-ability/practical classes, very little was done to reform the school. Tracking was so obvious, said Foley, that "Mexican political activists were fond of saying that Anglos had to be retarded before they were placed in the practical sections."[96] In ethnically "integrated" schools, the social, cultural, and academic climates were organized around an ideology so obvious that it became an insult to white students to be placed in classes with Mexican American students.

SEARCHING FOR A SCHOOL ETHNIC COMMUNITY COMPROMISE

Brownfield Mexican American parents were becoming more resentful at school officials because very little was being done to construct social and academic environments that would allow their children to flourish. COPE began an aggressive campaign to support a reform agenda that would bestow respect on Mexican American students. Within a few days, COPE multiplied its size from a small group of parents to approximately 550 dues-paying members.[97] As the group grew in size and political cohesion, it asserted its agenda more confidently against the local educational power structure. One concern was the lack of communication between Mexican American parents and the schools. Petitioning for a "community liaison" to improve ethnic relations, Marcos Santillana, a COPE member and a prominent entrepreneur, argued that the position would "strengthen communication between Mexican Americans and the school district."[98] In addition, the group reminded school officials that the use of Title I funds fell within federal guidelines to hire a community liaison. The board hesitated but was persuaded by Mexican American leaders to authorize the position.[99] Mary Guerra, a native of Brownfield and one of the few Mexican American women in the community with a college degree, was asked to fill the position by Mexican American leaders. In accepting the position, Guerra pledged to serve all poor people in the community. It was unjust to exclusively serve the Spanish speaking, she said, but it just happened that most poor people in "the area are Mexican Americans."[100]

Because racial/ethnic tension between Mexican American and white communities was escalating throughout the Southwest, the federal government encouraged school districts to use community relations specialists to soothe ethnic tension. Susan Navarro Uranga, from the U. S. Commission on Civil Rights, advocated that districts serving large Mexican American communities utilize relations specialists because they could "serve as a link between the people and the power structure." Uranga noted that Mexican American communities often relied on these individuals to bridge the communication gap.[101] But depending on how community relations specialists were used and what political orientation they held, individuals in these positions were viewed as buffers, ombudspeople, revolutionaries, sellouts, or apologists for those holding power.[102] In most cases, community relations specialists became intermediaries with vaguely defined roles. Most struggled to keep "lines of communications open" between schools and minority communities. Despite the need to improve school and Mexican American community relations, said Uranga, "most school systems have not established this type of liaison with the barrio." She found that "84 percent of the surveyed districts did not use community relations specialists at all."[103] In 1968, California had more than 1,000 school districts, but only 84 community relations specialists were employed. More important was the fact that most eligible school systems waived the opportunity to employ them and, as a result, the "Mexican American community [was missing] the type of communication and involvement" that such professionals were able to provide.[104]

Mary Guerra, the new community advocate for the Brownfield school system, and several Mexican American parents began to prioritize the reforms they wanted implemented immediately. Although their children faced numerous problems at all grade levels, they chose to focus on the schooling of LEP children in the primary grades. As a result, Mexican American leaders began to rally around the establishment of a bilingual-bicultural elementary school because their children were failing to benefit from mainstream curriculum and pedagogy. As they presented the idea of a bilingual-bicultural school, two board members seemed receptive while the rest staunchly opposed it because, they said, the district lacked the funds to support the project.[105] The bilingual-bicultural school, however, evolved into a larger discourse around Mexican Americans wanting to hold a stake in the education of their children, the desire to sustain a sense of cultural identity for their children, and, in the broadest sense, their inclusion in the decision-making structure.

Carrying out a petition drive to demonstrate to the school board that Mexican Americans supported the bilingual-bicultural school, COPE gathered 3,373 signatures in the community. When the issue came up for discussion, more than 300 people, mostly Mexican Americans, attended the school board meeting to support the proposed school. In their presentation to the school board, Mexican American leaders pushed for a bilingual-bicultural elementary community school that would serve preschool children, the limited English proficient, school dropouts, and the elderly. They also wanted to train parents so they could serve as classroom aides, to use older students to tutor younger children, to start an adult program (the idea was for members of the adult community to teach classes or share knowledge with others), to start a hot breakfast and lunch program, and to create parent council committees with the power to organize the school's curriculum and hire personnel.[106]

Although two board members were open to the bilingual school concept, the rest refused to consider it. One board member, Dr. Kim Barnes, said she needed more evidence to convince her that a bilingual-bicultural school would enhance learning opportunities for the limited English proficient. "After hearing tonight's presentation," she said, "being against the idea of a bilingual-bicultural school would be like being against motherhood." There were "many general concepts and very valid feelings," Barnes continued, "but little in terms of actual facts to convince me that this program would be better."[107] School board members resisted the bilingual-bicultural school concept because it went against the traditional curricular and pedagogical convention of the school district and community, they were unwilling to share power with Mexican American leaders, and they seemed to question Mexican American parents' sophistication in dealing with complex educational issues.[108]

But several Mexican American parents had successfully rallied support from the community and, more importantly, had contributed to the research and writing of a proposal to implement such a program. Though several members of the Mexican American community were instrumental in mobilizing the community, school officials saw Guerra, the community liaison, as a major influence.[109] Considering her a threat to the local educational power structure, school board members began to rethink her position as a paid employee in the district and began to talk about how to eliminate the position. Some Mexican Americans were perplexed as to why school officials were calling Guerra's role as a community advocate into question because, in their minds, she had been performing a commendable job. One Mexican American parent said school officials wanted "to fire Ms. Guerra" because they were "displeased with her success in the program."[110]

Mexican Americans resented the school board's plan to eliminate the community advocate position. It was this mechanism that had finally given Mexican American parents a voice in school affairs. More than 150 Mexican Americans attended a board meeting. One parent, Lazaro Olivas, claimed that the real reason the school board wanted to eliminate the position was because Guerra was discovering their misdeeds. Board members, however, explained that their goal was to make better use of Title I funds. Mexican Americans maintained that the position not only fell within Title I guidelines, but also that it was difficult to establish a dialogue with school officials about the plight of the Mexican American without a community advocate. Guerra said Mexican Americans were "being given just lip service" by school officials who were plotting a course of conduct that purported to promote the success of Mexican American students but rarely followed through. For some time school officials had been saying that they were interested in what Mexican American parents had to say, said Guerra. But after listening to what Mexican American parents wanted, local policymakers usually "present something else."[111]

One board member said Guerra had "done a good job in the community with the parents" but that she "had strayed far from the guidelines [and caused] much friction throughout the community."[112] One of the paradoxes of this period was that the U. S. Commission on Civil Rights attempted to encourage Mexican American parents in their communities to participate in school affairs while local educational power structures fought hard to maintain the status quo. Seeking a Mexican American voice in educational policy and school reform stirred up defensive feelings from the local school district and also produced some anxiety within the white community. If Mexican American activists were going to reform the schools, it was indeed going to involve conflict, power politics, and ethnic struggle.

WHITE BACKLASH TO MEXICAN AMERICAN DEMANDS

It was strange that white residents had not challenged earlier allegations made by the local newspaper, individual Mexican American parents, and VISTA worker Nate Warran that the Brownfield schools were inadequately serving Mexican American youth. But as soon as Mexican American parents became organized, cohesive, and openly critical of the local educational power structure and demanded specific reforms, some white members of the community began to respond. One way to explain this initial silence was that most white parents saw the Mexican American community as inert, a weak threat to the status quo of the schools, and that Mexican American parents lacked the capacity to muster local reform. The fact that Mexican American parents had united and made specific demands, however, made many white residents extremely nervous. The level of their anxiety was demonstrated by a letter written to the editor about the feelings of many people in the community concerning the Mexican American demand for educational reform. In this letter, Mr. and Mrs. Gus Gensen offered Mexican Americans three alternatives to their discontent: (1) "Finance and construct their own school(s)," (2) "Go back to Mexico and attend one of their choice," or (3) "Continue to attend one of our very fine, high-quality local schools and let the big, bad Anglos pick up the tab."[113]

The Gensens first attacked the bilingual-bicultural school Mexican American parents wanted to establish. Citing the program as un-American, they looked to the local Japanese American community to demonstrate that other American minorities were able to "make it" in school and society without bilingual-bicultural education. After World War II, the Gensens wrote, Japanese-American children "must have felt out of place and very uncomfortable" in school. They were denied opportunities to speak Japanese and "as for their culture and history, it would have been the last thing on earth that any school system would have considered teaching in class." The American public school, according to the Gensens, did not hinder Japanese American parents from doing a commendable job raising their children and, of "all races and cultures, they have the highest percent of people in the professions: Some of the most successful farmers and businessmen in the state." Rhetorically asking Mexican American leaders how the Japanese American community was able to succeed, the Gensens answered: "Consider—HARD WORK, MANY HOURS OF STUDY, GREAT FAMILY PRIDE AND A LARGE RESPECT FOR LAW AND ORDER." With a backhanded slap at the Mexican American leadership, they advised them to stop criticizing the schools and to assume more responsibility for the failure of their children. The Brownfield schools, they said, were doing "everything possible to keep ALL youngsters (including yours) in school so that they can some day get a better job and . . . become responsible citizens." For the Gensens, Mexican Americans were the ones who were being "prejudiced against the very country and people who have opened their doors to you." If Mexican American leaders were truly interested in improving their station in American life, the Gensens told them to stop complaining "and take a few lessons from the 'Japs'!"[114]

Although the Gensens' invective was explicitly addressed to Mexican American leaders, it was read as a character assault on the entire Mexican American community. Their letter suggested that Mexican American children were unable to thrive in school because their parents were indifferent to education or hard work and lacked family pride or respect for law and order.[115] At this juncture, more people entered the debate, manifesting their differences in politics, values, and, within this context, notions of how the school ought to serve the Mexican American child. Local reporter Ben Quarny was the first to respond to the Gensen's letter, calling into question the remark about Anglos picking up the tab for the schooling of Mexican American children. The Gensens assumed that white residents were the only ones who were supporting the schools financially. Quarny reminded the Gensens that Mexican Americans, whether they were U. S. citizens, permanent residents, or migratory laborers, all contributed to the local economy in one capacity or another. Moreover, he continued, for Mexican Americans to construct their own schools was both unconstitutional and discriminatory.[116]

As Mexican American leaders demanded their fair share of educational resources, a structural-economic tension further divided the community along ethnic lines. Local residents Ramon and Maria Martinez noted that it was offensive for the Mexican American community to have to beg for educational opportunities that were rightfully theirs. Given their exclusion, they said, Chicanos no longer should ask; instead, "WE DEMAND. We take what's rightfully ours. Remember," they added, "this is 'Occupied Mexico.' " The Martinezes warned "[Gus and Doris Gensen] and all racists like them" to be more cautious about making such ludicrous remarks.[117]

Some teachers may have supported Mexican American activists, but they remained silent because they feared reprisals from the local school administration. One teacher, however, spoke out in defense of the Mexican American community. Joy Olin said she understood the frustration Mexican American parents felt. "As an experienced teacher," she said, "I feel that parent involvement is of vital importance if I am to be successful in teaching any child. Textbooks, learning aids, audiovisual equipment, and most recent teaching techniques are of little value if there is no positive relationship between the home and school." She urged teachers, school administrators, and the board to "truly listen to their suggestions, for until we do," she concluded, "we will continue to fail their children."[118] But school officials held strong assimilationist ideologies about academic success. In their view, other immigrants, the Slavs, Portuguese, Japanese, and Italians, had come to Brownfield and been transformed into full-fledged Americans without special educational programs. For many educators and the white community, the Mexican American people appeared difficult, uncooperative, and absolutely recalcitrant.

Educational professionals saw Mexican Americans as foreigners and reasoned that they ought to be satisfied with what they had because it was superior to what they would have received in Mexico. For example, one teacher asked what the dropout rate was in Mexico and what percentage went on to college. American public schools have always dealt with linguistically and culturally diverse children, another teacher said, but Mexican American parents were expecting too much from the schools. Asserting a standard brand of meritocratic individualism, another resident said, "Yes, our school system needs improving. I agree with you." But not to the extent Mexican American activists were proposing. Others reminded Mexican Americans that they "chose to live in America" and that they needed to "meet the challenge with [some] integrity."[119]

Many white residents who had not experienced discrimination were disturbed by the Mexican Americans' reform agenda because conventional wisdom had led many of them to the comfortable belief that schools were doing a commendable job. They believed that if schools provided everyone with the same curriculum and pedagogy, schools were somehow equal. Mexican American parents, however, suggested that offering the same thing to all students was not necessarily a meaningful example of educational equality. As the debate continued, Mrs. Jeff Rolin warned the larger community that if COPE's reform demands were met, residents would probably never vote in favor of another bond election again. It was unfair, Mrs. Rolin said, to give special attention to one ethnic group over another. The desire to maintain one's culture was commendable, she noted, but not for it "to be transplanted here."[120]

While most Japanese Americans seemed reluctant to be drawn into the Gensens' debate, one prominent Japanese American community member, Ben Osaka, spoke out in defense of the Mexican American community. He resented the Gensens' politics of using the Japanese American model minority stereotype "to put down another." From Osaka's perspective, the comparison revealed Mr. and Mrs. Gensens' "racist attitude." They lacked understanding of the real issues involved in the schools, and they seemed unwilling to "understand the real reason why COPE is proposing such a necessary program." But Leonard Yamasaki, another Japanese American resident, disagreed with Osaka, arguing that it was wrong for Mexican Americans to ask for something they were able to obtain on their own.[121]

The message the Gensens and others like them were trying to convey to the community was that despite past discrimination, Japanese Americans were able to succeed because the American public school was the great equalizer. Within this context, American educators had a long history of insisting that public schools were meritocratic and that everyone was "given an equal chance to develop their abilities and rise in the social hierarchy."[122] The notion that success was based on ability and effort rather than inherited privilege attached to race/ethnicity was presented as a definitive logic. As a case in point, Brownfield resident J. Tovic talked about how Dr. Ishimura was able to make it in the United States because of persistence and hard work. Ishimura had arrived as a total stranger in Brownfield, said Tovic, but he "did not rush for help, demand endless assistance from bilingual teachers, special counselors and all sorts of other privileges that seem to be in vogue and great demand today."[123] For many white residents, Dr. Ishimura (and other successful immigrants) were the exemplars of Horatio Alger's observation that if one works hard enough, he or she will be able to succeed.

Mexican American demands for educational reform unfolded into a broader discussion of social policy. Because the reform agenda included free breakfast and lunch for the children, many white residents became resentful because they thought many Mexican Americans were already indulged in government assistance. When Mexicans arrive in Brownfield, one resident said, "the very next day they are on welfare." The resident asked members in the community if anyone could "find a way for me and my family to relish in some of the luxuries Mexican Americans have, I would appreciate it." Mexican American parents seeking educational reform were portrayed as welfare recipients who were draining the local economy.[124]

Bolstered by the ideological projection that Mexican Americans were receiving too much government assistance, some white residents lashed out even harder. Turning his attention to a small federal housing project that rented to low-income families, Jeff Rolin complained that it "was a great injustice by allowing [Mexican] families with four, six and seven children to be grouped together" in government housing. Insinuating a need for population control, he proposed that "if you have four children when you rent, you have no more than four when you move." He said it was his "inalienable right as a heavily burdened taxpayer to protest" because his tax dollars were "going for welfare, subsidized housing and federal aid to education under Title I." He gave his "sympathy . . . to the school board and teachers, because certain interest [groups were] getting pushy."[125]

Although a widening national consciousness was finally acknowledging that many school systems were failing to provide Mexican American youth with equal educational opportunities, the school systems were unwilling to change.[126] The problem was that many educators and the lay public took it for granted that all immigrant groups, including Mexican Americans, wanted to assimilate into the mainstream. The local white community continued to frame the Mexican American schooling experience in a way that ignored social, cultural, political, and economic power divisions that differentiated Mexican Americans among themselves.[127] That is, they refused to acknowledge that the Mexican American experience was different from those of the previous immigrant groups that had settled in Brownfield. Janet Holden, Karen Gibs, and Angela Swet argued that Mexican Americans ought to be treated like the rest of the people in Brownfield. Everyone in the community has Mexican friends, they said, but the ones who protested the loudest were the "lazy" ones who were unwilling to work and thought everyone owed them a living because of past injustices. If American life seemed harsh and unfair, these women said, Mexican American leaders should "go find a country that will let you speak the language of your choice, support you with welfare checks and provide housing for you and your children." They condescendingly told Mexican Americans that if they found such a place, "let the rest of us know . . . because by then you must have gone to heaven! God would be the only one who could possibly afford and put up with this." As they referred to the original letter that spurred the debate, they said, "[t]hree cheers to [Gus and Doris Gensen] . . . we're all behind you 100 percent so stick to your guns."[128]

As the newspaper debate came to a close, one resident, Harvey Gold, challenged those who were criticizing Mexican American leaders for demanding local school reform. Speaking directly to the subject of the bilingual-bicultural school, Gold asked what difference it made what language was used in school if the real purpose of education was to educate children. Given the burden of a language barrier and a school system that was unresponsive to the Mexican American community, Gold said it was easy for him to understand why so many Mexican American children were failing in school. He urged the white community to "withhold judgment about 'them' and about how [Mexican Americans] ought to take better advantage of the fine educational opportunities we provide." Mexican American students, "much to everybody's surprise, quickly get the idea that Anglos are not really interested in educating them. "What Mexican American students receive in school," he continued, was "his education thrown down at him like slop to the hog." Gold cautioned school authorities to stop wasting taxpayers' money "by perpetuating a course of conduct and policy which admittedly purports to educate, but does not actually educate a significant [number of Mexican American] students who go to school."[129] What was particularly important about Gold's letter was that he did speak for some white residents and teachers who saw the district as assimilationist, intolerant, and unwilling to share power with Mexican American parents.

CONCLUSION

As Mexican Americans began to challenge the Brownfield schools they realized they had to form a united front in order to bring about some reforms. The civil rights proequality climate, the local liberal newspaper, the Warran report, Mexican American parent complaints, and the high school student walkouts had some effect in the district. Moreover, federal and state funds (under Title VII) were becoming available for Mexican American children with linguistic needs. In a collaborative effort between COPE and school officials, for instance, a half-million dollar grant was awarded to the Brownfield district to create a pilot bilingual-bicultural elementary school. Although some school officials were lukewarm about the project and some white residents were hostile to the idea, federal funds were in place to begin the school.[130]

The grant became a symbolic act of victory for the Mexican American community because it forced the local administration to include them in the decision-making process; it gave them a greater sense of potency, self-worth, and control over some policy decisions that were bound to have an impact on their children's lives. Although Mexican Americans made some strides toward equality, they were mindful of their continued exclusion. For example, they lacked representation on the school board, and almost none were in positions of power. Tension with school officials and the white community made them realize that if they became cohesive as an ethnic group, if they rallied around a strong reform agenda, and if they found the financial means to support their ideas, they had the potential to bring about favorable changes.

COPE and other Mexican American organizations demonstrated that a small grassroots organization, with solid support from its ethnic minority constituency, was able to impact the way educational resources were distributed and educational policy was formulated. Contrary to determinist notions that viewed Mexican Americans as passive victims of dominant institutional and ideological structures, they demonstrated the capacity of a powerless minority group to organize and mount a serious campaign for educational justice. Even though change was slow, their united efforts eventually forced a reluctant white educational power structure to take seriously the needs of their children.

FOUR

The Irony of Year-Round Education

The preceding chapter described the mobilization of Mexican American parents in the Brownfield community. In keeping with the civil rights fervor of the 1960s and 1970s, Mexican American discontent with schools emerged in the district and expressed itself in several ways. The Brownfield educational power structure was challenged by parents who had traditionally been on the margins of school and society. As we saw, Mexican Americans were concerned about recalcitrant educational policymakers who refused to incorporate the Spanish language into public school curricula and pedagogy. Finding themselves in the midst of unfamiliar power struggles, educational professionals were pressed to include Mexican American voices in the decision-making process, to create schooling environments that would allow Mexican American children to thrive academically, and to implement a bilingual-bicultural elementary school. Despite the demands of Mexican American parents, educational professionals were resistant to share power with them and seemed uncertain about taking on some responsibility for the failure of their children. Between 1968 and 1971, Mexican Americans made definite calls for educational reform and, in a very small way, provoked some concessions through political action.

Across the Southwest, scholars were linking the Mexican American struggle for equal education with both bilingual education and community control of schools.[1] While these issues brought some attention to Mexican Americans, they also downplayed other problems being encountered in schools and communities. Few scholars have examined reforms and movements that lay outside the Mexican American struggle for bilingual and bicultural education.[2] One educational movement that became controversial but was rarely linked to the Mexican American community was year-round education. Before the 1970s, the literature on year-round education focused primarily on the most efficient use of space and on cost effectiveness in relation to white middle-class students in urban and suburban environments. Few studies explored the Mexican American response to year-round schooling during this period of analysis.

This chapter examines the political context of Brownfield's year-round school program and the Mexican American response to it during the early 1970s. Two general questions guide this chapter: First, if school authorities in Brownfield were aware that the traditional nine-month school calendar with a three-month summer vacation was historically designed to serve agrarian interests in the United States, why were the lifestyles of Mexican migrant parents downplayed in the debate on year-round schools? Second, how did Mexican migrant parent resistance to year-round education in Brownfield differ from the portrayal given in conventional accounts?

THE EVOLUTION OF YEAR-ROUND SCHOOLS

The history of year-round education in the United States from the early twentieth century to the 1970s indicates that the idea has always been controversial. Since the Buffton, Indiana, school system experimented with the concept between 1904 and 1915, proposals have consistently been met with intense public criticism and, more often than not, have vanished into the obscurity of old filing records. School systems became interested in the concept during the early twentieth century for a variety of reasons. Newark, New Jersey, for example, wanted to serve non-English speaking immigrant children throughout the year; Omaha, Nebraska, was interested in offering vocational training on a year-round basis; and Buffton, Indiana, wanted to institute curricular reforms. Most school systems, however, were driven by space efficiency and cost effectiveness. In 1925, at least thirteen U. S. school systems were experimenting with the extended-year schedule. By 1955, the Chattanooga, Tennessee, school district was the only one left. Although several large urban schools systems, such as Houston, San Diego, and Atlanta, considered implementing the concept during the first half of the twentieth century, year-round education was almost nonexistent by 1956.[3]

There are two ways to explain national resistance to year-round education during the early twentieth century. First, reforming the traditional nine-month calendar conflicted with a host of schooling traditions that had become part of American life. Communities rejected the concept because most plans clashed with athletics, extracurricular activities, summer camp, and other social activities. Second, the timing was bad for year-round school reform, based on concerns of space and cost. Most school systems in the nation were enjoying widespread financial support from the American public. Even during the Depression, "public schooling remained remarkably stable in funding. The Depression did not deflect much of the long-term institutional expansion from 1920 to 1950."[4] Government support, public confidence, and established cultural traditions, then, prevented the year-round school movement from becoming a significant reform.

But the late 1960s brought dramatic changes to U. S. public schools. Due to the postwar increase in births, enrollments soared, and schools began to experience serious financial difficulties. As a consequence, many professionals looked for strategies to manage enrollment growth without having to build new schools. A small cadre of educational professionals and concerned citizens began to rethink the traditional school calendar. They pointed out that the traditional calendar "was established when America was largely an agrarian society and youngsters were needed at home during the planting and harvesting time,"[5] and in the summer had "to help with the crops."[6] Advocates also noted that the United States had become an industrial giant and, by the late 1950s, a suburban society. They claimed, accordingly, that the nine-month school calendar with a three-month summer vacation had become obsolete.

Given the fiscal constraints many public school systems were experiencing, year-round school advocates criticized the professionals for failing to make effective use of schools and facilities. They claimed that educational plants were left "idle 25% of the time" and that trained teachers were being used ineffectively.[7] For example, Deputy Executive Secretary of the American Association of School Administrators William Ellena pointed out that for "years the schools' front doors were padlocked during July and August. Buildings stood idle . . . [and] teachers were out of work. . . . The American people held tenaciously to the old school calendar suited to our earlier agrarian life."[8] But the "time has come," declared Atlanta Superintendent John Letson, "to move from discussions to action and to tackle realistically the job of arranging the school year in accordance with the needs of today rather than yesterday."[9]

In addition to space efficiency arguments, advocates pointed out that year-round schooling created a less competitive local labor market for working-age youth during the summer months, and that parents did not have to be fundamentally confined to the traditional summer vacation season. Finally, as the president of the Minneapolis Board of Education, George Jensen, said, the "long, hot summer is a period of retrogression through idleness and boredom. . . . [The] manner in which the traditional school calendar was structured was an open invitation to mischief and vandalism."[10] Advocates made a concerted effort after 1960 to convince the American people that year-round schooling was "Not Just Adding Days" in order to use schools and their facilities more efficiently.[11]

Although the year-round school logic was becoming more sophisticated after 1960, it continued to be controversial. Most professionals were nervous because it conflicted with athletics, extracurricular activities, and vacation schedules. But "practically all of the opposition to the extended school year," said James Farnsworth of the Michigan House of Representatives, "stems from a single source . . . [the] reluctance of parents to consider a major change in the present vacation practices."[12] Insofar as resistance was coming from white middle-class families who were reluctant to alter their vacation schedules, advocates were adamant about convincing this segment of the population that their vacation options would be enhanced rather than restricted. In the words of Farnsworth, many "citizens are realizing that fall and spring, in addition to being the traditional hunting and fishing season are far better times to travel than mid-summer."[13] In a major speech given before a Year-Round Education National Seminar, George Jensen discussed social and ecological issues that would appeal to the American public. He talked about the "wall to wall people on the highways, on the lakes and streams, in the national and state parks, at the resorts and in the restaurants and motels during June, July, and August, the traditional vacation months."[14] Although they also pointed out some curricular advantages for "at-risk" students, Jensen and other advocates explored the limits and possibilities of year-round schooling primarily from a middle-class perspective.

Year-round school reform became more successful after 1960, but it failed to have a major impact in U. S. public schools. The number of systems experimenting with the concept increased from virtually none in 1956 to about 76 (out of 16,500 in the United States) in 25 different states by 1974.[15] Despite several well-functioning model programs the reform was still not able to garner widespread support from the American public. Americans chose to circumvent the year-round school concept and use alternative strategies instead to cope with problems in their communities.[16]

YEAR-ROUND EDUCATION COMES TO TOWN

Before 1960, Brownfield was seen as a desirable place to live, and its schools were well supported by the community. Its high school had an esteemed academic record, and numerous Brownfield high school graduates earned their college degrees and returned to the district to teach. Funding was so solid that all bond initiatives or tax increases had been passed since 1936.[17] But by the mid-1960s, Brownfield experienced dramatic demographic shifts, and some of the schools became overcrowded.

Consistent with the statewide trend, the district also began to lose economic support from its community. Indeed, every bond initiative and proposed tax increase was rejected between 1966 and 1971.[18]

As year-round school programs began to proliferate during the late 1960s, school officials in Brownfield began to look to this concept as a solution to their problems. They formed an ad hoc advisory committee to study the extended school year, they solicited external expert opinion to inform their decisions, and, on the surface, they attempted to include input from the larger community. School officials appeared to be operating under the *status congruent* power model, which depended "on a thorough investigation of relevant facts before reaching important decisions."[19] In other words, they claimed to be open to new ideas, including various perspectives in the decision-making process.

School officials brought in educational professionals from other school systems that were experimenting with year-round schools to share their insights with principals, teachers, and concerned citizens. But it was difficult to determine if year-round education was appropriate for the Brownfield community because most school systems experimenting with the concept were located in urban and suburban settings. Brownfield had a large Mexican American student population (33.1 percent in 1972) and served more than 1,200 Mexican migrant students.[20] In the list of U. S. school districts considering year-round programs, Brownfield had the largest Mexican migrant population.[21] Cognizant that Brownfield differed from the national year-round school norm, one board member asked visiting experts what effects they thought the reform would have on Mexican migrant youth. Experts were unfamiliar with the schooling realities of Mexican migrant students, but they hypothesized that such students would probably benefit from the nontraditional calendar.[22] Their hypothesis was based on the notion that year-round schooling would improve the Mexican migrant attendance record because it would require them to attend school during the summer months. How the concept would potentially affect the Mexican migrant family had not yet become a focus of their discussion.

Pushing the initiative forward, school officials proclaimed that year-round education was the district's only solution to its overcrowding crisis. Aware that the year-round school concept had a history of national resistance, school officials made certain to consider only the most reputable designs. By the late 1960s and early 1970s, school systems were able to choose from about thirty extended school year patterns. The general structure of most programs, however, "fit into 3 or 4 categories."[23] The most popular programs involved a four-quarter system, a structure in which students attended three of the four quarters throughout the year. By having students in school year-round, this design meant that school attendance in any one quarter was about 75 percent of the district's total enrollment, thus reducing overcrowding. John McLain, chairperson of the Pennsylvania state committee on year-round education, noted that this design not only became appealing to many school systems because it reduced overcrowding, but also because it avoided the construction of new schools.[24]

As an alternative to the four-quarter plan, the 45–15 program was probably the most prominent in the United States. Implemented by the highly touted Valley View school system in Lockport, Illinois, in 1970, the schedule called for alternating periods of forty-five days in school and fifteen days off throughout the year. This plan "was so successful," said Jensen, that the Illinois Department of Education was in the process of making a " 'how to do it' sound and color film . . . for general distribution."[25]

Not all school systems used the 45–15 plan, however. The modified four-quarter plan consisted of about fifty school days each quarter, with three weeks between quarters. One week of each break was devoted to parent conferences, teacher in-service, and team planning. The philosophy of this program was driven to improve the quality of education, not the space efficiency or cost effectiveness concerns that drove so many. The operational cost of this program, however, was fifteen percent higher than the traditional schedule.

Another design was the eleventh month plan, which had an entirely different philosophy. Its goal was for students to complete the traditional twelve years of education in ten, a strategy to graduate students as soon as possible. The last design was the flexible all-year school plan. This plan intended to meet the needs of communities in a rapidly changing, technologically advanced society. It was designed to operate throughout the year "with no beginning and no ending of the school year—with both instruction and time individualized."[26]

Brownfield school officials eventually zeroed in on the 45–15 plan. They pointed to space efficiency and cost benefits and noted that parents and students were given frequent vacation breaks. They saw it as a way to reduce the loss of learning during the summer months and to limit summer vandalism while providing some teachers with the opportunity to earn more money. In an attempt to present a balanced view in the community, school officials also acknowledged the plan's drawbacks: There would be problems coordinating activities with schools that operated on a traditional schedule, problems coordinating vacations, problems with after-school care for families with children in different schools with different schedules, and problems with student transfers from year-round to non-year-round schools. Also, the plan would increase administrative costs, force teachers to pack up every forty-five days, and jeopardize teacher training programs during the summer months.[27] It is noteworthy that, in

[handwritten annotations: "what was the remainder population specifically consider immigrant middle upper class Mexican families did consider family life they fam..."]

their list of advantages and disadvantages, nothing was mentioned about how the concept would <u>affect Mexican migrant families.</u> Brownfield officials, it seems, were merely following the conventional discourse that was mainly focusing on white middle-class families and children in urban and suburban communities. For instance, when year-round school experts at the national level raised questions about how it would affect rural and agricultural communities, this was usually discussed within a certain narrow, historical context. <u>That is, experts took it to be sufficient that most families did not need their children for the harvest season or that "Junior doesn't have to go home to bale hay anymore."</u>[28] *ok*

School officials in Brownfield recognized an inherent financial contradiction in year-round schooling. While the district had the potential to save large amounts of money by limiting school construction, year-round schooling required an increase in operating costs. Proponents also maintained that the rejection of school bond initiatives and tax increases since 1966 had created overcrowding conditions in some of the district's schools that could not be dismissed. To continue business as usual, the local press wrote, meant that the quality of schools would decline: There would be more split sessions; less state money allocated to the district; and an increase in class size.[29] But if year-round education was the district's only solution, the process and speed used by educational policymakers in reaching their decision was nonetheless problematic for some members of the community.

One of the themes that almost always ran through the year-round school literature was how controversial the concept became if it was forced on the public. Experts frequently advised school systems "anticipating a change to year-round operation . . . to include students, parents, and teachers in the decision process."[30] In the Metro Atlanta area, where a sizable plan was implemented, Gillis described how school officials "realized that this program could not be developed in isolation from the community."[31] School officials involved parents, teachers, civic groups, and church organizations in order to win support from the community. As Atlanta experimented with the 45–15 year-round plan, Gillis "found that involvement of all those concerned has tended to lessen the negative aspects" in the schools and community.[32]

Other experts recommended allowing at least two years from the start of discussions about year-round education to its actual implementation, providing time for community residents to think of it as their own idea, involving teachers, and keeping community members informed at all times. It was urgent, the experts warned, to let "everyone know about it as each step is taken down the road toward the first day of school."[33] School officials in Brownfield were inspired by a local survey that indicated

people in the community were open to the idea of experimenting with
the nontraditional schedule.[34] The survey seemed to correspond with an
emerging national trend that was showing more Americans interested in
the year-round school concept. At the national level, Jensen cited a *Phi
Delta Kappan* publication that found that 53 percent of Americans supported year-round education, 41 percent disapproved, and 6 percent had
no opinion.[35] Other studies showed a similar pattern.[36] However, the
largest study on parental attitudes toward year-round education showed
the opposite. Most Americans, according to this study, still rejected the
idea.[37] How Americans perceived year-round education remained relatively vague in the mid-1970s.

Although the Brownfield survey may have shown community interest,
a group of Mexican migrant parents, Los Padres Unidos, immediately
challenged the plan. Members were concerned about their children's having
to attend school during the summer months. This presented a serious
problem because a significant number of parents depended on the earning power of their children during those months. School officials were
forced to explore the impact of year-round schooling on the Mexican
migrant community, but they focused on the children and ignored effects
on their families. For example, although most teachers were lukewarm
about the concept, some supported it because, in their opinion, it would
give Mexican migrant children more schooling opportunities. One teacher
said that the Brownfield schools had always served Mexican migrant
children, who only attended school part of the year because of the nature
of seasonal agricultural labor. The teacher also believed the proposed 45–
15 year-round plan would provide a structure to serve Mexican American
migrant children better because school terms would begin several times
during the year. More important, the teacher said, the fifteen-day session
breaks could be used as an opportunity for schools to serve those in
need.[38] Teacher views corresponded with Jensen's idea that the 45–15 plan
would better serve at-risk students because it would avoid forcing them
to repeat a full year's work; deficiencies would be discovered and rem-
edied every forty-five days. Jensen wrote that if "he cannot make up his
work during the 15 schoolday recess his classmates are having, then he
simply does his 45 days work over at much less cost to him in lost
self-esteem and far less cost to the district in dollars."[39]

Although it was commendable that experts in the field and some
Brownfield teachers saw some possibilities for at-risk students during the
fifteen-day session breaks, they did not fully understand the economic
reality of Mexican migrant families. Many such families were dependent
on the earning power of their children for survival during the summer
months. According to Carter and Segura, even with these supplemental

incomes, they earned "less than the federal poverty minimum" and they lived in conditions that were "probably worse than for any other group in the nation."[40]

Los Padres Unidos were becoming more concerned with the proposal and began to raise more questions about the 45–15 plan. The superintendent directed his attention to the group because its members were starting to voice their concerns publicly. But, like most superintendents in the United States during the 1960s and 1970s, he "found it difficult to communicate and understand the sentiments of the poor and underprivileged."[41] The Brownfield superintendent thus devised a plan that would give migrant children attending middle school (students between twelve and fourteen years old) the opportunity to work during the fifteen-day session breaks throughout the year to make up for income lost during the summer months. He was convinced that something could be worked out to disarm the problem and advance equity for the migrant family.[42]

Contrary to what school officials expected, Los Padres Unidos refused to accept the superintendent's migrant student work proposal. They remained skeptical that his program would resolve the problem because they distrusted the school administration's intention to act in their best interest. But Los Padres Unidos lacked political power in the community. They were not in a position to negotiate because most members were poor and lacked a strong command of the English language. In an attempt to strengthen their stance on the issue, Los Padres Unidos began to seek the support of the Communidad Organizada Para Educación (COPE). COPE, however, was put in an extremely sensitive position because it was already on record as endorsing the year-round school initiative. COPE members were originally receptive to the district's 45–15 plan because they were led to believe the initiative would include a bilingual-bicultural community school. They did not know, however, that the plan was viewed by the school administrators as the only way to end the double school sessions and that the proposed bilingual school might be jeopardized if the plan was not implemented.[43]

After considering some of the plan's potential effects on Mexican migrant families, COPE withdrew its endorsement. It seemed that the organization wanted to avoid the risk of ethnic polarization; it claimed that local professionals were failing to consider the economic situation of Mexican migrant workers, especially those working in the fields. Moreover, COPE found no evidence that the local year-round study commission or school administrators had studied their specific problems before advancing the 45–15 plan. COPE was also disturbed that school officials had not asked for the organization's endorsement until after it had been accepted as a solution to the district's overcrowding problem. COPE recommended an analysis of the plan that went beyond cost and space efficiency factors before they would endorse the initiative.[44] Although year-round school experts at the national level were constantly urging local policymakers to include multiple perspectives in their communities, COPE pointed out that the sole Mexican American involved in the study commission was only able to participate on a part-time basis. COPE felt that this level of participation was tokenism and that it undermined real Mexican American participation in the plan.[45] Los Padres Unidos and COPE resented their exclusion from negotiating a reform that was bound to have significant consequences for their lives.

The superintendent saw COPE's withdrawal as a "political move rather than an educational one" and asserted that the year-round program was more "beneficial to the Mexican American child" than the traditional schedule.[46] In an attempt to evoke support from the Mexican American leadership, he attempted to link the impending pilot bilingual-bicultural elementary school with the 45–15 plan. He said Mexican American activists were shooting themselves in the feet because the 45–15 year-round program would make space available for the bilingual-bicultural school.[47] But COPE discovered from state authorities that the bilingual school would open regardless of the year-round school outcome.[48] Mexican American leaders accused the superintendent of using the bilingual-bicultural school as a lever to win their support for the 45–15 plan.[49] COPE saw the bilingual school as a needed reform that stood on its own and took offense at the suggestion that its withdrawal of support was politically motivated. As the organization saw it, it was the superintendent who was playing politics.

The superintendent lashed out at Mexican American activists, claiming that his plan not only offered their children more schooling opportunities but had the potential to break the cycle that forced their children to work in the fields during summer months.[50] He felt his proposal had the potential to improve migrant children's lives by exposing them to employment opportunities other than agricultural labor.

The local press rallied behind the school administration and proclaimed that year-round education was good for everyone in the community. In the face of difficult economic challenges, the press listed the district's options:

1. Find $7.5 million to build new schools for the following year.
2. Continue the double sessions that were common up to the third grade and expand them to the fourth and fifth grades for the following year (according to a district study, students forfeited one instructional day per week under the double session).

3. Adopt a year-round plan that used school plants more efficiently, eliminated double sessions, and made possible a bilingual-bicultural elementary school for the limited English proficient.[51]

Mexican American leaders continued to assert that the initiative would negatively affect migrant families. Despite that claim, school officials made a unanimous decision to move the 45–15 plan forward. In a school board meeting, Mexican Americans and school officials heatedly discussed the effects of year-round schooling on the Mexican migrant family and its children. The superintendent pledged to Mexican American leaders that migrant children would have the opportunity to work during the fifteen-day vacation breaks throughout the year to make up for lost income. He publicly stated that he would stand by his promise because, he said, if he renegotiated, he would be finished as a superintendent in the district.[52]

But other dimensions of the year-round school debate were missing from the mainstream press. In a local bilingual newspaper, Mexican American activists expressed apprehension about school authorities asserting such domination over their lives. If they agreed to support the student work proposal, it would be the school administration, instead of the Mexican seasonal migrant workers, who would determine whether the family needed their children's help.[53] In addition to their concern about power and control, Mexican Americans also pointed out other conflicts. They feared that Mexican migrant students enrolled in the high school, which maintained a traditional schedule, would have to care for their younger siblings participating in the year-round plan during the fifteen-day session breaks. This situation, they said, had the potential to exacerbate the dropout rate that was already a serious problem at the local high school.[54] The superintendent's student work proposal seemed progressive and well-intentioned, but the issues overlooked were too substantial for Mexican Americans to leave their resolution to others.

To demonstrate to the school administration that Mexican Americans looked unfavorably upon the 45–15 year-round plan, a gathering of 300 to 400 protesters, most of them Mexican Americans, marched to the district office.[55] The protesters became agitated, resulting in a disturbance during which a smoke bomb was tossed through a window of the school district office building. The demonstration was ineffective, because the year-round plan continued. The disturbance, however, did result in some compromise. The year-round initiative was reduced in scale to a model that included four elementary schools, grades kindergarten to sixth, and one junior high school. The press felt that school officials had reached a reasonable compromise with Mexican leaders because the number of students attending double sessions was reduced.[56] Some Mexican American activists were unsatisfied with the results of the protest and began to press for a boycott. Standing firm behind the board's decision, the superintendent said that if Mexican Americans boycotted, the district would simply continue standard practices. He discouraged a boycott because it would accomplish nothing more than disrupting the children's education.[57]

Brownfield school officials ratified the 45–15 plan, but it still needed state authorization. Aware that the year-round initiative had become a heated issue in the Brownfield community, California State Superintendent Wilson Riles gave it special attention. Riles was known as a year-round school supporter and he had predicted that most California public schools would become "year-round schools within 10 years or less."[58] Nevertheless, he ordered school officials in Brownfield to: (1) identify and provide alternate schools for students whose parents preferred the traditional school year plan; (2) provide transportation to students electing a traditional school year plan on the same basis as to any other student in the district; (3) establish a bilingual school for the 1972–1973 school year; and (4) publicize these conditions in the Brownfield school system and community.[59] Riles, in effect, ordered policy adjustments that made year-round schooling optional and, more important, ensured that school officials would have to follow through on the pilot bilingual-bicultural elementary school.

School officials came to terms with state guidelines and policy adjustments, but some board members "expressed dissatisfaction with the establishment of a bilingual school as a condition to the approval of the year-round pilot program."[60] State Superintendent Riles had basically shifted the year-round school debate from one attempting to make the bilingual-bicultural school dependent on the 45–15 year-round plan to one that made the 45–15 year-round plan dependent on the bilingual-bicultural school. Giving conditional approval on July 1, 1972, Riles mentioned in a letter to school officials that he was especially impressed with the fact that out of the students participating in the "five schools . . . only 58 students requested alternative assignments."[61] Notwithstanding Riles's policy adjustments, Mexican American activists continued to protest and organized a "boycott school" that met in the basement of a local church.

COPE persuaded one of its members, a local Mexican American woman with a teaching credential, to accept the position of teaching and administering the school. She accepted the job because she opposed the 45–15 year-round plan and because she did not want "children of boycotting families to miss out on their education."[62] The boycott school, however, did not generate widespread support from the Mexican American community. In fact, only about fifty students participated, whereas 1,930 students enrolled in the year-round program.[63] Table 4.1 shows year-round school enrollments for Fall 1972. As we can see, the percentage of

Table 4.1. *Year-Round Schools in Brownfield, Fall 1972*

School	Enrollments	White	Mexican American
Patroni	428	54.7	37.7
Pumpkin	313	60.3	34.1
Libre	505	52.4	41.3
Esconde	291	54.0	39.6
Montañas, Jr. High	395	58.1	37.4
Total	1930		

Source: The Brownfield School District, *School Board Minutes,* July 18, 1972, p. 356. Racial/ethnic percentages were obtained from the Brownfield School District, *Racial/Ethnic Distribution,* October 2, 1972.

Mexican American students participating in the year-round elementary schools ranged from 37.3 percent to 41.3 percent. They made up 37.4 percent in the junior high school program. In the elementary schools white students made up the majority, ranging from 52.0 percent to 60.3 percent. At the junior high school, whites made up 58.1 percent.[64]

One would have expected more support for the boycott school, given the number of Mexican American parents attending school board meetings, the newspaper articles in the Spanish bilingual newspaper focusing on the issue, and the 300 to 400 protesters who marched to the school district office. One way to explain the small number of Mexican migrant families participating in the boycott school is that the number of migrant students (twelve- and thirteen-year-olds) participating in the plan was quite small. For example, of the 395 students enrolled in the district's year-round junior high school, approximately 150 (37.4 percent) were of Mexican origin. Even if all 150 Mexican-origin students had been migrants (which they were not), the number would have accounted for only 8 percent of the district's 1,200 migrant students. In addition, Mexican migrant parents realized that California state policy allowed them to choose between the traditional and year-round plans.

It was indeed interesting that school administrators saw the boycott school as a sweeping failure because its enrollments were small, it lacked widespread support from the Mexican American community, and it failed to reopen in the fall. Mexican American leaders however, saw the function of the boycott school through a different lens: It was never intended to be a permanent institution but was a symbolic act of protest that called attention to their exclusion from those policymaking decisions that were bound to have significant effects on their lives.[65] After the 45–15 plan had been in operation for several months, the director of the program said Mexican migrant children were benefiting from the program, particularly because it had boosted their attendance record. Under a traditional schedule of 181 school days from September to June, for example, Mexican migrant children attended an average of 116 days. Under the 45–15 plan, their attendance record increased to an average of 146 days.[66] But an improved attendance record failed to impress Mexican American leaders. They had always been mindful that year-round education had the potential to improve their children's school attendance. With this in mind, they countered the improved attendance argument by claiming that the amount of time spent in a classroom did not by itself necessarily guarantee high-quality education.[67]

A year later, school officials downplayed Mexican American resistance to the year-round plan and asserted that the once-vocal Mexican American opposition had disappeared. From their perspective, the year-round school protest was unsuccessful because the boycott school did not reopen in the fall, it had a peak enrollment of less than fifty participants, the larger Mexican American community gave little support to the boycott, and teachers who had opposed the plan admitted that children were learning and seemed happy with the new calendar. The changes that made parents nervous, one school official observed, had been taken in stride by their children. One study noted that resistance gradually declined and, presumably, year-round schooling was now supported by the Mexican American community.[68]

CONCLUSION

The Mexican American response to year-round schooling in Brownfield supports the claim made by other researchers that public schools had difficulty sharing power with poor and minority groups.[69] In Brownfield, Mexican American leaders became suspicious of offers made by school officials because their proposals for reform were typically ignored, resisted, or watered down. And because year-round schooling bypassed the needs of Mexican migrant families and was created at the national level by a professional elite that was interested in space efficiency and cost effectiveness, COPE and Los Padres Unidos, with the help of high-level state officials, had to assess the effectiveness for their children on their own. First, they were nervous about supporting a plan that mandated their children's attendance during the summer months, and, second, they were disturbed that their participation was sought only after decisions had been made.

Their response to the 45–15 plan was influenced by a legacy of suspicion and mistrust created by prior encounters with the local educational administration. Just before the initiative became a topic of discussion, the Mexican American community had mobilized and demanded curricular and pedagogical reforms. After years of exclusion, they had demanded to know how the district qualified for federal funds, how funds were distributed, how various committees were formed, and how educational policies were shaped in general. As the Mexican American community had pressed for local reform, they realized that, if they united, they had the potential to bring about some changes. But they were realistic about their capacity to reform the schools, and mindful of their exclusion from educational policymaking bodies such as the school board, the central administration, and other positions of power.

COPE was heavily criticized by school officials for initially endorsing the year-round school initiative and then withdrawing its support. But its turnabout was a response to the district's minimal effort to explore how the plan was going to affect Mexican migrant agricultural workers. Furthermore, COPE was disturbed by the superintendent's attempt to manipulate the process by linking the year-round program to the bilingual-bicultural school. Los Padres Unidos suspected that the initiative, imposed by the local educational power structure, might be used to control them rather than to offer their children more opportunities in school. They did not trust educational policymakers' assertions that the plan was going to improve their children's attendance, give them the opportunity to either work or catch up on their studies during the fifteen-day session break, and expose them to job opportunities other than agricultural field work. Deep-seated norms in the district worked against Mexican American participation because the administrative structure, like so many, dictated that all educational policy decisions were technical matters best settled by experts.

School officials have historically succeeded in imposing educational innovations on people with less power and influence. But what differentiated Brownfield from other instances of year-round school resistance in the United States was that Mexican migrant agricultural workers had to gauge the effects of year-round school on their children's attendance, the economic impact of their decision to participate or not in the year-round program, and how much they were able to trust programs created by school administrators who had little interest in sharing power with them. Although school officials portrayed Mexican migrant resistance (that is, the boycott school) in the community as a failure, a more accurate account was that Mexican migrants realized their options in the schooling process and, at the same time, decided they would cautiously respond to the aspirations of local activists. They recognized that state policymakers were giving them the opportunity to participate in either the traditional school calendar or the 45–15 year-round plan.

Educational policymakers failed to understand that year-round schooling had different effects on different groups. What seemed appropriate and beneficial to some groups was not necessarily true for others. As we saw, the concerns of white middle-class parents were very different from those of Mexican migrant workers. White parents were mostly concerned with vacation schedules and other technical matters; whereas, Mexican migrants were concerned about the earning power of their children during the summer months. Formal mechanisms to guard the well-being of all groups were absent, especially those groups in the most vulnerable positions. If school officials had included all voices in the community, especially migrant parents, they would have perhaps experienced less resistance to the reform.

Finally, it was ironic that year-round school experts neglected to consider the lifestyles of Mexican migrant agricultural workers. This was particularly significant because the group represented a segment of the U.S. population that continued to rely on their children's assistance in farm work, one of the reasons the traditional school calendar was established in the first place. Another irony was how year-round school consistently trumpeted the need to incorporate as many special interest groups as possible in the decision-making process. But although school authorities in Brownfield tried to be inclusive in creating a year-round program, they did not include all groups in their communities in the process. To this end, Mexican American activists and Mexican migrant parents had to confront the initiative in small groups, deciphering it through their own historical experience, in their own terms.

FIVE

Mandated Bilingual Education Comes to Town

In the last chapter we examined the Mexican American migrant parent response to year-round education. As we saw, Brownfield was one of the few school districts in the nation serving a large Mexican migrant population that experimented with the concept. Mexican parents challenged the implementation of the 45–15 year-round plan because they were excluded from the decision-making process and because the design jeopardized the livelihood of the migrant family. Many depended on the earning power of their children during the summer months, but most year-round school studies focused primarily on middle-class concerns in urban and suburban environments. The previous chapter gave special attention to how Mexican migrant resistance differed from conventional concerns.

Let us now shift our attention to the next controversial issue in Brownfield. This chapter examines how the Brownfield school system and community responded to mandated bilingual education. The mandate became controversial both because it provided a curriculum and pedagogy in Spanish for Mexican American limited-English-proficient (LEP) children, and also because the reform raised a number of issues relating to immigration, language policy, patriotism, demographic changes, and ethnocentrism. More important, the mandate inadvertently called for the incorporation of ethnic minority groups into a profession (education) that traditionally excluded them. Educators began to wrestle with a state directive that was bound to have dramatic implications for the ways public schools functioned. Although numerous studies have examined the politics of bilingual curriculum and pedagogy at the federal and state levels, the politics of its implementation at the local level has hardly been treated.[1]

THE POLITICS OF LANGUAGE

Throughout the history of American education, schools frequently became involved in ethnic issues as successive immigrant communities tried to use schools to maintain their language and culture. During the mid-nineteenth century, as a case in point, many German communities achieved political clout, aggressively resisted assimilation, attempted to preserve their cultural and linguistic identity, and created German-English bilingual schools throughout the Midwest. They were among the first to establish bilingual classes at the elementary school level. "In 1840," wrote David Tyack, "German citizenry persuaded the Ohio legislature to pass a law requiring school boards to teach German whenever 'seventy-five freeholders' demanded it in writing. The resulting schools were bilingual: at first children learned reading, grammar, and spelling in both English and German in the primary grades."[2] By 1875, the superintendent of the St. Louis schools, William T. Harris, defended teaching German in public schools. Harris "saw no conflict between Germans' desire to retain their 'family ties with the old stock' and their determination that their children be 'thoroughly versed in the language and custom of the country in which they are to live'."[3]

Unlike the first half of the twentieth century, when Mexican children attended segregated schools because of their so-called "language handicap," a national debate about bilingualism developed during the 1960s and 1970s. Bilingual education became a civil rights issue for Mexican Americans and a means to obtain respect for their culture, an instrument to fight discrimination against the non-English-speaking, and a device to integrate themselves into the educational profession. Mexican Americans, however, "were slow to emulate their European predecessors' demands for bilingual education."[4] Before the civil rights era, organizations such as the League of United Latin American Citizens (LULAC) and the American GI Forum stressed social, political, and economic justice and attempted to integrate into American life. LULAC placed special attention on ending *de facto* segregation in schools and job discrimination.[5]

But during the 1960s, the emphasis shifted from socioeconomic issues to broader educational objectives. Scholars focused on theories of alienation to defend bilingual education for children reared in environments where English was not spoken. Throughout this period educators began to hear that public schools confused, disoriented, and belittled Mexican American children.[6] Within this context, advocates claimed that bilingual education was essential for the Mexican American child to gain a new sense of pride. As I stressed in Chapter 3, Mexican American activists blamed their children's underachievement on negative teacher attitudes and culturally insensitive curriculum, and on the fact that children were falling behind academically in the early grades because they had a limited command of the English language. By the time children reached high school, the activists said, many had become discouraged and dropped out of school. Failing to see the relevance or economic benefits of their education, a significant percentage of these students left school to find employment.

The civil rights era indeed marked a new outlook toward Mexican American language minority children. As we have seen, Mexican American communities became energized; they felt deceived by schools and realized that equal educational opportunity made little difference if their children lacked an understanding of the language of instruction. Addressing this educational problem at the federal level, Congress started to promote new programs that would teach Mexican children in their native language while they learned English.[7] This is not to say that Congress fully understood what bilingual education was all about, because research on the subject was sparse and only a very small number of programs actually existed. The U.S. government was merely taking a political stance on an issue: Mexican Americans in public schools had been grossly neglected in the past.[8] Although Congress had not defined specific methods of instruction for those with limited English proficiency, new programs became eligible for funding under the new bill. Federal funds were provided to local school districts to support innovative and experimental programs for non-English-speaking children and those who came from "disadvantaged" backgrounds.[9]

Proponents began to transform bilingual education from simple curricular innovations into specific instructional methods. They pressed officials of the U. S. Department of Education, Office for Civil Rights, to put out a policy statement affirming public school responsibility for LEP children. In 1968, President Lyndon B. Johnson signed the Bilingual Education Act into law; thus the U. S. government made its first commitment to addressing these students' language needs. But it was not until May 25, 1970, that the federal government entered a national debate: Stanley Pottinger, director of the Office for Civil Rights (OCR), sent a memorandum to "school districts with more than five percent national-origin-minority group children" informing them of their responsibility under Title VI of the Civil Rights Act, which outlawed discrimination in federally supported programs. "[D]istricts must take affirmative steps," ordered Pottinger, "to rectify the language deficiency in order to open its instructional program to these students."[10]

Although hundreds of school districts were made aware of their responsibility to the language-minority child, most ignored the commission's statement and carried on business as usual. The statement failed to significantly impact local educational policy. The Chinese community in San Francisco, however, challenged its school administration on the issue. The U. S. Supreme Court, in *Lau v. Nichols* (1974), stated that failure to provide non-English-speaking Chinese students a comprehensible education denied them equal educational opportunities. *Lau* stands out as a landmark case on the road to bilingual education. It was not enough, said Justice William Douglas, to merely provide "students with the same facilities, textbooks, teachers, and curriculum, for students who do not understand English are effectively foreclosed from any meaningful education." In other words, equal resources were no longer seen as providing equality of opportunity for youngsters unable to speak English. Public schools were thereafter required to take "affirmative steps" to rectify the deficiency.[11]

The *Lau* decision affirmed Pottinger's May 25th memorandum by arguing that federally funded school districts had to provide students of foreign origin with limited English proficiency the services that would give them equal access in schools. *Lau* did not prescribe a specific remedy, and it did not mandate bilingual education. The decision merely stated that steps had to be taken to make schooling comprehensible to the child with limited English. Proponents in many states, nevertheless, used *Lau* to strengthen their case for mandated bilingual education. By 1975, "*Lau* remedies" were created to help school districts comply with the ruling; they provided technical guidance and attempted to clarify ambiguities in the decision. But what was important about the *Lau* remedies was the institutional belief that English-as-a-second-language (ESL) programs were inadequate by themselves. More importantly, *Lau* remedies in many cases informed school districts that native language instruction was a necessary component. Even though some school districts were given the option to forgo the use of native language instruction, the burden was put on local policymakers to develop alternative programs that were consistent with the *Lau* remedies. In other words, the burden of providing an acceptable alternative to bilingual education continued to rest at the local level.[12]

Although the *Lau* remedies helped implement bilingual education on a voluntary or exploratory basis, such education was now becoming mandatory in some states.[13] In 1976, California became one of the first states in the nation to mandate bilingual education. The state enacted Assembly Bill AB–1329, requiring bilingual education in school districts serving LEP children. This bill created political unrest in many school systems and communities.[14] Although there was an enormous amount written both for and against bilingual education, few studies have documented the way in which special interest groups resisted or supported mandated bilingual education.

Scholars broadened the campaign for bilingualism and biculturalism into a general critique of American society—in particular, that the melting pot had never worked. Americanization, they said, had injured Mexican Americans and other ethnic minorities whose history in the United States was one of continued cultural and economic degradation. Far from serving these newcomers, public schools had always been prone to reinforcing existing racial, ethnic, and social class hierarchies. Those immigrants who had gained middle-class status during the early twentieth century had done so not because of schools, but in spite of them. Critics of bilingual education claimed that it "might have gained wider acceptance if its advocates had been content to describe bilingual education as no more than a transitional bridge to assimilation."[15] The argument went on to say that academicians linked bilingual education with bicultural education and bicultural education with cultural separation. By doing so, the academicians supposedly alienated the great mass of conservative and middle-of-the-road voters who continued to compose the majority of the American electorate. Biculturalists, the argument went on, misjudged the temper of the nation as a whole. They assumed that the United States was in a state of spiritual malaise, that a sense of disenchantment had struck at the very heart, soul, and spirit of the American people, and that public opinion was ready for a fundamental change. A widespread ethnic revolt, one transcending the Mexican American community, supposedly reflected a wider discontent with the white, Protestant, Anglo-Saxon establishment on the part of other white ethnics and their descendants. This assumption was in fact mistaken because the bulk of middle-class Americans were satisfied with their institutions.

CHANGING CONCEPTS OF BILINGUAL EDUCATION

The call for bilingual education grew louder in California as the number of Mexican American schoolchildren unable to speak English rapidly increased. Like other communities, Brownfield was experiencing dramatic growth. The town, for example, grew from 14,569 in 1970 to 23,543 in 1980. Whites increased 26.6 percent from 1970 to 1980 (from 9,500 to 12,034), while Mexican Americans increased 127 percent (from 5,069 to 11,509). The ethnic ratios in Brownfield's total population changed substantially. Whites, who accounted for 62.2 percent of the community in 1970, dropped to 51.1 percent in 1980. At the same time, Mexican Americans grew from 34.7 percent to 48.8 percent.[16] School enrollments fluctuated between 1971 and 1979; in fact, they slightly declined from 12,998 to 12,598. Racial/ethnic composition of the school district, however, changed. White enrollments dropped from 64.6 percent in 1971 to

50.3 percent in 1979, while the Mexican American portion rose from 30.8 to 44.3 percent.[17]

The exact number of Mexican LEP students enrolled in the district during the early 1970s is uncertain; by 1975, they numbered approximately 2,093. More compelling were their percentages at individual schools, ranging from 9.2 to 83.0 percent.[18] The Brownfield school system was indeed representative of the kinds of changes that were occurring in many agricultural communities across the state. But contrary to conventional wisdom that large inner-city school systems were the only ones being challenged by AB–1329 (the mandated bilingual education bill), medium-sized school districts such as Brownfield were also struggling with the new legislation.[19] Given the Mexican American struggle to establish the pilot bilingual-bicultural school in Brownfield during the early 1970s, one would have expected vehement opposition to mandated bilingual education from educators in the district. More striking was the Mexican American strategy to assure that bilingual education would be enacted in Brownfield. They became less vocal, less confrontational, and mindful that school officials had to implement the reform. Within this context, they let the law work for them instead using the confrontational tactics of the late 1960s and early 1970s.[20]

As it did in other locales in the state, bilingual education in Brownfield met resistance by some whites, some educational administrators, and some school board members. As a case in point of local opposition, one local citizen, J. Crawlings, said the bilingual education mandate was going to have far-reaching implications for the schools and community. From Crawlings' perspective, bilingual education was being forced on the community and it was going to "tempt the infestation of this area with more people from Mexico" and "aid in the deterioration of our society as we know it." He considered leaving Brownfield because he did not want his children to grow up in a bilingual-bicultural town. He implored white residents "to revert back a few years to a time when anyone could feel at ease to walk downtown on Thursday evening or Sunday afternoon."[21]

Responding to the letter, one white resident noted that Crawlings was the epitome of the "fear and prejudice" that people in Brownfield held toward Mexican Americans. If bilingual education was such a burning issue that it was compelling some people to think about leaving Brownfield, that was Crawlings' option, "and if he feels that strongly," wrote the resident, "maybe he should."[22] More people began to enter the mandated bilingual education debate. While many educators were generally nervous about the mandate and opposed it, others came to favor the reform. Paradoxically, a group of liberal white school teachers began to complain that the pilot bilingual-bicultural school was the only site in the district that was providing bilingual instruction to the LEP child. Although the board claimed that more bilingual teachers had been added to the district (six at the elementary level and one at the high school), white teachers responded that what had been added was nothing more than ESL programs. Asserting that very little was being done to serve the LEP child, teachers told board members that the district's "bilingual efforts [were] not enough." Several white teachers and Mexican American parents, in fact, told the board that "until bilingual education is given support, it will continue to be an unwanted stepchild." White teachers had a vested interest in supporting the new legislation: They were becoming frustrated because they lacked the skills to work with the non-English-speaking child. They testified in a school board meeting about having to rely on bilingual (migrant) teacher aides to serve these children.[23]

Given the anti-bilingual education climate in the district and community, board members were astonished that White teachers were calling for more bilingual programs in the district. The school board was split on the issue. One board member supported its expansion but believed it was "unrealistic to expect 100 percent compliance." He said that "while I am saddened that compliance is not better, I am surprised there is as much as there is." Another member, the first and only Mexican American to be elected to the board, was more optimistic. He believed that the problem with bilingual implementation was not so much with teachers but rooted with school principal resistance. "[U]ntil we get the principals on the ball," he said, "we're not going to comply."[24]

Officials of the California State Department of Education began pushing school districts throughout the state to comply with the bilingual education mandate. Billy Richmond, Brownfield's superintendent, accepted responsibility for the district's problems, claiming that the district was noncompliant because of a "a poorly outlined plan of commands from the district level to the schools." If the district was going to reach compliance, he said, a Bilingual Education Master Plan needed to be drafted as soon as possible. As a way to deflect pressure from special interest groups in the community, the administration and school board formed a Bilingual Advisory Committee.[25]

THE STRUGGLE FOR A BILINGUAL EDUCATION MASTER PLAN

School districts with large LEP enrollments began to feel pressure from the California State Department of Education.[26] Like many other school systems in the state that were raising questions about bilingualism, people in Brownfield were concerned about the district's ability to comply because there was a lack of bilingual curricula and a serious shortage of bilingual teachers. Concerning bilingual pedagogy, some people believed in using the students' primary language as the mode of academic instruction, with an ESL component. Others called for a program using both languages for academic instruction. Still others disagreed with the use of the native language and supported a full-fledged ESL program. The Bilingual Advisory Committee recommended the first two models: the use of the primary language with an ESL component and the use of English and Spanish interchangeably. School officials were astonished to discover that the Bilingual Advisory Committee recommended an extensive augmentation of bilingual education in the district. The committee's recommendation meant that about one-third of the district was going to be "fully bilingual."[27]

The district's assistant superintendent supported the Bilingual Advisory Committee's recommendation, but he anticipated resistance from the white community because it meant some schools were going to use Spanish as the mode of instruction during the primary grades. He was surprised that "for so long the emphasis in school had been on learning English. [N]ow there is acceptance and even encouragement to learn Spanish." But before the Bilingual Advisory Committee made further recommendations in the master plan, policymakers needed to know how many LEP students were enrolled in the district in order to determine the extent of the bilingual program in the district. To find this out, committee members recommended testing in October for language dominance (basic written skills for Spanish-speaking students). Other recommendations were to evaluate programs, to inform parents of the bilingual education mandate, to explain the options available to them, and to establish bilingual advisory committees reflecting the ethnic composition of each school.[28]

Although Mexican American parents refrained from pushing school officials to implement the Bilingual Master Plan as soon as possible, they did say that LEP children were dropping out of school at a rapid rate because they were unable to keep up academically with their English-speaking peers. "[If] bilingual education is more available," they said, "the drop-out rate will lessen."[29] One survey taken in 1975 revealed that LEP enrollments at the high school level dramatically decreased in the later years. Out of 174 Mexican American limited English-speaking (LES) students enrolled at Brownfield High, for example, 41.3 percent were in the ninth grade, 26.4 in the tenth, 17.2 in the eleventh, and 14.9 in the twelfth grade. Of the school's 101 non-English-speaking (NES) students, 78.8 percent were in the ninth grade, 10.8 in the tenth, 4.9 in the eleventh, and 5.9 in the twelfth grade.[30]

In trying to comply with the bilingual directive, the Brownfield school system was confronted with the challenge of hiring enough bilingual teachers. School administrators and white teachers began to express interest in organizing seminars and workshops about bilingual education. Board members were less than mindful that a significant number of white teachers had been requesting more assistance from the district to help them work with LEP students. The district's Coordinator of Curriculum started to organize "survival skills" workshops and seminars for teachers working with LEP children. These classes provided basic information about bilingual curricula, pedagogy, and teaching strategies.[31]

As the district drew closer to a Bilingual Master Plan draft, a group of white parents and teachers, calling themselves Concerned Citizens for Education (CCFE), sought to defeat the expansion of bilingual education in the district because, they believed, it was harmful to their children.[32] At a school board meeting, CCFE presented a petition with 1,200 signatures indicating parents wanted to stop the expansion of bilingual education in the district. The group alerted school officials that if their complaint was downplayed, they would gather "5,000 more signatures." Many parents "applauded almost every speaker who told the board that bilingual education was going to disrupt classrooms and cause innumerable problems." CCFE told school officials that bilingual education "was a costly, time-consuming program that was alienating parents, frightening students and confusing teachers." One parent captured the sentiment of the audience by asking why the district was suddenly "catering to Mexicans."[33]

Even though only a few board members supported the Bilingual Education Master Plan, many local citizens believed there was a conspiracy to make all schools in the district bilingual. Facing an angry crowd of white parents, one board member asked the CCFE group to understand that the board was not responsible for mandated bilingual education but that they were "simply carrying out the law." Because most parents at the meeting were white, the Mexican American board member suggested that the next meeting be held in both languages so that Mexican American parents could "have their say too." One white parent cynically responded that she also wanted a bilingual meeting "but only to prove how unworkable it would be."[34]

CCFE protested the spread of bilingual education for many reasons. Their first criticism was the way in which the district was counting LEP students. This count was very important because the number of LEP students determined the extent of bilingual education in the district. CCFE's point of contention was that migrant LEP students were being counted in October, but that many left the following month, so that they should be excluded from the district's survey. In addition to demanding to know what budget categories were going to fund bilingual education in the district, CCFE also asked what arrangements were being planned for parents who elected to remove their children from bilingual school settings.[35]

Like most other school systems in the state, Brownfield's was given a two-year grace period to comply with the bilingual mandate from the state. By September 1979, the Brownfield district was expected to have a bilingual program in place. While there was a serious concern over the difficulty of recruiting enough bilingual teachers to meet the district's demand, the assistant superintendent claimed that the district needed to work harder toward that goal.[36] Many white teachers seemed to support the assistant superintendent; they wanted the opportunity to become bilingual. Of the approximate 500 teachers in the district, about 100 (20 percent) volunteered to learn Spanish. Some of these teachers wanted to earn bilingual certificates in order to participate in the district's bilingual program. They believed that white teachers "should be given an opportunity . . . to prove they could become bilingual." They were realistic about learning a second language and understood that the process required an enormous amount of work. Some said that if their efforts were going to help their students learn better, then "the effort was worth it." In December 1977, the district had fewer than twenty bilingual teachers. School administrators projected that 80 to 100 would be needed by fall 1979 to meet state compliance.[37]

But there was a faction of teachers who were offended by the state mandate. Unlike those who were willing to become bilingual, these teachers sought transfers to nonbilingual schools. One CCFE member said that many teachers and community members wanted to know more about the bilingual education concept. As it was, the move toward compliance felt as though "something so foreign was being forced down our throats." Believing that mandated bilingual education was fundamentally wrong, one teacher said it was outrageous to have to learn another language because, she asked, "Whose country is this?"[38] While these teachers understood that it was their right not to have to learn another language to keep their jobs, they resented those who were willing to learn Spanish and teach in bilingual settings. But the problem was more complicated than learning another language, one teacher said. There was a "strong undercurrent of fear" that some teachers were going to be eliminated even though board members had assured them they were not in danger of losing their jobs because they were not bilingual.[39]

As we saw in the previous chapters, there was tension between the schools, the white community, and Mexican American parents. But with the mandated bilingual education issue, tension also evolved between the central administration and the CCFE group. Part of the problem, according to the CCFE, was that the central administrators were too anxious to implement the Bilingual Master Plan. The assistant superintendent, in fact, became a major player in the move to execute part of the plan during the middle of the academic year. He took a strong stand on the issue because, he said, the district needed to comply by September 1979. Some board members, teachers, and community members challenged him, arguing that mid-year change was an inconvenience for students and the larger community. What follow are short excerpts from two opposing views from school board members. "To move children around just to satisfy one phase of this law," the first said, "to me seems wrong." The other stated that "Anglo and Mexican American parents [will] determine the scope of bilingual education in Brownfield by deciding how many children [will] stay in proposed classes." One board member proposed that "parents should be told as soon as possible . . . so the district will know how many classes actually need to be set up."[40]

Concerned Citizens for Education asked central administrators, especially the assistant superintendent, why they were so adamant about implementing the program. Nearby school districts with similar demographics, the group said, were not taking such drastic measures to meet compliance. One parent said Brownfield was rushing "into this thing that nobody knew about."[41] Even though the CCFE group knew that the Bilingual Master Plan was targeted at only a few schools in the district, they were concerned that some schools were going to require "bilingual classes at every grade level" because, according to a 1977 district survey, the LEP population was soaring. Moreover, the survey noted that "about half of the children who [qualified] under the new law for bilingual instruction were not receiving it."[42]

As the Bilingual Education Master Plan debate continued, an attorney from a legal aid organization came to a board meeting to remind board members that "children who need bilingual instruction are to be receiving it now," that it was the right of parents to have their children in a bilingual class, and that if the district failed to comply there were "legal remedies available."[43] As legal activists warned the district of its responsibility to its language-minority population, CCFE continued to challenge the mandate in general and its implementation during the middle of the school year in particular. A group of liberal white teachers and Mexican American parents, however, confronted the CCFE group. They said there was no basis for CCFE's criticism because most of them had never been to a bilingual class. One teacher from the pilot bilingual schools told CCFE that it was "immoral not to let Spanish-speaking children learn until they understood English." The group of liberal white teachers and Mexican American parents proclaimed that there was no quality in an educational system where more than forty percent of Mexican American youth left school before graduation. Challenging CCFE's allegations that bilingual education was alienating parents, frightening students, and confusing teachers, the liberal white teachers and Mexican American parents said it was the existing educational structure that was harming the language-minority children because they were not able to understand the language of instruction. Schools that rejected the student's linguistic background, they continued, negated their cultural identity, eliminated their motivation to learn, marginalized them, and created discipline problems for everyone in the schools and community. From their perspective, mainstream schooling was confusing LEP children and frustrating teachers because they were unable to communicate with them.[44]

CCFE then shifted its strategy in order to stop the spread of bilingual education. Instead of challenging the local schools, they sought to challenge state officials. CCFE (and a couple of board members) arranged a special meeting in Sacramento to ascertain whether the Brownfield school district was following procedures. They asked Assemblyman Peter Chacon (coauthor of AB–1329) whether it was legal to implement part of the Bilingual Master Plan in the middle of the year. Chacon responded that "it was very foolish to set up bilingual classes in the middle of the school year." Back in Brownfield, CCFE told the central administration and the rest of the board that state officials "were very surprised by some steps Brownfield administrators have taken." But the assistant superintendent responded that he had also been in close contact with state officials and that they had never told him that "the district should slow its efforts down." From the assistant superintendent's perspective, it "seemed reasonable . . . that laws should be carried out as soon as possible."[45]

Despite the information that school board members and CCFE obtained from the state, there were still questions about midyear implementation and whether Mexican migrant LEP children qualified for the district bilingual survey. To assure CCFE that the district was following state guidelines, the assistant superintendent invited Guillermo Lopez (one of the state's top bilingual education officials) to clarify some of the issues. In a school board meeting, Lopez informed educators and community members that midyear changes were appropriate and that migrant LEP students were to be "included in the data used to determine how many bilingual classes the district must form."[46]

Lopez assured board members they were moving toward bilingual compliance and commended administrators for their efforts. Some teachers, administrators, and members from the CCFE group, however, challenged Lopez on the migrant LEP count issue. The superintendent presented a hypothetical situation to Lopez, asking him what the district ought to do in a predicament where twelve migrant LEP students were in a bilingual class, but ten of them had left the area temporarily. The question was whether the district was still obligated to continue a bilingual class. Lopez authoritatively replied that "whether the students leave because they are migrant or because their parents take them out of the class, the program has to continue until new language tests are taken." One CCFE member asked what responsibility the district had to parents who were unwilling to let their children participate in bilingual education. Because many of the town schools were expected to implement bilingual classes, the member asked: "[C]ould they be put in another classroom or do they have to be bused to another school?" Lopez did not answer because, he said, the situation depended on local educational policy. He said that it was not the role of the state to micromanage schools. Within the context of AB–1329, it was the responsibility of schools to offer LEP students better schooling opportunities. This was an issue of choice, however, and the question needed an answer. The assistant superintendent stepped up and said that if parents chose to remove their children from a bilingual class, "the only choice as I see it is to transfer the child to another school." Parents responded negatively to the assistant superintendent because they wanted their children to attend their neighborhood schools.[47]

Because Guillermo Lopez had reinforced what Brownfield's assistant superintendent had been claiming all along, CCFE said that he had "just confused things." From the perspective of the CCFE group, "there was so much anger and confusion" that Lopez merely clouded the issue at the meeting.[48] Looking back on the mid-1970s, Lopez remembered the meeting with Brownfield educators and community members. From his perspective, what was taking place in Brownfield "was typical of what occurred throughout the state." He recalled many "angry faces and uptight people" in Brownfield. The problem was that bilingual education appeared "foreign and un-American and that we were casting allegations upon the existing system." In his analysis, people in Brownfield were unreceptive to the bilingual mandate.[49] Lopez was partially correct that many communities were nervous about bilingual education. As one bilingual teacher in Brownfield observed, white residents felt that bilingual education was "a shadow descending over the land, they [the white community] see Brownfield becoming a Spanish-speaking town."[50]

Some board members came to realize that mandated bilingual education was indeed a radical proposition. One board member said that "what may be reasonable to the administration may not be reasonable to citizens who have not yet caught up with the impact of such legislation."[51] Because the central administration was adamant about making midyear changes, some white residents believed some board members and administrators were "deliberately implementing this program now as a pressure tactic to get more people into the bilingual program."[52] Special interest groups began holding "private meetings" with board members to discuss the details of the Bilingual Master Plan. As one board member said, it was unethical to hold private meetings because one ran into the danger of establishing policies without everyone present. Given the power of some special interest groups, the board member said, it was "unfair to give special attention to any one group." But other board members disagreed, maintaining that it was "perfectly permissible for board members to have private meetings as long as [each member made] it clear he is speaking as an individual." A third board member said "that I would certainly be available to meet with a group as a representative of my personal opinion." One board member said he did not favor any group in particular, mentioning that he had already met with the Chicano Leadership Council (a group that supported bilingual education). Another board member said she/he "would not meet with Concerned Citizens for Education, a group opposed to some aspects of bilingual education, because I don't think we should be associated with special groups even by inference."[53]

The problem with private meetings was that some people were acting on the information that was being discussed. For example, one board member criticized other members of the board for going to Sacramento with CCFE on their "special fact-finding mission" to determine if the district was acting correctly. If board members continued to function in that manner, he said, every time the district ran into a difficult problem they would begin making decisions as experts rather than basing their decisions on public information.[54]

A part of the Bilingual Master Plan was implemented in the middle of the school year. Although the reform began to bring some changes to several schools, it was surprising that of the district's 500 teachers, only ten requested transfers to nonbilingual schools. Moreover, schools within the town that traditionally lacked bilingual classes were now offering them. Some elementary schools were beginning to offer bilingual classes in various grades; others were offering them at all grade levels. For example, one school in the center of Brownfield that traditionally served white children was now offering bilingual education to seventy first graders. There were some schools that were offering bilingual and English-only classes at every grade level. Of all the district's schools, only two were fully bilingual.[55]

White parents wanted school officials to accommodate English-only classes. The assistant superintendent reminded parents that they ultimately had the choice of selecting bilingual or nonbilingual placement, but he also pointed out that white students in smaller schools who wanted to be in English-only classes faced an obvious disadvantage. He gave an example of a school in the district that had an enrollment of 166 students, was fully bilingual, and was unable to accommodate English-only classes. Larger schools with more space, he continued, did allow for both bilingual and English-only curricula and pedagogy at each grade level.[56]

Although part of the Bilingual Master Plan was implemented, the district faced an enormous amount of work to comply with the law. Local educators and the larger community knew the plan was going to be approved because it was policy and because a new generation of teachers was supporting it. Although Mexican American parents did not become confrontational, they diplomatically informed the board that they had the "power to decide if bilingual education is a success in the Brownfield schools," and that their "decision can make the difference between allowing the non-English-speaking children in this district their rights to the full benefits of a good education or preventing them from their rights."[57]

In the recent past, board meetings had been crowded, tense, and political. Some white parents had vigorously pressured the district to stop the spread of bilingual education. At the meeting where the Bilingual Education Master Plan would be either adopted or rejected, only a small number attended. The plan was approved by a three to two vote. "The swift and easy adoption of the plan," the local press noted, "was in contrast to the drama and even anger which had been a visible part of the preceding months' discussions."[58] After the plan was approved, board members explained why they voted as they did: "All children should have a language facility," one member said, "or education becomes irrelevant." The second said the district needed it, the "law requires it and it's a start." The third said "I could see no alternatives. I agree with the concept that each child should get what he needs to be a functioning member of society." The fourth member promised to try to change the law because she/he did not "support mandated bilingual education." The fifth member rejected mandated bilingual education in its entirety, noting that the Brownfield school district was going to suffer from bilingualism just as the Canadians.[59]

CONCLUSION

The implementation of the Bilingual Education Master Plan was a victory for those who believed LEP students were going to receive better schooling opportunities. But there were those who continued to believe that bilingual education was going to "breed mediocrity" and reduce the quality of education for white students.[60] The implications of the Bilingual Master Plan had far-reaching consequences in the district. As Mexican American enrollments continued to grow in the southern part of the district, white enrollments began to decline. Many white parents rejected bilingual education and this began to affect the racial/ethnic composition of some schools. One CCFE member observed that integrated bilingual classes were difficult to establish because white parents fled. "The Anglos ran," she said, "they didn't want that. There were very few Anglo students in bilingual classes." In some schools, it "was almost all Mexican."[61]

The Mexican Americans' struggle for equal schools rallied around a national and state discourse. That is, they relied on the *Lau* decision and AB–1329 to execute reform rather than on the confrontational tactics reminiscent of the late 1960s and early 1970s. They watched white liberal teachers and school officials push the Bilingual Education Plan through. This dual emphasis was articulated within a single preoccupation, to provide bilingual education to Mexican American LEP students without taking on criticism from the larger white community. The Mexican American community learned that state support was crucial in its struggle for equal education. They also learned that in order for local reform to be successful, they needed the support of teachers and white residents. Contrary to determinist notions that social-cultural minorities lacked understanding of hegemonic politics in dominant institutions and ideologies throughout the United States, this case demonstrated the capacity of Mexican Americans as citizens to influence their historical trajectory, using state laws to provide equitable schooling for their children.

SIX

Self-Interest and Compliance in the Desegregation Process

Bilingual education was enacted in California public schools because of federal policy, state legislation, and, in Brownfield, the support from a progressive mix of educators within the local educational power structure. Mandated bilingual education catalyzed a new formula for local school governance in which school authorities were forced to assume more responsibility for the language-minority child. This mandate meant curricular and pedagogical opportunities for those who had traditionally been educated under a "sink or swim" educational philosophy. The Brownfield school district, however, was experiencing profound changes: Mexican American population growth, relative to whites, was becoming an obvious and distinctive trend. Within this context, school segregation became an important issue in the schools and the larger community. This chapter will look at the politics of school desegregation, the Mexican American trend in the Southwest during the 1960s and 1970s, and the Brownfield experience. Why was the Brownfield school administration able to push a controversial Bilingual Education Master Plan through but unable to integrate Mexican American students from Brownfield with white students from the Atherton community?

THE EVOLUTION OF SCHOOL DESEGREGATION

School desegregation has been one of the most emotionally charged issues the United States has faced in its history. It became oversimplified, however, into its most basic emotional forms, and the terms "integration" and "busing" by themselves infuriated even the most liberal parent during the 1960s and 1970s. The political terrain surrounding this issue resounded with a confusing barrage of attacks, allegations, and retractions. The desegregation debate was undertaken at a variety of levels: The courts sought to use judicial orders to employ busing to integrate; the executive and legislative branches of government and elected officials proposed constitutional amendments to restrict busing; parents generally opposed the idea; and social scientists debated desegregation effects on educational equality. Given the nation's educational history of local control, there were fundamental questions about the federal government and the courts restructuring American public schools. Conflict developed between the branches of the government as well as between minority and nonminority people.[1]

When the U. S. Supreme Court struck down *de jure* segregation in *Brown v. Board of Education* (1954), it did not articulate how desegregation should take place, it did not insist on immediate change, and things remained almost the same for more than a decade. Although revisions in *Brown* subsequently gave more direction on how to desegregate racially segregated schools, the Supreme Court assigned responsibility to the lower courts to work things out. Between 1954 and 1964, only a small number of schools were desegregated. By 1965, in fact, ninety-four percent of African American students in the South were still attending all-black schools.[2] The survival of segregated education was the result of Southern school systems' continuing to assign children to schools according to race and, more important, the lower courts' unwillingness to force public schools to integrate.

After the Civil Rights Act of 1964, however, the tempo of Southern school desegregation began to change. The Justice Department started to press for desegregation litigation, providing communities with judicial strength to confront recalcitrant educational policymakers at the local level. After President Lyndon B. Johnson pushed the Elementary and Secondary Education Act (ESEA) in 1965, he raised the stakes for Southern school systems because the act denied federal aid to segregated schools. In subsequent years, the Department of Health, Education, and Welfare (HEW) Office of Civil Rights (OCR) convinced many Southern school districts to reform their student assignments in a manner that resulted in more integration.[3]

School desegregation in the South was gradually increasing, but it was insufficient. Part of the problem was that many communities had the "freedom of choice" desegregation plans to integrate their schools. As a result, the Supreme Court in 1968 ruled in *Green v. County School Board of Education of New Kent County* that such plans were no longer satisfactory. That is, the court in *Green* considered student assignment plans wherein students were given the choice to attend African American or white schools to be ineffective. Addressed here was the issue that most students chose to attend the schools identified with their own racial background. *Green* challenged school systems to eliminate race-based student assignment and forced them to do away with single-race schools. In the course of the *Green* decision, a growing number of Southern school systems resorted to a form of geographic attendance zones and boundaries in order to circumvent the new constitutional requirement.[4]

Student assignment based on geography was unable to fully desegregate schools in many urban areas because there were high levels of residential segregation. From *Green* arose the question of whether the Fourteenth Amendment could force urban school systems to assign children to schools outside their immediate geographic areas in order to overcome residential segregation. For the next three years the U. S. Supreme Court remained relatively silent on this issue. The Supreme Court's silence, however, generated some problems. The lower courts, as a result, interpreted *Green* differently from place to place: Some judges dismantled residential segregation, crossed district boundaries, and achieved some desegregation. Others ignored *Green*, left schools as they were, and carried on business as usual.[5]

Public schools needed to take affirmative steps to integrate racially segregated school systems. By 1971, the *Swann v. Charlotte-Mecklenburg Board of Education* decision declared that busing could become a means to achieve "the greatest possible degree of actual desegregation."[6] Also, transporting children to schools outside their immediate geographical area was an acceptable remedy for past racial discrimination and thereby legitimized the use of busing. But *Swann* also held that courts could order desegregation outside district boundaries only if it were proven that schools were intentionally segregating and in doing so, in part, due to governmental actions. Intentional segregation was simple to prove in Southern school districts because it had been legally sanctioned until 1954. After the HEW/OCR had investigated hundreds of school systems in the South, and negotiated with thousands of them, it imposed court-ordered desegregation on more than 150 districts. To ease the process, Congress passed the Emergency School Aid Act in 1972 to help school districts desegregate: Special programs were funded, materials were purchased, and special staff were employed in newly integrated settings.[7] In most cases, efforts to desegregate were directed at the American South.

Legislators subsequently turned their attention to the North. But unlike the Southern experience, where educational apartheid was legislated, Northern and Western states did not have recent histories of legal segregation.[8] For the first time, however, the Supreme Court took up the question of whether school boards outside the South were deliberately segregating their schools: In 1973, *Keyes v. School District No. 1* in Denver, Colorado, opened the door to desegregation efforts in urban school systems across the United States.[9] *Keyes* looked at urban school systems that engaged in some actions designed to segregate students of color (i.e., mostly Mexican American and African Americans) in portions of their districts. As a result of *Keyes*, many urban school system began to lose large numbers of white students to the suburbs or to private schools. Almost every major city in the United States experienced an "out-migration" of whites to the suburbs and "in-migration" of mostly Blacks and Hispanics to the cities.[10]

The nation's changing demographics made the integration of urban schools systems extremely difficult, especially in the North. That is, whereas urban school districts in the South generally included entire metropolitan areas, the suburbs, and some rural areas, Northern urban school districts were traditionally separated from suburban and rural areas. This separation created numerous problems for the federal government in the northern and western parts of the nation: Integration became virtually impossible without crossing school district boundaries. With the election of Richard Nixon in 1972, the political landscape began to change, and a more conservative administration began to take hold. In 1974, the *Milliken v. Bradley* case ruled that the courts could not order busing across school district boundaries. The *Milliken* case prevented interdistrict remedies unless it could be proven that district lines had been drawn in a manner to preserve segregation, or local government officials had taken other action that contributed to that segregation.[11] Although this type of segregation existed, it was extremely difficult to prove. For the first time, the Supreme Court declined to define school desegregation laws as it had done in *Green, Swann,* and *Keyes.* The *Milliken* case may have presented sharp limitations to integration, setting back desegregation policies, but hundreds of school districts across the United States used busing as a means to integrate their schools.

School desegregation, however, did not assure integration. A new problem called "second-generation discrimination" evolved. This phenomenon generally meant that white and minority children were kept in separate classes within desegregated schools. Better known as segregation within desegregated schools, the most common form involved tracking minority youth in special programs such as special education, or compensatory classes (Title 1), or placing minority students in low-level courses and white students in high-level ones. In addition to curriculum differentiation, the term also took into account other forms of segregative experiences. According to some studies, African Americans were overrepresented by twenty percent in special education courses. Evidence suggests that more than ninety percent of school districts in the South were placing African American students in special education classes in disproportionate numbers. Circumventing integration, about seventy-five percent of school districts had more than one-hundred percent overrepresentation of African Americans in those classes. At the same time, African American students were underenrolled in advanced college preparatory courses and programs for the gifted and talented.[12]

But whether school desegregation was taking place in the American North or South, the process was not necessarily ensuring equal educational opportunities for African American youth. Some school districts were making important strides, achievement was rising, and race relations were improving. Conditions in other school systems were unfavorable; recalcitrant schools and communities resisted desegregation, racial tension increased, and little headway was made. One issue had become unequivocally clear by the late 1970s: School desegregation (that is, busing) was coming to a gradual standstill. Some branches of the government, along with social scientists and educational professionals, began to rethink the concept, to question its value, and to turn to other alternatives to integrate public schools.

MEXICAN AMERICAN SEGREGATION IN THE 1960s AND 1970s

The school desegregation debate up to this point was generally being discussed within a Black-White context. This parameter was understandable because the federal government, for the most part, was trying to dismantle the dual system of education in the American South. But even though the discourse began to move away from the South into other regions of the country, most Americans continued to think of school desegregation as a Black-White issue. The desegregation literature reflected this attitude, as social scientists, policymakers, and educational professionals wrote very little about the Mexican American experience.[13] As we saw during the civil rights era, Mexican Americans became a significant force, especially in the Southwest, in their struggle for equal education. Several national policies had attempted to provide better schooling opportunities for Mexican American children. Congress tried to stimulate the development of bilingual-bicultural education, the U. S. Department of Health, Education, and Welfare struggled to prohibit certain forms of cultural and linguistic discrimination, and the Supreme Court mandated that public schools needed to provide better schooling opportunities for students with limited English proficiency. At the same time, the courts, especially in *Keyes* in Denver, gave attention to the isolation of Mexican American youth. But what seemed obvious in the desegregation process (mixing African American and white children together in the same schools) raised powerful opposing impulses when Mexican American students were concerned. Unlike the African American experience, educational policymakers saw the integration of Mexican Americans as a political nightmare because the linguistic needs of these children as well as their color had to be considered.[14]

While the courts, federal policymakers, social scientists, and educators had successfully shown that segregation was inherently unequal for African American children, they now had to improve the experience of Mexican Americans, whose problems were even more perplexing. Mexican Americans were challenging the schools during the early 1970s, as various Hispanic groups worked through the courts and administrative agencies to reform local conditions. Throughout the 1970s, the *Keyes* case had the most compelling effect: It was responsible for making the Supreme Court decide how Mexican American children must be treated. For example, in a district with a sixteen percent African American and twenty-five percent Mexican American student population, the court was forced to determine whether only African Americans should be desegregated or whether the illegal segregation of Mexican Americans should be acknowledged. Put another way, *Keyes* called into question the Denver Public Schools' strategy of integrating Mexican American with African American students and calling it desegregation. The Court had to define Mexican American students as Caucasians and integrate them with African Americans or redefine their ethnic status (as a protected ethnic minority group) and integrate them with everyone else.[15]

The *Keyes* case held that there was enough evidence to support the fact that African American and Mexican Americans suffered similar treatment. The Court said, "there is also much evidence that in the Southwest Hispanos and Negros have a great many things in common. Though of different origins, Negros and Hispanos in Denver suffer identical discrimination in treatment when compared with the treatment afforded to Anglo students." The Court, however, also recognized that the educational needs of Mexican Americans were different from those of African Americans.[16] Before *Keyes,* the desegregation of Mexican Americans had been relatively inconsistent. In places such as Houston, for example, educational professionals allowed schools to count Mexican Americans as whites for desegregation purposes. In other parts of Texas, school districts defined Mexican Americans as a separate ethnic minority group and desegregated accordingly. *Keyes*, in short, settled the question of how public schools were to treat Mexican Americans in the desegregation process in the United States. It simply stated that the Mexican American educational experience was similar to the African American and that they should be accorded the same rights, and the U. S. Supreme Court agreed.[17]

Richard Valencia has noted that the segregation of Mexican Americans in the Southwest has always been persistent, pervasive, and disproportionate.[18] As we saw in Chapter 1, Gilbert Gonzalez asserted that by "the mid-1930s . . . 85 percent of surveyed districts in the Southwest were segregated in one form or another, some through high school, others only through the fifth grade."[19] Three decades later, large percentages of Mexican American students continued to attend minority schools. In 1968, the U. S. Commission on Civil Rights conducted a study to find out the extent of Mexican American school segregation in the Southwest. The commission discovered that, in addition to being disproportionately distributed in the Southwest, Mexican American students were also unevenly distributed among school districts. The uneven distribution, in general, reflected the concentration of Mexican Americans in certain geographic areas of the states surveyed. However, in many cases, their proportion in districts and schools bore little resemblance to their proportion in the communities where the districts and schools were located.

Table 6.1 shows the numbers and percentages of Mexican Americans in predominantly Mexican American school districts across the Southwest during the late 1960s and early 1970s. Although the commission found that Texas had the greatest number of Mexican American students in predominately Mexican American districts, conditions in California were just as deplorable. Of the fifty-seven California schools districts that had 50 to 100 percent Mexican American enrollments, five were almost all-Mexican American. Compared to Texas and California, enrollments in Arizona and Colorado were relatively small: Arizona had fifteen school districts that were 50 to 100 percent Mexican American and none that

Table 6.1. *Mexican American Pupils in Predominantly Mexican American Districts*

	Districts 50–100% Mexican American			Districts 80–100% Mexican American			
State	No. of Districts	No. of Pupils in Districts	Percent of Total Mex-Am. Enrollment in State	No. of Districts	No. of Pupils in District	Percent of Total Mex.-Am. Enrollment in State	Mexican American Total State Enrollment
Texas	94	291,398	57.7	31	107,140	21.2	505,214
Calif	57	54,741	8.5	5	5,149	.8	646,282
NM	31	38,891	37.8	9	17,117	15.6	102,994
Ariz	15	12,125	16.9	0	0	0	71,748
Colo	9	6,568	9.2	2	1,736	2.4	71,348
SW	206	403,723	28.9	46	131,142	9.4	1,397,586

Source: U. S. Commission on Civil Rights (1971), *Mexican American Education Study. Report I: Ethnic Isolation of Mexican Americans in Public Schools of the Southwest*, p. 22.

were 80 to 100 percent Mexican American. Colorado had nine districts that were 50 to 100 percent Mexican American and two that were 80 to 100 percent Mexican American.

One of the more notable findings of the mid-1970s, wrote Gary Orfield, was "that there was a slightly higher proportion of Hispanic than of black children in predominantly minority schools."[20] Although Orfield was referring to a national demographic trend, changes were quite dramatic in the West, as the percentage of Mexican American children in predominantly minority schools had increased from 48.5 percent in 1970 to 56.3 percent in 1974.[21] In another study conducted by Orfield, the percentage of Latino students in predominately white schools in the West, most of whom were Mexican American, dropped from 58 percent in 1968 to 32 percent in 1984, a 44.8 percent loss within a 16-year period. Moreover, the percent of Latino students in the West in 90 to 100 percent minority schools increased from 12 percent in 1968 to 23 percent in 1984, reflecting a 91.7 percent gain within this same period.[22] In sum, there was sufficient evidence that Mexican American students, as a whole, were becoming more isolated from their white peers.

As we saw in Chapter 1, schooling environments for Mexican American children during the pre-*Brown* era were extremely poor. Separate schooling was generally the rule, observed Gilbert Gonzalez. "Inadequate resources, poor equipment, and unfit building construction," he said, "made Mexican schools vastly inferior to Anglo schools."[23] Even though some conditions had improved during the late 1960s and 1970s, many things had remained unchanged. Similar to the "second-generation discrimination" phase many African American youth experienced after schools were desegregated, two primary forms of segregation within desegregated schools developed for Mexican American youth. The first obvious form was tracking. Jeannie Oakes has defined tracking as a process whereby students are sorted into categories to assign them into taking certain types of classes. Students, she claimed, were often identified as "fast, average, or slow learners and placed into fast, average, or slow classes." Unlike the pre-*Brown* era, when students were often openly assigned to classes and schools according to race, decisions were now being made according to achievement test scores or teachers' estimates of student academic potential. In some cases, students were placed according to what seemed appropriate to their future lives.[24]

But the other form of tracking, which differed from the African American experience, was based on linguistic difference. Policymakers at the local level typically separated Mexican American LEP students (and other language minority groups) from their white peers. To the extent that Spanish-speaking children generally scored lower on standardized tests, the results usually meant placement into courses for the educable mentally retarded (EMR), low track courses, or classes that supposedly met their linguistic needs.[25] In Texas, Mexican American students were twice as likely to be placed in special education classes as were their white peers, and in California, they were almost two-and-a-half times as likely as whites to be placed in such classes.

The point here is that Mexican American students have traditionally been tracked into low-ability courses and underrepresented in high-ability classes. Table 6.2 shows the distribution of Mexican American and white students in low, medium, and high-ability placements. According to this study, most Mexican American and white students were placed in medium (average) ability classes. There was a sharp difference, however, between low- and high-ability placements: Mexican Americans were overrepresented in low-ability and underrepresented in high-ability classes. Conversely, white students were underrepresented in low-ability classes and overrepresented in high-ability classes. Put another way, one in three Mexican American children was assigned to low-ability classes, while one out of seven white students was assigned to such classes. In contrast, one out of four white students was assigned to high-ability classes and one in seven Mexican American students was so assigned. But the table also indicates that the difference in the assignment of white and Mexican American students was strong despite the ethnic composition of the school. In schools that had less than twenty-five percent Mexican American enrollments, thirty-six percent of Mexican American students were enrolled in low-ability courses and 10 percent in the high-ability ones. Comparative figures for white students were fifteen percent in low and 23 percent in

Table 6.2. *Percent Distribution of Chicanos and Anglos in Each of the Specified Ability Group Levels*

Percent of School Composition That Is Mexican American	Student Ethnicity	Low	Medium	High	Mean
0–24.9	Chicanos	34.4	53.6	10.0	100.0
	Anglos	14.6	62.1	23.3	100.0
25.0–49.9	Chicanos	36.2	55.2	8.6	100.0
	Anglos	15.5	62.2	21.9	100.0
50.0–100.0	Chicanos	30.2	50.4	19.4	100.0
	Anglos	12.6	43.8	43.5	99.9
Total	**Chicanos**	**33.3**	**52.7**	**13.9**	**100.0**
	Anglos	**14.6**	**59.1**	**26.3**	**100.0**

Source: U. S. Commission on Civil Rights (1974), *Toward Quality Education for Mexican Americans*, Report VI, Table VIII, p. 23.

high courses. Within the context of school segregation within desegregated schools, educators found ways to keep Mexican American students, as much as possible, apart from their white peers.

LANGUAGE SEGREGATION IN DESEGREGATED SCHOOLS

As we saw in Chapter 1, educators had always separated the Mexican American LEP student from the educational mainstream. The separation was based on the notion that Mexican children needed to improve their competency in English before mixing with white children. The defendants in *Del Rio v. Salvatierra* in Texas (1931), *Alvarez v. Lemon Grove* (1931) in California, and *Delgado v. Bastrop* (1948) in Texas all sought to show, to some degree, that the Mexican Americans' limited English proficiency justified the use of separate classrooms or, in some cases, separate schools. A few decades later, as we saw in Chapter 5, *Lau* (1974) brought forth a new ruling about the responsibility of public schools to the LEP child. Within this context, researchers and policymakers began to examine the legal ramifications of policies stemming from the joint application of the Supreme Court's ruling in *Lau* and *Brown*. For example, *Brown* made it unlawful to segregate children based on race. *Lau* placed Mexican American children in school settings where they were forced to address an additional host of background needs. Given the legal forces behind these cases, a new form of school segregation began to unfold.

By the mid-1970s, a small group of researchers, policymakers, and educators pointed to a potential "conflict between bilingual education (although not mandated by *Lau*) and school desegregation."[26] While the group recognized that bilingual education and desegregation were both essential elements in the schooling process for a significant number of Mexican American language-minority youth, the issue became more complicated than originally anticipated. For example, Perry Zerkel maintained that bilingual education and desegregation had different, if not opposite, meanings. Desegregation generally meant "scattering Black students to provide instruction in 'racially balanced settings,'" he said. "Bilingual education, on the other hand, has usually meant the clustering of Spanish-speaking students so they could receive instruction through their native language."[27] Even if bilingual education and desegregation were not completely conflicting remedies, Zerkel concluded, "they were not fully compatible."[28] One of Zerkel's important points was that bilingual education and desegregation conflicted because they competed with one another in school systems with limited resources.

Educators seemed to understand the multiplicity of school desegregation. Mixing minority students in order to reach racial/ethnic balance was controversial but relatively simple to conceptualize. Integrating Mexican American LEP students with their white counterparts, however, was more complicated. For many policymakers responsible for school desegregation, the language issue complicated the process. One year after the *Lau* decision, Jose Cardenas found that many school systems in the Southwest were pitting the educational needs of Mexican American LEP children (bilingual education) against the desegregation process. These children, he reported, were in "either segregated bilingual education or integrated without bilingual education."[29] For many educators, it was becoming an either/or situation. Depending on one's educational philosophy, for example, educational policymakers were circumventing the implementation of bilingual education by scattering LEP children throughout their districts in the name of desegregation. Others who opposed mixing Mexican American and white children in the same classrooms used the opportunity to segregate Mexican American LEP youth in bilingual classes, thus continuing the familiar historical practice of separating Mexican children from their white peers because of language difference.

Many desegregation experts were examining the process within the context of race and ethnicity, ignoring the isolation of students with limited English proficiency. The more astute researchers, however, suggested that successful desegregation plans "preserve[d] existing bilingual programs."[30] By the late 1970s, bilingual education and desegregation had become serious enough problems that the California State Department of Education sponsored a conference on them. California possessed one of the largest LEP enrollments in the nation, so scholars, educational policymakers, and representatives from different levels of government attended the conference. After discussing the potential conflict between desegregation and bilingual education, most participants acknowledged that these issues "in effect, looked at two different but valid definitions of equality."[31] Presenters were optimistic that "integrated education and bilingual education [were] partners in the social enterprise."[32] Most of those attending concluded that bilingual education and desegregation could work without risking the needs of the language-minority child.

Educational professionals were aware that many school systems were either using bilingual education to segregate the language-minority child or dismantling bilingual education in the desegregation process. In many cases, school systems took on an either/or approach, ignoring the overall obligation to educational equality.[33] For example, many desegregation plans endangered bilingual education programs because they assigned students throughout their districts without considering their language needs.

Breaking down bilingual programs was easy to accomplish, wrote Peter Roos. "If all children in need of bilingual education programs were dispersed without consideration of that [language] need, it is unlikely in most communities that there would be sufficient numbers of children in any school or area to justify separate classes for comprehensive bilingual-bicultural instruction."[34] Roos understood the delicacy of the issue: On the one hand bilingual education could not justify language segregation, but on the other, there needed to be enough LEP students in the same classroom to establish a program. The controversial Boston public school system, in its reconciliatory negotiations with the court, became an exemplary case where bilingual education and desegregation were simultaneously considered. Although it was not always carried out in practice, in theory a specific number of LEP and English-speaking students were assigned in consecutive grades in order to establish and maintain linguistically integrated bilingual classrooms.[35] The issue was that true integration for the language-minority child needed to be carefully thought out. It was very easy for schools to appear ethnically integrated on paper, but beneath the facade of desegregation there was the risk of reverting back to the same historical problem—linguistic segregation.

DESEGREGATION IN BROWNFIELD
DURING THE LATE 1960s AND EARLY 1970s

During the 1960s and early 1970s, educational professionals in Brownfield understood that ethnic isolation was becoming an issue. But in the face of the struggle Mexican Americans in the district were making to achieve equal education, the professionals did not seem to give desegregation much public attention. Prior encounters between Mexican American parents and the district regarding the pilot bilingual-bicultural elementary school, year-round education, and state-mandated bilingual education seemed to deflect attention from the segregation issue. Ironically, the most powerful push for ethnic integration in the Brownfield schools did not come from the local educational power structure or the Mexican American community. The California State Department of Education was persistently pressing all school systems in the state to "ethnically balance" their schools. But there was a lag between push and response in Brownfield, even though the state had labeled several of its schools "racially isolated" in 1967.[36] Table 6.3 shows the schools in which Mexican American enrollments ranged from 37.3 to 71.7 percent during this period. Total minority enrollments, including Asian children, ranged from 46.2 to 79.5 percent.

Table 6.3. *Racially/Ethnically Segregated Schools in the Brownfield School District in 1967*

School	Total Enrollment	Percent White	Percent Mex-Am	Percent Other	Percent Total Minority
Pumpkin	321	53.8	37.3	8.9	46.2
Libre	652	57.0	37.1	5.9	43.0
Blanca	449	51.4	43.6	5.0	48.6
Corridor	700	48.7	40.2	11.1	51.3
Bird	602	41.1	53.1	5.8	58.9
Harvard	280	23.2	71.7	5.1	76.8
Esconde	191	12.5	69.1	10.4	79.5

Source: California State Department of Education (1966), *Racial/Ethnic Survey*, Sacramento, California.

Federal and state officials began to slap desegregation orders on most large urban school systems in California. According to Nathaniel Colley, of the Western Regional School Desegregation Projects, the "Los Angeles City Unified School District alone [had] 550 racially imbalanced schools. San Francisco had 114, San Diego 91, Oakland 72, Fresno 49, San Bernardino 42, San Jose 42, and Sacramento 33."[37] While the segregation issue was highly visible in most urban school systems, the problem was prevalent in medium-sized rural/suburban school districts like Brownfield. As early as 1971, for example, the superintendent in Brownfield notified the school board that some of their schools were being identified as "racially imbalanced" by the state. New desegregation policies were now stipulating that if there was a deviation of more than fifteen percent above or below the average district distribution, schools were deemed segregated.[38] According to this policy, Brownfield had eleven schools that were regarded as racially imbalanced. Like other school systems in the state, Brownfield officials were required to submit a "desegregation report" to the state by January 15, 1972, to demonstrate how local officials were going to "prevent and eliminate" racially and ethnically segregated schools.[39]

But unique geographical factors began to inhibit Brownfield's ability to comply with state desegregation guidelines. For example, the distance between the Atherton schools and the Brownfield schools (eight to thirteen miles) was seen as a serious barrier to district desegregation. Given the distance between the communities, the issue became an opportune focal point for those who opposed integration. Although this geographical issue provided a nonconventional excuse to limit integration, busing as a potential remedy was becoming a politically volatile alternative. The differences in class and ethnicity between Atherton and Brownfield, however, were sufficient to cause serious problems in the district. The local newspaper, in fact, began to highlight the busing issue between Brownfield and Atherton. Like many other communities across the nation that were beginning to take up the issue of desegregation, busing was going to be unacceptable to parents as an option. For decades, the press noted, busing was the daily experience of many students from Brownfield's rural communities. When "kids ride a bus to school where their classmates are the same color that's called transportation," one reporter noted. But "[W]hen kids ride a bus to a school where many of their classmates are another color, that's called busing." In other words, busing students to school from rural communities into Brownfield had been unchallenged in the past because it was simply done to transport children to school. Busing to achieve integration, however, was a different matter. Liberal newspaper reporters advocated integration in Brownfield so that the younger generation would grow up "without the racial hang-ups of their parents. . . . [B]using" the reporter wrote, was "the only way to achieve that."[40] But a large faction of white citizens in Brownfield, as we have seen in previous debates, were not as liberal as its journalists.

Integrating Atherton with Brownfield began to receive attention. School officials sought ways to limit the process, asking state officials whether desegregation was obligatory if distance was an issue. The superintendent seemed lukewarm about integrating Atherton and Brownfield and urged state officials to carefully examine "the geographical abnormalities of the district" because, he suggested, there were actually two districts within one. He requested that state officials regard Brownfield as a unique case, to consider desegregation to be exclusive to Brownfield (excluding Atherton), and to accept "whatever proposal the district submits for improving ethnic balance."[41] It was indeed ironic that as Mexican American children were becoming increasingly isolated in some of the Brownfield schools, several board members refused to acknowledge that segregation was a problem in the schools. They were baffled that the state was pushing an issue that was not being challenged by the larger community. Some board members admitted that there were "minority problems" in the schools, but maintained it was not a result of segregation. One board member claimed that reaching ethnic balance in the district was a low priority for both Mexican Americans and whites because, he said, "Mexican Americans are more concerned about what's going on in the classroom, on the quality of their education."[42] This was a false distinction, however, because ethnic isolation was quite relevant to Mexican Americans. Even though Mexican Americans were not actively challenging the district's lax efforts to integrate per se, their separation through ethnically homogeneous schools was a disturbing issue to them.[43] The issue was that Mexican Americans were in conflict with the educational power structure and the white community during the early 1970s over numerous educational policies and practices.

SEGREGATION IN THE LATE 1970s

By 1978, the California State Board of Education (CSBE) had made significant desegregation revisions in its policies and applied more pressure on public schools. Segregated school districts in California were being notified of their "constitutional obligation to take reasonably feasible steps to alleviate the racial and ethnic segregation of minority students." But like those in many other states, California's officials did not stipulate specific remedies; they left it to local school authorities to decide what constituted "reasonably feasible steps." Some districts worked hard to desegregate their schools; others submitted token and gradual desegregation plans that brought about very little change.[44] One issue of contention for many communities in California was the new legislation that no longer required a percentage above or below the district minority student average. The new legislation waived the numerical policy to control segregation, and it gave local school boards some leeway to determine for themselves what constituted a segregated school. Rather than relying only on minority percentages, the new desegregation policy actually called upon districts to consider more complex factors. Thus, local school district officials needed to look at: (1) the number and percentage of minority students enrolled in each school compared with the entire district, and the changing trends in ethnic enrollment over the preceding five years; (2) the racial and ethnic composition of administrative, instructional, certificated, and other classified staff in each school; (3) the attitudes and perceptions of school administrators, district staff, and the community regarding the "minority" status of each school; (4) the quality of buildings and equipment; and (5) the participation in extracurricular activities by the various minority groups attending each school.[45] Moreover, state officials ordered offending districts to submit desegregation plans no later than January 1, 1979.[46]

Even though the new state guidelines were more elaborate, their multiplicity suggested that local officials still had some leeway to decide which schools were "segregated" and what solutions they thought were appropriate. State commands became tough-sounding, they made their power threateningly felt, notifying local officials that they needed to "eliminate segregation regardless of community sentiment." They also warned local policymakers that if segregated education persisted, "the courts then [had] the authority to draw up a plan and carry it out."[47] The Brownfield superintendent seemed torn between his responsibility to the state and his allegiance to the white community in Atherton and other rural white communities.

Anticipating that the state would order busing as a means to integrate, he claimed that "forced busing would not be acceptable" to most community residents.[48] He pushed for desegregation within the Brownfield schools, including its southern rural communities, but became determined to exclude Atherton from the plan. He called for school closures (two of the district's predominantly segregated "Mexican" schools) and sought to construct another site west of Brownfield to draw white students in from the southwestern rural communities. Some school officials, however, saw the superintendent's proposals as radical: They were too complicated, argued the Director of Elementary Education, who envisioned a "community uproar when residents learn school districts are under State orders to desegregate."[49]

The school district had been confronting one issue after another. As one resident put it, dealing with desegregation was extremely difficult because they "had not recovered from the Bilingual Education Master Plan." Desegregation within Brownfield was one issue; integration between Atherton and Brownfield, one school board member said, was unacceptable. In fact, the board member said, if the Atherton community was "told their children had to go to school in [Brownfield] their first reaction would be to break away and form their own district."[50] Feeling pressure from the state and the community, local authorities looked for ways to desegregate the district without incorporating the Atherton schools. This search meant a plan that excluded long-distance busing. Authorities gravitated toward the "zone concept" by which the state permitted local officials to redraw school boundaries if this would "promote maximum racial and ethnic balance in segregated schools." But critics complained that the zone method would actually reinforce segregation because Atherton and Brownfield would be treated as two distinct school systems.[51]

As in other areas where desegregation became controversial, state officials in California recommended that all school districts involve their communities in the process as much as possible. In Brownfield, the Community Desegregation Advisory Committee (CDAC) was formed to assist the school board and to demonstrate to the state that the district was making a concerted effort to desegregate its schools. One middle school teacher, however, noted that CDAC members were "politically appointed" by the school board. As a result, he said, "you had committee appointees who represented the point of view of the Board [or] people who had north end perceptions [and] people from [Brownfield] who were from the old guard." Of the thirty members that made up CDAC, nineteen were white, eight Mexican Americans, two Asian, and one African American. Moreover, even though the CDAC functioned in an advisory capacity, white members seemed to have more influence, due to their positions within the community's social, economic, and political structures.[52]

But not all members of the school board and CDAC thought alike. To distinguish their political differences, I will use the terms "Pluralists" and "Conservatives."[53] To begin, Pluralists challenged the politics of the zone method, insisting that it was unethical to omit Atherton from the district's desegregation proposal. Conservatives countered that the zone concept was a legitimate way to satisfy the state's criteria to integrate racially imbalanced schools. Whether it was permissible or not, Pluralists maintained that Mexican American enrollments were too large in Brownfield to integrate the schools and called for two-way busing between Brownfield and Atherton. Ironically, even Conservatives on the school board acknowledged the difficulty of integrating the Brownfield schools, noting that "you have to get the majority students from somewhere if you expect to balance the schools." It was blatantly clear to one Conservative board member that it was a "sham and fraudulent to cut one section of the district out." Yet, they were vehemently opposed to a plan that would bus Atherton students to the Brownfield schools.[54]

It was extremely difficult for the school board and CDAC to reach a consensus.[55] But under the strain of the state's deadline, the district forged a working definition of a segregated school, which took account of a complex set of variables: student achievement, student-teacher ratio, the use of special funding, personnel, location of schools, student mobility, and educational facilities. In other words, if a school had a "high" ethnic minority population, low student achievement, was federally funded, had low minority participation in extracurricular activities, and was located in one of the oldest and poorest sites in the district, the school was considered "segregated." However, school authorities were unable to agree on the minority percentage above or below the district average that would qualify a school as ethnically imbalanced. And so the whole complex formula for defining a segregated school was rendered ineffectual.[56]

Pluralists wanted to maintain the "fifteen percent above or below" criterion, but the Conservatives wanted to raise the ratio to twenty-five percent. They claimed that the fifteen percent guideline "would lead to long distance busing" and force the district to integrate too many schools. But Pluralists insisted that "anything over the fifteen percent definition would still mean an identifiable problem at schools excluded from the definition of segregation."[57] After much deliberation, board members tentatively agreed on the fifteen percent guideline to designate imbalanced schools.[58] In 1979, nine schools in Brownfield (out of fourteen) failed to satisfy the fifteen percent criterion. These schools ranged from 65.4 to 96.0 percent minority. To the extent that the Atherton area was not part of the desegregation plan, the ethnic composition of its five schools ranged from 92 to 98 percent white.[59]

Pluralists contacted some Mexican American parents, especially those who were leery of the district's desegregation plan, to seek out their opinions. Mexican American concerns were different from those of the white community: Whereas white residents allegedly objected to long-distance busing, Mexican American parents feared the treatment their children would face in the Atherton schools. Ethnic tension was already a problem in some of its schools, and some Mexican American parents felt that busing their children to Atherton schools would exacerbate the situation. Brownfield's Mexican American school board member said that part of the problem was class differences between the two communities. From his perspective Mexican American parents would have been received unfavorably by the community and the schools in Atherton. "It would have been very awkward," he said," for Mexican American parents from [Brownfield] to attend meetings in [Atherton]."[60]

Despite the increasing segregation in the Brownfield schools, a powerful conservative white bloc staunchly opposed the inclusion of Atherton in the desegregation process. As a result, Conservatives succeeded in negotiating a plan that limited busing within the Brownfield southern schools. The idea was that integrating some of Brownfield's southern rural schools, which had larger percentages of white students, would effect some desegregation.[61] As a result, policymakers began to discuss the possibility of school pairing, adjustment of attendance boundaries, reorganization of grade structures, and school closures in Brownfield.[62] But Pluralists complained that these strategies would mean token desegregation because substantive desegregation would not come about "without involving the [Atherton] area fully." Pluralists reminded Conservatives that school districts needed to take reasonable steps to end minority isolation and that the Brownfield schools had "been warned about heavy minority concentrations by State and Federal officials."[63]

The California State Board of Education had laid down a set of complex and ambiguous desegregation standards, but they ultimately bestowed on local officials the responsibility to design their own methods to integrate their schools. Nevertheless, state officials clearly expected all districts to reduce racially imbalanced schools. Because Conservatives failed to construct a plan that excluded the predominantly white Atherton schools, Pluralists began to push this issue harder. One Pluralist in CDAC called the desegregation proposal a "band-aid measure" that was going to make matters worse. Conservative board members, however, reminded everyone that desegregation was going to take place because they were indeed going to shut down two of Brownfield's most ethnically segregated schools. With this strategy, Conservative board members claimed they were taking meaningful steps toward equalizing conditions for Mexican American students. Pluralists, however, countered that closing down the two segregated schools would not yield significant change, that the situation would merely distribute Mexican American students within the southern rural schools that already had a significant number of Mexican Americans.[64]

Fearing court-ordered desegregation, white residents in the southern rural schools soberly began to review their options. Ironically, while their sentiments ran against the plan to bus elementary level children to the Brownfield town schools, "[white] parents wouldn't mind having minority children bused in to make the school more racially balanced." They made it clear that "we just don't want to lose our children from [our community]."[65] Realizing that the desegregation discourse was leading to one-way busing (minority children to white schools), Pluralists met with Mexican American parents. Together, they voiced the concern that the desegregation plan was discriminatory because it proposed busing Mexican American students out of Brownfield while permitting white students to remain in their neighborhood schools. La Coalición—a local Mexican American political group—called for a more equitable plan: If Mexican American students were going to be moved, they said, then "an equal number of Anglo children should be bused." But Atherton residents stood firm against busing their children to the Brownfield schools.[66] One school board member cautioned Atherton residents that if they continued to resist integration, there could be a danger and "a real possibility that the courts [would] desegregate the [Brownfield] schools if the district [did] not." He noted that the district was already under strict orders from the state to desegregate and that they only had a few months to obey the order.[67]

At a district meeting, Atherton parents raised the historically familiar proposal to separate into two districts because Atherton and Brownfield were such distinct communities. Atherton parents favored deunification with "loud and prolonged applause" after the question was raised. Some Conservatives supported deunification, but others pointed out that "the courts [would] not allow de-unification where desegregation [was] an issue." Even though distance was the focal point for many Atherton parents, other considerations were raised in some board meetings. Atherton parents simply told board members to "consider the number of parents in the audience that won't have their kids in any of these [Brownfield] schools." One ex-CDAC member recalled how Atherton parents "resisted their children having to alter a lifestyle to facilitate a responsibility to the district as a whole." The dilemma for many Atherton parents was that their identity was not wedded to the district and, as a whole, they did not see themselves as part of Brownfield.[68]

Vocal Atherton residents were cognizant that school officials were under severe pressure from the state to submit a desegregation proposal. But they also warned school officials that "any large moves for forced integration . . . would lead to large numbers of children being taken from the public schools and put into private schools."[69] Other Atherton residents, concerned about the extent to which the state might intervene, expressed a more pragmatic interest in negotiating a limited participation in the desegregation plan. Like Brownfield's rural southern community, they indicated a willingness to allow some Mexican American students to be bused to the Atherton schools but "only with reassurance that none of their children would be moved away from [their] neighborhood" schools. In this case, Atherton residents were willing to discuss the desegregation process but only on their own terms.[70]

One middle school teacher recalled a point of contention: Conservatives were determined to devise a one-way busing plan. The local press observed that "when school busing to achieve racial balance comes to [Brownfield], children in the upper-income [Atherton] areas will remain in their neighborhood schools while minority children in town are moved."[71] For Pluralists, the desegregation plan was unquestionably biased. One resident called it "unconscionable because it involved [Atherton] so little," and one Mexican American parent said it was "grossly inequitable." Conservatives, however, insisted that busing Mexican American students was the only way desegregation was going to come about. And because part of the desegregation proposal called for school closure of two predominantly Mexican American elementary schools, they reasoned that moving Mexican American children was inevitable, that one was unable to "close these schools without moving minorities" to other schools. The desegregation plan proposed shifting 1,802 children within the Brownfield and southern schools.[72] But after noting where students were going to attend school, very little was going to change. Pluralists found that the number of segregated schools was going to be reduced by only one.[73]

As school officials continued to modify the desegregation plan, very little change was taking place. To the extent that Mexican American children were going to be moved within Brownfield and its southern rural communities, Pluralists claimed the plan was ineffectual because it was moving Mexican American children several blocks (except for one elementary school in the eastern foothills) away to other schools. One Mexican American woman in the CDAC complained that "we are just shifting kids around but not to the [Atherton] area." A Japanese American CDAC member voiced the same concern, noting that it was very frustrating. "[W]e don't seem to know what the objectives are," he said, "[i]n some areas there are no changes. We are shuffling people around but are getting nowhere." Anita Jones, the only African American woman in the CDAC, said white people had been running from integration for decades. "Eventually," she said, "they are going to confront the issue. The time is now. If someone wants to pay for private school, that is all right, it should not become an overriding factor in our decision."[74]

Jones recalled how divided CDAC was. "You had people who wanted to go full steam ahead and some who were obstructionists who kept putting up road blocks." But she also pointed out that the obstructionists were very articulate and that they were part of the power structure in the white community. Moreover, continued Jones, "[Atherton] residents had the full support of the district office." To characterize the politics of desegregation in Brownfield, she said Atherton and some school officials "were very much in bed together. They had an agenda. The agenda basically was the status quo. [Atherton] people did not want change."[75]

One board member reminded Conservatives that the whole idea behind desegregation was not only to integrate but to achieve equality whether they agreed with it or not. One Conservative board member concurred that quality education was in fact their priority but that "quality education [was] not necessarily integrated education."[76] According to Jones, Conservatives were determined to circumvent integration between Atherton and Brownfield. From her perspective, "the bottom line was that they simply did not want to integrate the schools. They didn't want to change the ethnic make-up of the [Atherton] schools." Jones recalled one strategy school officials used to manipulate district boundaries. There was a small enclave of Mexican migrant families living between Atherton and Brownfield, at about equal distance from both areas. Had these Mexican American children been sent to the Atherton schools, she said, "it could have made a difference in integration." The enclave, however, was zoned as part of the Brownfield schools.[77]

Conservatives felt significant political pressure from Pluralists to revise the desegregation plan because it was unequivocally clear Mexican American children were going to participate disproportionately in the plan.[78] In order to avoid allegations of discrimination, the board recommended that the district: (1) develop an exchange program between different schools with high proportions of minority and majority students; (2) ensure that busing was voluntary; (3) equalize school facilities for minority students; and (4) set up an ongoing committee to reassess and recommend changes in the desegregation plan and to see that resegregation would not occur.[79] On the surface, the district appeared to be seriously engaged in an effort to integrate Mexican American and white children. But the July 1980 enrollment figures showed that little integration between Atherton and Brownfield came about. One Conservative claimed that only minimal change was brought about because busing white students from Atherton to Brownfield would "never work with a community so much opposed to it."[80]

Proposition 1, the 1979 state constitutional amendment that limited the use of mandatory busing, had serious effects for policymakers across California. Many Atherton residents were optimistic that the district would be omitted from the desegregation process. Moreover, the superintendent maintained that the state could only force the district to bus white children to Brownfield if segregation was a result of clear discriminatory intent. Intentional segregation was not the case in the area, he said, because "housing patterns, rather than government action, have caused racial isolation in . . . [Brownfield]. We haven't been aiding and abetting the situation," he said. The district had not "deliberately built schools in the center of heavily minority areas to isolate minority students."[81] But Pluralists reminded Conservatives that intentional discrimination in Brownfield would be rather simple to prove because decisions made in the mid-1960s and early 1970s did produce segregated schools. One Mexican American parent said that if a desegregation lawsuit was brought about, complainants would "only have to point to [the Atherton] High School and [the Atherton] Jr. High School. They were built where only white people live. If someone took it to court and said these schools were built here recently so that the people in this area wouldn't have to mix with Mexicans, it would be hard to prove that wasn't the reason the schools were built where they [are] located."[82]

Some Conservatives denied that the district's historical record showed that schools had been built in predominantly white communities. One board member, an attorney, warned that allegations of *de jure* segregation were a serious matter because "at least one or two schools in the district will be considered deliberately segregated." He suggested that "if the issue of segregation in [Brownfield] comes before the court, the district may be found [guilty] of *de jure* segregation. The very existence of [Atherton] High School would probably constitute *de jure* segregation."[83] A white woman from CDAC added that according to court precedents, if school districts had an opportunity to alleviate racial isolation but failed, the case could be considered *de jure* segregation.

The inequality of Mexican American school segregation was palpable, according to Anita Jones. Jones noted that, as a child, she had attended "one of those separate but equal schools [in Louisiana]." She said that "I can tell you it was anything but equal. As a black mother," she continued, "I anticipated that Mexican Americans would have many of the same problems blacks have had in this country. I went into this committee thinking we could deal with the situation like we would with blacks. But blacks never had problems coming from a totally different culture and speaking a different language like [Mexican Americans]."[84] Jones also understood that school authorities had glib justification for not pushing integration between indigent Mexican-American and privileged white children from Atherton. While it somehow seemed more acceptable that people were basing their decisions on what was best for everyone involved—especially those "poor Mexican kids"—Jones felt that Conservatives were mainly interested in keeping the Atherton schools as they were. Using such superficial rationales, she said, was "a lot better than saying we do not want the Mexicans coming over here to our schools."[85]

Segregation deepened in the Brownfield schools during a short interval when communication between the state and the district waned. In late 1979, however, the OCR generated and published the nation's 100 worst segregation offenders. Brownfield was ranked 81st on the list. The Brownfield superintendent immediately challenged the OCR report, calling it "unbelievable, unprofessional, absolutely ridiculous." He did not contest that Brownfield had "racially isolated schools;" his point was that if the federal government had "just called, they could have found that we've been working hard to improve the situation."[86] The report was generally criticized for sampling only 6,069 school systems in the nation's 16,000. OCR apologized to school authorities in Brownfield, acknowledging that the survey was perhaps a bit premature and that it should have not been released. Nevertheless, they said, the survey did help determine where OCR was going to conduct desegregation compliance reviews for the following year.[87]

Although school officials in Brownfield realized that Proposition 1, the amendment that limited mandatory busing, would not provide the legal means to circumvent desegregation between Atherton and Brownfield, Conservatives sought to buy time by waiting for more concrete information from the courts. The superintendent continued to claim that the district was doing everything possible to integrate its schools. While the scope of this study ends in 1979, segregation had intensified in some schools, remained the same in others, and declined in still others during the early 1980s.

Table 6.4 shows the desegregation plan and the racial/ethnic composition in Brownfield between 1980 and 1985. Four schools were deemed racially isolated, five were being monitored, and fourteen schools were considered nonisolated. We also can see that by the mid-1980s Mexican American enrollments in the Atherton schools actually increased, due to the district's integration plan. In some of the Atherton schools, for example, minority (mostly Mexican American) enrollments in Ocean View Elementary School increased from 9.5 percent in 1980–81 to 36 percent in 1984–85, and in Menchaca Elementary School increased from 4.3 to 26 percent during the same period. Most of the other Atherton schools remained predominantly white, especially River Elementary, Atherton Junior High, and Atherton High. The problem was that the plan stipulated that "a school shall be considered racially isolated when the total minority student population is in excess of 80% of the school's total enrollment."[88] School authorities adopted the policy that "the district shall alleviate minority isolated schools according to a reasonable and feasible timetable." By 1985, the district had four schools that were officially segregated; five schools were being monitored, ranging from 73 to 75 percent minority; and five others were considered nonsegregated, but ranged from 60 to 68 percent minority.

Table 6.4. *Brownfield School District Desegregation Plan: Minority Percentage, 1980 to 1985*

School	1980–81	1981–82	1982–83	1983–84	1984–85
RACIALLY ISOLATED					
Bird K-6	97.0	97.4	97.9	97.6	99
Libre	83.4	88.1	84.2	83.8	84
Blanca	80.3	83.2	81.7	83.2	83
Esconde	75.1	79.9	78.8	82.0	81
TO BE MONITORED					
Alliance	97.3	77.8	74.7	77.7	75
Corridor, Jr.	80.3	79.0	79.4	78.8	76
Corridor Elem.	74.2	79.7	78.9	79.3	79
McDonald	74.6	79.7	78.9	79.3	79
Bird Jr.	68.0	70.6	69.6	71.0	73
NONISOLATED					
Patroni	60.0	64.3	61.4	64.5	62
Atherton Jr.*	7.3	6.3	9.0	9.9	11
Romer	30.2	30.9	32.3	31.6	28
Haley	25.1	24.4	32.4	32.4	31
Pumpkin	53.7	48.9	46.6	56.8	60
Ocean View*	9.5	26.7	33.2	32.3	36
River*	10.3	8.6	7.6	11.7	15
Montanas	64.0	58.7	59.4	67.9	68
Exitor K–6	51.8	53.7	66.2	64.4	63
Exitor 7–8	46.8	34.5	48.7	52.6	58
Menchaca*	4.3	7.0	28.5	29.6	26
Atherton High*	7.0	7.8	9.2	9.5	8
Alternative	26.7	27.4	23.5	29.5	29
Brownfield High	59.5	61.8	64.7	65.2	66

Source: The Brownfield School District, *The Desegregation-Integration Plan*, 1985-87, p. 5.

*Schools part of Atherton area

CONCLUSION

Those who struggled for an equitable desegregation plan in the district came to think of it as a frustrating and strenuous task. Although a small percentage of Mexican American children were bused to some of the Atherton schools, most remained in Brownfield by virtue of the district's definition of segregation. School officials planned out two strategies to entice Mexican American children to the Atherton schools. Known as the Enrichment and the Basic Skills Plus Programs, the district did persuade a significant number of Mexican American students to attend Ocean View and Menchaca elementary schools. Except for the Alliance Magnet Elementary School, which did show the most significant gain of white students (about twenty-five percent) in the Brownfield area, ethnic isolation was largely sustained in the Brownfield schools. Decades after the *Brown* decision, desegregation continued to be controversial in the late 1970s, the 1980s, and the 1990s.

SEVEN

Summary and Conclusion

This book has briefly documented the Mexican American struggle for equal education during the civil rights era. The Southwest was examined in general and the Brownfield community in particular. Chapter 1 recounted Mexican American educational experiences during the pre-Brown era in order to situate the 1960s and 1970s in context. Specifically, we saw how school segregation, Americanization, vocational education, and psychometrics affected Mexican American children. Public schools began to systematically sort Mexican American students into curricula that were differentiated from those for white students. Also, the results of IQ tests were being used to affirm theories of intellectual inferiority wherein much educational and social science research tended to portray Mexican Americans as a burden to U. S. society.

In addition to the Mexican Americans' presumed intellectual inferiority, educators and the American lay public viewed them as lazy, amoral, dirty, stupid, disease ridden, and deviant. It was not surprising, then, that educational professionals went to great lengths to segregate Mexican American children in separate classrooms or in entirely separate schools. Educators across the Southwest repeatedly maintained that segregating Mexican youth during the elementary grades was in their best interest in order to remedy their cultural and linguistic deficiencies. Most Mexican children, however, were placed in separate facilities despite their command of the English language or their level of assimilation. In retrospect, we see that Mexican Americans faced some of the same educational challenges as southern and eastern European immigrants. A more accurate portrayal of their schooling experience, however, pointed out its similarity to that of African Americans.

The early twentieth century was indeed a period when educational reformers were trumpeting the need to assimilate all immigrants. But it was also an era when the same reformers became relatively silent about integrating Mexican immigrants into U. S. society. Their silence was partly due to the fact that the Mexicans' inferior and low castelike status was seen as a fixed condition that public schools were unable to reverse. Whether Mexican children attended urban, suburban, or rural schools, they were generally kept apart from white children and disproportionately channeled into classes or schools where the manual arts were stressed. Throughout the literature on Mexican American education, conventional wisdom held that Mexican youth were best suited for manual labor. As a response, public schools attempted to match their presumed destinies with specific curricular and pedagogical practices.

Chapter 2 provided a brief history of the Brownfield Community and politics of school district consolidation. The case study began when school consolidation became a political issue in the area, when the number of small school districts was called into question, and when some unification took place in 1946. As a response to the consolidation that came about, groups of people became nervous about losing their influence in school district affairs. As a result, in 1948, unification was voted down. To the extent that consolidation continued to be a hot topic of discussion throughout the nation during the 1950s, the reform was reconsidered in the Brownfield area during the early 1960s. After vigorous debate, a vote was taken in 1964; the decision to unify the whole area into one school system won by a small margin. Some suburban communities were reluctant to unify, but they supported the reform because they benefited from Brownfield's economic infrastructure: It offered a tax-base advantage to surrounding communities. In addition, there was pressure from the state to consolidate. One of the inconsistencies in the unification literature was that experts pronounced that by 1960 the reform was no longer championed by educational progressives. If this account was an accurate representation of the movement across the nation, then the Brownfield community was an anomaly, because the issue was vigorously debated up to the mid-1960s.

In all, consolidation inadvertently produced better schooling opportunities for Mexican American children in Brownfield because there was now an institutional possibility (although it did not immediately occur) for them to attend a range of schools in the newly formed school district. That is, the Mexican American community now had a legitimate claim to schools that historically had not served them. The reform, however, also created unintended consequences by paving the way for a serious debate about educational equity, integration, power, and control. The consolidation movement, as a byproduct, came to have progressive consequences for the Mexican American community that were altogether apart from the typical claims of the reform.

During the late 1960s, when the nation's moral vision was imbued with a sweeping sense of change and possibility, the legislative and executive branches of the federal government gradually began to attend to the needs and rights of the Mexican American people. President Lyndon B. Johnson, for example, launched a serious campaign to end poverty and tried to raise the educational achievement level of disadvantaged youth. Within this context, Chapter 3 looked at how Brownfield Mexican Americans started to call for better schooling opportunities for their children. Ironically, a few white journalists in Brownfield believed that poverty and educational inequality had no place in the midst of affluence, that everyone deserved an equal chance to succeed, and that its schools were failing to properly serve Mexican American youth. It was suggested in the local press that everyone, despite ethnic background, deserved better schooling opportunities in order to rise in the community's socioeconomic structure. Cognizant that federal funds were available for disadvantaged youth, the local press held that establishing better schooling opportunities for Mexican American children would benefit everyone in the community. But reforming the schools to meet the special needs of Mexican American youth failed to become a priority after unification because most educators were resistant to change. School officials, moreover, were more interested in devising new areas of authority, with careful allocations of powers and functions within the new district.

As a result of the proequality climate in California, the liberal views of the local newspaper, the Warran report (noting that something needed to be done about insensitive high school teachers and the high schools' culturally irrelevant curriculum and pedagogy), and a few Mexican American parents who had been complaining to the school board all along, increasing numbers of Mexican American parents started to challenge the school district more aggressively. In addition, federal and state funds were specifically targeting the needs of Mexican American children, especially those with limited English proficiency (LEP). By 1971, the Mexican American community had formed a united front and made several demands to the local school board: They sought curricular and pedagogical reforms; they wanted to be included in the decisionmaking process; and they wanted the district to establish a new bilingual-bicultural elementary school. These demands, however, triggered a passionate reaction from school officials and the white community. Many white residents believed that the plight of Mexican American children was the result of a cultural orientation that did not value education, rather than the structure of the school.

Contrary to conventional wisdom that Mexican American parents were indifferent about their children's education, Communidad Organizada Para Educación (COPE) collaborated with some school officials. This cooperative effort was awarded a half-million-dollar federal grant to start a pilot bilin-gual-bicultural school in the district. The grant became a turning point in the local politics of education because the educational power structure was now obligated to include Mexican American parents in some decision-making processes. In a break from the historical past, the bilingual-bicultural school engendered in Mexican American parents a greater sense of potency, self-worth, and control over policy decisions that were bound to have an impact on their children. Although Mexican Americans made some progress toward being included in the decision making process, they were mindful of their continued exclusion from the most powerful decision making bodies.

Mexican American parents came to learn that a small grassroots or-ganization, with solid support from its ethnic minority constituency, was able to have some effect on the distribution of educational resources, the formulation of educational policy, and the expenditure of funds in the schools. Contrary to determinist notions that viewed them as passive victims of dominant institutional and ideological structures, Mexican American parents made it clear that they possessed the capacity to orga-nize and mount a serious campaign for educational justice. Although change was slow, their united efforts eventually forced recalcitrant edu-cators and board members to take seriously the educational needs of minority children.

Throughout the Southwest, scholars, educational professionals, and the news media were associating the Mexican American struggle for equal education with bilingual-bicultural education. While the quest for appro-priate curriculum and pedagogy did bring some attention to Mexican Americans, other concerns were overlooked in the process. Chapter 4 examined the politics of year-round education and its impact on Mexican migrants. As we saw, year-round schooling became extremely controver-sial in the United States, but it was not a reform item that was particularly associated with Mexican American communities. The literature on year-round education up to the 1970s focused primarily on the most efficient use of space and on cost effectiveness within the context of white middle-class students in urban and suburban environments. Few studies had explored how Mexican American communities responded to year-round schooling during this period of analysis.

In Brownfield, the response of Mexican Americans to year-round schooling supported the claim that public schools had difficulty sharing power with poor and minority groups. Mexican American parents became distrustful of offers made by school officials because minority proposals for reform had typically been disregarded, rejected, or watered down. The plan for year-round schooling was created at the national level by a professional elite that was mostly interested in space efficiency and cost effectiveness and ignored the needs of minorities, so Mexican American parents had to confront the initiative on their own. They challenged a plan ordering their children to attend school during the summer months and were disturbed that their participation was sought only after decisions were made. *This is a repeat of the chapter!*

COPE was criticized by school officials for initially endorsing the year-round school initiative and then withdrawing its support. But its turnabout was a direct response to the district's minimal effort to explore how the plan was going to affect Mexican migrant agricultural workers. In addition, COPE was annoyed by the superintendent's attempt to manipulate the process by linking the year-round program to the bilingual-bicultural school. Los Padres Unidos and other Mexican American activists suspected that the initiative, imposed by the local educational power structure, might be used to control them rather than to offer their children more opportunities in school. They distrusted educational policymakers' assertions that the plan was going to improve their children's attendance, give them the opportunity to either work or catch up on their studies during the fifteen-day session break, and expose them to job opportunities other than agricultural field work. Deep-seated norms in the district worked against Mexican American participation because the administrative structure, like so many aspects of the establishment, dictated that all educational policy decisions were technical matters best settled by experts.

Educational professionals have historically succeeded in imposing educational innovations on people with less power and influence than they had. But what differentiated Brownfield from most other instances of year-round school resistance in the United States was that Mexican migrant agricultural workers had to gauge the effects of year-round school *repeat!* on their children's attendance, the economic impact of their decision to enroll their children in year-round schools, and how much they were able to trust programs created by people who had little interest in sharing power with them. School officials evaluated Mexican migrant resistance (that is, the boycott school) in the community as a failure, but a more accurate accounting revealed that through this action Mexican migrant parents realized their options in the year-round school process. Parents discovered that state policymakers gave them the choice to participate either in the traditional or in the 45–15 calendar.

One of the ironies of the year-round school controversy was that the experts neglected to consider the lifestyles of a segment of the U. S. population that depended on their children's assistance in agricultural labor, one of the reasons the traditional school calendar had been established in the first place. Another irony was that the literature on year-round education consistently trumpeted the need to include as many people as possible in the decision-making process. In Brownfield, educational policymakers failed to understand that year-round schooling had different effects for different groups. What seemed appropriate and beneficial to some groups was not necessarily that way for others. Formal mechanisms were absent to guard the well-being of all groups, especially those in the most vulnerable positions. As such, Mexican Americans were excluded from the process and had to confront the initiative in small groups, deciphering it through their own historical experience, in their own terms.

Chapter 5 examined the impact of state-mandated bilingual education in Brownfield. In contrast to the many communities where Mexican American activists were pressuring school districts to comply with Assembly Bill 1329, which mandated bilingual education in districts serving LEP students, Mexican American parents in Brownfield toned down their demand for bilingual education because central administrators took on an unusual role. That is, central administrators, the assistant superintendent in particular, initiated an aggressive campaign to implement bilingual education in the district as soon as possible. As a result, tension escalated between the central administrators and white parents. A group of mostly white parents (Concerned Citizens for Education—CCFE) organized and challenged the district administration. The group was especially concerned about the district's action to include migrant students in the computation on which bilingual classes were formed. It challenged this issue because migrant LEP students were enrolled for only part of the school year. The issue being challenged was CCFE's concern that migrant students would increase the number of bilingual classrooms in the district. CCFE's other issue of contention was the district's intent to implement part of the Bilingual Education Master Plan during the middle of the school year. Many white parents (and some teachers) believed that bilingual education was being imposed on them too quickly, that not enough was known about the reform, and that bilingual education was ultimately going to breed mediocrity in the schools and reduce the quality of education for white students.

The implementation of the Bilingual Master Plan had far-reaching consequences in the district. As Mexican American enrollments continued to grow, especially in the southern part of the district, many white parents began to reject bilingual education. This rejection inadvertently affected the racial/ethnic composition of classrooms and schools. As one Concerned Citizen for Education observed, integrated bilingual classes were difficult to establish because white parents were transferring their children to other schools, and, as a result, some schools were becoming almost 100 percent Mexican American.

Brownfield took the lead in establishing bilingual education in the area. Although bilingual curricula and pedagogy were generally new and undeveloped at the time, some school sites did become places where minority parents and students felt they were a part of their schools. How bilingual education affected the educational achievement of the Mexican American child is largely beyond the scope of this book. Ostensibly, bilingual programs reduced the psychological and mental withdrawal of some Mexican American students; bilingualism gave them a sense of pride, and, as some educators observed, they learned to value their Mexican heritage.

In contrast with the late 1960s and early 1970s, when the Mexican American community had relied on confrontational tactics in their struggle for equal education, in the late 1970s they learned that legislative and judicial support was crucial to achieve their goals. They also became aware that the cooperation of teachers and white residents was essential. With this new understanding, Mexican Americans began to see that they could gain power to affect educational history.

Unlike the support given by central administrators for bilingual-bicultural education, resistance was their reaction to school desegregation—especially between Brownfield and its surrounding affluent communities. Chapter 6 focused on this issue. As we saw, educators resisted busing white middle-class students from Atherton to Brownfield. Educators as well as the white community struggled to keep Atherton out of the desegregation debate. Given the district's geographical abnormalities, critics of desegregation proposals consistently stressed distance between Atherton and Brownfield. But after the U. S. Commission on Civil Rights named Brownfield as one of the nation's most segregated school districts, some white parents came to accept that some integration was inevitable. However, most white suburban (and rural) parents were willing to participate in the desegregation process only so long as their own children were allowed to remain in their neighborhood schools.

Resistance to an equitable desegregation plan frustrated some members of the district's Community Desegregation Advisory Committee. They believed that integration would only come about when the Atherton schools fully participated. Even though a small percentage of Mexican American children was bused to some of the Atherton schools, most remained in Brownfield by virtue of the district's definition of racial/ethnic isolation. Educational policymakers created "enrichment" programs in schools around the Atherton area to entice Mexican American parents to send their children there, and a significant number attended two of these schools. But ethnic isolation was largely sustained in Brownfield, except for a few schools that kept a significant number of white students. Desegregation continued to be controversial in the late 1970s, the 1980s, and reached national attention by the mid-1990s. True integration between these communities became so explosive that Atherton deconsolidated from the Brownfield schools and formed its own district.

Mexican Americans were unable to make significant changes in the Brownfield schools during the 1960s and 1970s because they lacked political power. They were marginalized from the political infrastructure of the community, they had minimal representation on the school board (just one Mexican American), and they rarely held positions of power in the central administration. In most cases they were unable to influence educational policy decisions that were certain to have an effect on their children. Even though some federal policies, state mandates, and court decisions worked in favor of creating equal schools for Mexican Americans, change was extremely slow and, in some schools, conditions remained virtually unchanged. The political impotence of Mexican Americans was a major problem in their struggle, and, as this study has demonstrated, as long as Mexican Americans are being denied their rightful place in American society, they will continue to resist the existing educational system.

+ On one hand the Mex-Amer struggle was as I expected b/c MA had little political power & representation but I learned
- Year Round edu & how it actually affected Mex-Amer → although it seems as y the reason for not thinking g this is two-fold (a) just plain unaware b) unwilling to share power)
This situation made me realize that there are some situations at home that teachers can't change but must take into consideration 1) we can't assume that everyone lives like we do → This is why it is the teacher/school's resp to learn about cultures rep in schools & have them represented in the school board & other policy making bodies
- Interesting to see how the state y Cali supported Mex Amer w/ decision allowing for choice
- Mex Amer fought for more than equal ed in the Year Round issue—

[Handwritten annotations:]

They realized that imp[ortant] decisions were deliberately being made w/o them and they aimed to put a stop to it (boycott) or at least make people realize that they knew what was going on

+ Bilingual Ed Battle -> I am not surprised at the backlash/resistance from the mainstream white community but I am surprised that people weren't expecting white teachers to be on the side of education -> made me realize what was missing from this text

- Donato writes from an outsider's position. Where are the perspectives of white teachers? Mex-Amer parents? Mex-Amer students? School board members?
- Donato's structure is repetetive -> repeats almost exactly same words -(who's this written for?)

Notes

INTRODUCTION

1. See, for example, Harvard Educational Review (1969), *Equal Educational Opportunity* (Cambridge: Harvard University Press); Jencks, C. (1972), *Inequality: A Reassessment of the Effects of Family and Schooling in America* (New York: Harper and Row); Mosteller, Frederick, and Moynihan, Daniel P. (1972), *On Equality of Educational Opportunity* (New York: Random House); Gross, Ronald, and Gross, Beatrice (eds.) (1969), *Radical School Reform* (New York: Simon and Schuster); Levine, D. M., and Bane, Mary Jo (eds.) (1975), *The "Inequality" Controversy: Schooling and Distributive Justice* (New York: Basic Books); Kozol, Johnathan (1967), *Death at an Early Age: The Destruction of the Hearts and Minds of Negro Children in the Boston Public Schools* (Boston: Houghton Mifflin); Kluger, Richard (1975), *Simple Justice: The History of Brown v. Board of Education and Black America's Struggle for Equality* (New York: Vantage Books); Willie, Charles, and Greenblatt, Sharon (eds.) (1981), *Community Politics and Educational Change: Ten School Systems Under Court Order* (New York: Longman); Monti, Daniel, J. (1985), *St. Louis School Desegregation and Order in Urban America* (Columbia: University of Missouri Press); Grant, Gerald (1988), *The Wonderful World We Created at Hamilton High* (Cambridge: Harvard University Press).

2. The Brownfield community, its school system, and individuals are pseudonyms.

3. Burma, J. H. (1954), *Spanish-Speaking Groups in the United States* (Durham: Duke University Press).

4. Gutierrez, Armando, and Hirsch, Herbert (1974), "The Militant Challenge to the American Ethos: Chicanos and Mexican Americans," in F. Chris Garcia (ed.), *La Causa Politica: A Chicano Politics Reader* (Notre Dame: University of Notre Dame Press), p. 86. Also see Roberts, Kenneth (1928), "The Docile Mexican," *Saturday Evening Post*, February 18.

5. *Independent School District v. Salvatierra*, 33 S. W. 2d 790 (Tex. Civ. App. San Antonio, 1930), cert. denied, 284 U. S. 580 (1931); Alvarez, Robert (1986), "The Lemon Grove Incident: The Nation's First Successful Desegregation Court Case," *Journal of San Diego History* (Spring): 116–135.

153

6. *Mendez v. Westminster School District,* 64, F. Supp. 544 (S. D. Cal. 1946), 161 F.2D 744.

7. For 1960s movements, see Muñoz, Carlos, "The Politics of Educational Change in East Los Angeles," in Alfredo Castaneda *et al.* (eds.) (1974), *Mexican-Americans and Educational Change* (New York: Arno Press); Navarro, Armando, "Educational Change Through Political Action," in Alfredo Castaneda *et al.* (eds.), *Mexican-Americans and Educational Change* (New York: Arno Press).

8. San Miguel, Guadalupe (1987), *Let Them All Take Heed: Mexican Americans and the Campaign for Educational Equality in Texas, 1910–1981* (Austin: University of Texas Press).

9. Katz, Michael (1971), *Class, Bureaucracy & Schools: The Illusion of Educational Change in America* (New York: Praeger), p. 114.

10. California State Department of Education, *Racial/Ethnic Survey, 1967;* Brownfield School District, *Racial/Ethnic Survey,* 1979.

11. Trueba, Henry, Rodriguez, Cirenio, Zou, Yali, and Cintron, Jose (1993), *Healing Multicultural America: Mexican Immigrants Rise to Power in Rural California* (New York: The Falmer Press), pp. 3–4.

12. "Discrimination: School Bias Toward Mexican-Americans," *School & Society* (November 1966): 94, 378.

13. Parsons, Theodore W. Jr. (1965), "Ethnic Cleavage in a California School." Doctoral dissertation, Stanford University.

14. Sanchez, George, I. (1940), *Forgotten People* (Albuquerque: University of New Mexico Press); Manuel, Hershel T. (1965), *Spanish-Speaking Children of the Southwest: Their Education and the Public Welfare* (Austin: University of Texas Press).

15. Carter, Thomas (1970), *Mexican Americans in Schools: A History of Educational Neglect* (New York: College Entrance Examination Board), p. 19. Also see Carter, Thomas, and Segura, Roberto (1979), *Mexican Americans in Schools: A Decade of Change* (New York: College Entrance Examination Board); U. S. Commission on Civil Rights (1971), *Mexican American Education Study, Report 1: Ethnic Isolation of Mexican Americans in the Public Schools of the Southwest* (Washington, D.C.: GPO); U. S. Commission on Civil Rights (1972), *Mexican American Education Study, Report 3: The Excluded Student: Educational Practices Affecting Mexican Americans in the Southwest* (Washington, D.C.: GPO); U. S. Commission on Civil Rights (1974), *Mexican American Education Study, Report 6: Toward Quality Education for Mexican Americans* (Washington, D.C.: GPO).

16. Carter, *Mexican Americans in Schools,* p. 19.

17. Ibid., p. 12.

18. San Miguel, Guadalupe (1986), "Status of the Historiography of Chicano Education: A Preliminary Analysis," *History of Education Quarterly* 26: 553–554.

19. San Miguel, *Let All of Them Take Heed.*

20. Gonzalez, Gilbert (1990), *Chicano Education in the Era of Segregation* (Philadelphia: The Balch Institute Press).

21. Foley, Douglas (1990), *Learning Capitalist Culture: Deep in the Heart of Tejas* (Philadelphia: University of Pennsylvania Press), p. 17.

22. Trueba *et al., Healing Multicultural America,* pp. xi–xii.

23. Davies, Don (ed.) (1981), *Communities and Their Schools* (New York: McGraw-Hill); Fantini, Mario, and Gittell, Marilyn (1973), *Decentralization: Achieving Reform* (New York: Praeger); McCarty, Donald, and Ramsey, Charles (1971), *The School Managers: Power and Conflict in American Public Education* (Westport: Greenwood Publishing Corporation); Wirt, Frederick M., and Kirst, Michael (1972), *The Political Web of American Schools* (Boston: Little, Brown); Saxe, Richard W. (1975), *School-Community Interaction* (Berkeley: McCutchan); Peterson, Paul E. (1976), *School Politics, Chicago Style* (Chicago: University of Chicago Press).

24. Katz, Michael (1987), *Restructuring American Education* (Cambridge: Harvard University Press); Bowles, Samuel, and Gintis, Herbert (1976), *Schooling in Capitalist America: Educational Reform and the Contradictions of Economic Life* (New York: Basic Books); Bourdieu, P., and Passrow, J. C. (1977), *Reproduction* (Beverly Hills: Sage Publications); Willis, Paul (1981), *Learning to Labor* (New York: Columbia University Press); Spring, Joel (1972), *Education and the Rise of the Corporate State* (Boston: Beacon Press).

25. Gonzalez, *Chicano Education*, p. 27.

CHAPTER 1. SCHOOLING IN THE PRE-*BROWN* ERA

1. Tyack, David (1974), *The One Best System: The History of Urban Education in the United States* (Cambridge: Harvard University Press).

2. Katz, Michael (1971), *Class, Bureaucracy, and Schools* (New York: Praeger Publishers).

3. Addams, Jane (1902), *Democracy and Social Ethic* (New York: Macmillan).

4. Olneck, Michael, and Lazerson, Marvin (1988), "The School Achievement of Immigrant Children: 1900–1930," in McClellan, B. Edward, and Reese, William (eds.), *The Social History of American Education* (Urbana: University of Illinois Press).

5. Tyack, David (ed.) (1967), *Turning Points in American Educational History* (Waltham, Mass.: Blaisdell), see chapter 4, "Forming a National Character," pp. 83–115; Kaestle, Carl (1983), *Pillars of the Republic: Common Schools and American Society* (New York: Hill and Wang), see chapters 5 and 6.

6. Bullock, Henry Allen (1967), *A History of Negro Education in the South, From 1619 to the Present* (New York: Praeger); Bond, Horace Mann (1934), *The Education of the Negro in the American Social Order* (New York: Octagon Books).

7. Reynolds, Annie (1933), *The Education of Mexican and Spanish-Speaking Children in Five Southwestern States* (United States Department of the Interior. Washington, D. C.: GPO), p. 9.

8. Ibid., p. 9

9. Ibid., p. 9.

10. Manuel, Herschel T. (1930), *Education of Spanish-Speaking Children*, p. 90.

11. Kibbe, Pauline R. (1946), *Latin Americans in Texas* (Albuquerque: University of New Mexico Press), pp. 96–97.

12. Reynolds, *The Education of Spanish-Speaking Children*, p. 10.

13. Gonzalez, Gilbert (1974), "System of Public Education and its Function Within the Chicano Communities." Doctoral dissertation, University of California, Los Angeles.

14. Carpenter, Charles (1935), "A Study of Segregation Versus Non-Segregation of Mexican Children." Master's thesis, University of Southern California, p. 29.

15. Ibid., p. 30. Carpenter noted that the following districts had some "segregated districts composed of Mexicans, or Mexicans and other Foreigners": Azusa, Bakersfield, Bell, Compton, Huntington Park, Lanershim, Madera, Modesto, Monrovia, Montebello, Napa, Ontario, Pomona, Potterville, Redlands, San Bernardino, San Fernando, Santa Barbara, Santa Maria, Santa Monica, Van Nuys, Visalia, Whittier.

16. Penrod, Vesta (1948), "Civil Rights Problems of Mexican-Americans in Southern California." Master's thesis, Claremont Graduate School, p. 69.

17. Cooke, Henry W. (1948), "The Segregation of Mexican American Children in Southern California," *School and Society* 67: 417.

18. Van Norman Hogan, Milo (1934), "Study of the School Progress of Mexican Children in Imperial Valley." Master's thesis, University of Southern California, pp. 81–82.

19. Stanley, Grace (1920), Special Schools for Mexicans, *The Survey* 45: 715.

20. Burma, John (1970), *Spanish-Speaking Groups in the United States* (Durham: Duke University Press), p. 75.

21. Hendrick, Irving (1977), *The Education of Non-Whites in California: 1848–1970* (San Francisco: R & E Associates), p. 57.

22. Donato, Ruben, Menchaca, Marta, and Valencia, Richard (1991), "Segregation, Desegregation, and Integration of Chicano Students: Problems and Prospects," in Valencia, Richard (ed.), *Chicano School Failure and Success. Research and Policy Agendas for the 1990s* (New York: Falmer Press), pp. 35–36. "On January 23, 1927," wrote Donato *et al.,* "the Attorney General of California stated that Mexicans could be treated as Indians, thereby placing them under the mandates of *de jure* segregation."

23. Carpenter, *A Study of Segregation*, p. 80.

24. Ibid., p. 149.

25. Ibid., p. 80.

26. Meguire, Katherine H. (1938), "Educating the Mexican Child in the Elementary School." Master's thesis, University of Southern California, p. 52.

27. McClellan, Edward, and Reese, William (1988), *The Social History of American Education* (Urbana: University of Illinois Press), p. 161. McClellan and Reese found that "high schools were constructed at the rate of one per day between 1890 and 1920."

28. Treff, Simon Ludwig (1934), "The Education of Children in Orange County." Master's thesis, University of Southern California, pp. 26, 39.

29. Bishop, Hazel Peck (1937), "A Case Study of the Improvement of Mexican Homes Through Instruction in Homemaking." Master's thesis, University of Southern California, pp. 2–3.

30. Taylor, Paul (1934), *An American-Mexican Frontier: Nueces County, Texas* (Chapel Hill: University of North Carolina Press), p. 195.

31. Kaderli, Albert (1940), "The Educational Problem in the Americanization of the Spanish-Speaking Pupils of Sugarland, Texas." Master's thesis, University of Texas, p. 36.

32. Weinberg, Meyer (1977), *A Chance to Learn* (London: Cambridge University Press), p. 147.

33. Tyack, David (1974), *The One Best System: A History of American Urban Education* (Cambridge: Harvard University Press), p. 230.

34. Handlin, Oscar (1951), *The Uprooted: The Epic Story of the Great Migrations that Made the American People* (Boston: Little Brown).

35. Covello, Leonard (1958), *The Heart Is the Teacher* (New York: McGraw Hill).

36. Cubberley, Ellwood (1909), *Changing Conceptions of Education* (Boston: Houghton Mifflin).

37. O'Brien, Sara (1909), *English for Foreigners* (Boston: Houghton Mifflin).

38. Tyack, *The One Best System*, p. 241.

39. Hill, Merton (1928), "The Development of an Americanization Program." Master's thesis, University of California, Los Angeles, p. 1.

40. Treff, Simon (1934), "The Education of Mexican Children in Orange County." Master's thesis, University of Southern California, p. 16.

41. Bishop, "A Case Study of the Improvement of Mexican Homes," p. 6.

42. Manuel, Hershel T. (1934), The Educational Problem Presented by the Spanish-Speaking Child of the Southwest, *School and Society* 40: 694; Reynolds, *The Education of Spanish-Speaking Children.*

43. McWilliams, Carey (1943) "The Forgotten Mexicans," *Common Ground* 3: 68.

44. McDonaugh, Edward, C. (1949), "Status Levels of Mexicans," *Sociology and Social Research* 33: 455.

45. Ibid.

46. Gonzalez, Gilbert (1990), *Chicano Education in the Era of Segregation* (Philadelphia: The Balch Institute Press), p. 60.

47. Kliebard, Herbert (1986), *The Struggle for the American Curriculum, 1893–1958* (Boston: Routledge & Kegan Paul); Krug, Edward (1972), *The Shaping of the American High School, Vol 2: 1920–1941* (Madison: University of Wisconsin Press); Reese, William (1995), *The Origins of the American High School* (New Haven: Yale University Press).

48. Bowles, Samuel, and Gintis, Herbert (1976), *Schooling in Capitalist America: Educational Reform and the Contradictions of Economic Life* (New York: Basic Books), p. 194.

49. Kantor, Harvey (1988), *Learning to Earn: School, Work, and Vocational Reform in California, 1880–1930* (Madison: University of Wisconsin Press).

50. U. S. Congress, House, 63d Cong., ed. sess., 1914, "Report: Commission on National Aid to Vocational Education," in Lazerson, Marvin, and Grubb, Norton, (1974), *American Education and Vocationalism: A Documentary History, 1870–1970* (New York: Teachers College Press), pp. 116–132.

51. Ibid., pp. 30–31.

52. Krug, Edward (1964), *The Shaping of the American High School: Vol. 1* (New York: Harper & Row), pp. 243–244.

53. Lazerson, Marvin, and Grubb, Norton (1974), *American Education and Vocationalism: A Documentary History, 1870–1970* (New York: Teachers College Press).

54. Krug, *The Shaping of the American High School*, pp. 243–244.

55. Gonzalez, *Chicano Education*, p. 79.

56. Lazerson and Grubb, *American Education and Vocationalism;* see also Oakes, Jeannie (1985), *Keeping Track: How Schools Structure Inequality* (New Haven: Yale University Press).

57. Munsterberg, Hugo (1913), *Psychology and Industrial Efficiency* (New York: Houghton Mifflin).

58. Kliebard, *The Struggle for the American Curriculum*, p. 99.

59. Armour, Basil (1932), "Problems in the Education of the Mexican Child," *Texas Outlook* 16: 29–31.

60. Hill, "Development of an Americanization Program," pp. 195–196.

61. Ward, William L. (1931), "The Status of Education of Mexican Children in Four Border States." Master's thesis, University of Southern California, p. 73.

62. Pratt, Philip S. (1938), "A Comparison of the School Achievement and Socio-Economic Background of Mexican and White Children in a Delta Colorado Elementary School." Master's thesis, University of Southern California, p. 105.

63. Ibid., p. 107.

64. Meguire, Katherine H. (1938), "Educating the Mexican Child in the Elementary School." Master's thesis, University of Southern California, pp. 40, 52, 67.

65. Ibid., p. 72.

66. Whitewell, Inez M. (1937), "A Homemaking Course for Mexican Girls Who Will Be Unable to Attend High School." Master's thesis, University of Southern California, p. 82.

67. Bishop, "A Case Study of the Improvement of Mexican Homes," pp. 2–3.

68. McGorray, William E. (1943), "The Needs of a Mexican Community," *California Journal of Secondary Education* 18:349.

69. Hill, "Development of an Americanization Program," p. 189b.

70. Karier, Clarence (1975), *Shaping the American Educational State: 1900 to the Present* (New York: The Free Press); Violas, Paul (1973), *Roots of Crisis* (Chicago: University of Illinois Press), p. 120.

71. Bowles and Gintis, *Schooling in Capitalist America*, p. 196.

72. Kamin, Leaon (1974), *The Science and Politics of IQ* (Maryland: Erlbaum Associates).

73. Binet, Alfred, and Simon, Thomas (1911), *A Method of Measuring the Development of the Intelligence of Young Children* (Lincoln, Ill.: Courier Company).

74. Terman, Lewis (1916), *The Measure of Intelligence* (Boston: Riverside), p. 7.

75. Ibid., p. 12.

76. Spring, Joel (1972), "Psychologists and the War: The Meaning of Intelligence in the Alpha and Beta Tests," *History of Education Quarterly* 12: 3–15; see also Gould, Stephen J. (1981), *The Mismeasure of Man* (New York: W.W. Norton & Company).

77. Yerkes, Robert (1917b), "How May We Discover the Children Who Need Special Care," *Mental Hygiene* 1:252–259.

78. Brigham, Carl (1923), *A Study of American Intelligence* (Princeton: Princeton University Press), p. 182.

79. Gonzalez, *Chicano Education*, p. 62. Gonzalez maintains that more than 33 studies were produced between 1920 and 1930.

80. Sheldon, William H. (1924), "The Intelligence of Mexican Children," *School and Society* 19:142.

81. Garth, Thomas (1923), "A Comparison of the Intelligence of Mexican and Mixed and Full Blood Indian Children," *Psychological Review* 30:398.

82. Ibid., p. 401.

83. Garth, Thomas (1928), "The Intelligence of Mexican School Children," *School and Society* 27:794.

84. Ibid.

85. Garretson, O. K. (1928), "A Study of Causes of Retardation Among Mexican Children in a Small Public School System in Arizona," *Journal of Educational Psychology* 19:39–40.

86. Ibid., p. 40.

87. Florence Goodenough (1928), "Racial Differences in Intelligence of School Children," *Journal of Experimental Psychology* 9: 395.

88. Paschal, Franklin, and Sullian, Louis (1925), "Racial Differences in the Mental and Physical Development of Mexican Children," *Comparative Psychology Monograph* 3:73.

89. Haught, B. F. (1931), "The Language Difficulty of Spanish American Children," *Journal of Applied Psychology* 15:92.

90. Ibid.

91. Ibid., pp. 94–95.

92. Goodenough, *Racial Differences*, p. 393.

93. Drake, Rollen H. (1927), "A Comparative Study of the Mentality and Achievement of Mexican and White Children." Master's thesis, University of Southern California, pp. 46–47.

94. Pratt, "Comparison of the School Achievement," p. 100.

95. Ibid., pp. 103–108.

96. Cobb, Wilbur K. (1932), "Retardation in Elementary Schools of Children of Migratory Laborers in Ventura County, California." Master's thesis, University of Southern California, p. 1.

97. Ibid., p. 106.

98. Sanchez, George I. (1932), Group Differences and Spanish-Speaking Children—A Critical Review, *Journal of Applied Psychology* 16:550.

99. Barerra, Mario (1979), *Race and Class in the Southwest* (Notre Dame: University of Notre Dame Press), p. 75.

100. Ibid., p. 76.

101. McWilliams, Cary (1942), *Ill Fares the Land* (New York: Barnes & Noble), pp. 299–329.

102. Ibid., p. 234.

103. Ibid., p. 230.

104. Ibid., p. 234.

105. Gibbons, Charles, and Bell, Howard (1925), *Children Working on Farms in Certain Sections of the Western Slope of Colorado* (New York: National Child Labor Committee. National Information Bureau, Inc.), p. 111. Gibbons and Bell noted that when "the school is opened the children are hauled from the camp to a separate school [and] the school usually runs for six months but because of getting started so late, it was said, the school would probably not be in session that long for the year 1924–25."

106. Reynolds, "Education of Spanish-Speaking Children," p. 34.

107. Taylor, Paul (1929), *Mexican Labor in the United States: Valley of South Platte, Colorado* (Berkeley: University of California Press).

108. Colorado White House Conference on Child Health and Protection (1932), Report on the conference called by the Hon. William H. Adams, Governor of Colorado, January 14–16.

109. Gibbons and Bell, *Children Working on Farms*, p. 83.

110. Kibbe, *Latin Americans in Texas*, p. 176.

111. Manuel, *Education of Mexican and Spanish-Speaking Children*, pp. 117–118.

112. Ibid., p. 118.

113. Hayden, Jessie (1934), "The La Hambra Experiment in Mexican Social Education." Master's Thesis, Claremont College, p. 146.

114. Manuel, *Education of Mexican and Spanish-Speaking Children*, p. 72.

115. Ibid., p. 77.

116. Ibid., p. 76.

CHAPTER 2. THE EVOLUTION OF A COMMUNITY AND THE MAKING OF A SCHOOL DISTRICT

1. Gonzalez, Gilbert (1990), *Chicano Education in the Era of Segregation* (Philadelphia: The Balch Institute Press), p. 30.

2. Estrada, Leobardo, Garcia, Chris F., Macias, Reynaldo F., and Maldonado, Lionel (1988), "Chicanos in the United States: A History of Exploitation and Resistance," in Garcia, Chris F. (ed.), *Latinos and the Political System* (Notre Dame: University of Notre Dame Press).

3. Acuña, Rodolfo (1972), *Occupied America: The Chicano's Struggle Toward Liberation* (San Francisco: Canfield Press), pp. 101–102.

4. Ibid., p. 7.

5. U. S. Commission on Civil Rights (1972), *The Excluded Student: Educational Practices Affecting Mexican Americans* (Washington, D.C.: U. S. GPO), pp. 76–82.

6. Gann, L. H., and Duignan, Peter J. (1986), *The Hispanics in the United States: A History* (Boulder: Westview Press), p. 20. Most Californios were Mestizos, a mix of Spanish and Indian heritage. The term "Mexican/Californio," will be used to describe this population.

7. Pitt, Leonard (1966), *The Decline of the Californios: A Social History of the Spanish-Speaking Californians, 1846–1890* (Berkeley and Los Angeles: University of California Press), p. 95.

8. Camarillo, Albert (1984), *Chicanos in a Changing Society: From Mexican Pueblos to American Barrios in Santa Barbara and Southern California* (Cambridge: Harvard University Press), p. 13.

9. Pitt, *Decline of the Californios*, p. 97.

10. Ibid. See chapter 15, "The Second Generation, 1865–1890," pp. 249–276.

11. Gann and Duignan, *Hispanics in the United States*, p. 22.

12. Barerra, Mario (1979), *Race and Class in the Southwest: A Theory of Racial Inequality* (Notre Dame: University of Notre Dame Press), pp. 18–21.

13. Acuña, *Occupied America*, p. 105.

14. Rowland, Leon (1947), *Annuals of [Santa Rita] County*, p. 97. In Brownfield there were eight ranchos, totaling 86,180 acres. The land was granted to a number of "Hispanics": by the Mexican government between 1820 and 1843. Even though the U. S. Court confirmed the land grants between 1850 and 1876, by the late nineteenth century every rancho was either sold, taken by squatters, fetched by shady real estate deals, or confiscated by the courts. One Hispanic, for example, lost his 15,400 acre rancho to thirty-four squatters in a court dispute. He passed away while his case was pending and his wife was driven off her land prior to the court's decision. Koch, Margaret (1973), *[Santa Rita] County: Parade of the Past* (Fresno: Valley Publishers), p. 16.

15. Gann and Duignan, *Hispanics in the United States*, p. 21.

16. Pitt, *Decline of the Californios*, p. 87.

17. Gann and Duignan, *Hispanics in the United States*, p. 22; also see Barerra, M., *Race and Class*, p. 38, and McLemore, Dale, and Romo, Ricardo (1985), "The Origins and Development of the Mexican American People," in de la Rodolfo Garza, Bean, Frank, Bonjean, Charles, Romo, Ricardo, Alvarez, Rodolfo (eds.), *The Mexican American Experience: An Interdisciplinary Anthology* (Austin: University of Texas Press), p. 10.

18. McLemore and Romo, *The Origins and Development of the Mexican American People*, p. 11.

19. Camarillo, Albert (1984), *Chicanos in California: A History of Mexican Americans in California* (San Francisco: Boyd and Fraser), p. 32.

20. Ibid.

21. Acuña, *Occupied America*, p. 150.

22. Sowell, Thomas (1981), *Ethnic America: A History* (New York: Basic Books), p. 248.

23. Camarillo, *Chicanos in California*, p. 33.

24. Gann and Duignan, *Hispanics in the United States*, p. 34.

25. Camarillo, *Chicanos in California*, p. 45.

26. Bogardus, Emory S. (1919), *Essentials of Americanization* (Los Angeles: University of Southern California Press), p. 270. Bogardus presented a list of eight problems Mexican immigrants were facing in the United States. In the second, he asked "[w]hy do many Americans think of Mexicans as being barbarians?"

27. Ibid., p. 267.

28. Young, C.C. (1930), *Mexicans in California: Governor Young's Fact-Finding Committee* (San Francisco: Department of Industrial Relations), p. 95.

29. Ibid., p. 171.

30. Theobald, Paul, and Donato, Ruben (1992), "Children of the Harvest: The Schooling of Dust Bowl and Mexican Migrants During the Depression Era," *Peabody Journal of Education* 67: 30–33.

31. Samora, Julian (1971), *Los Mojados: The Wetback Story* (Notre Dame: University of Notre Dame Press), p. 40.

32. Hoffman, Abraham (1974), *Unwanted Mexican Americans in the Great Depression: Repatriation Pressures, 1929–1939* (Tucson: University of Arizona Press).

33. Ibid.

34. McLemore and Romo, *Origins and Development*, p. 16.

35. Camarillo, *Chicanos in California*, pp. 49–50.

36. Ibid.

37. Samora, *Los Mojados*, p. 41.

38. Manuel, Hershel T. (1965), *Spanish-Speaking Children in the Southwest: Their Education and the Public Welfare* (Austin: University of Texas Press), p. 19.

39. Ibid., p. 75.

40. Camarillo, *Chicanos in California*, pp. 50–51.

41. Quoted in Barerra, *Race and Class in the Southwest*, p. 122.

42. Cornelius, Wayne A. (1978), *Mexican Migration to the United States: Causes, Consequences and U. S. Responses* (Cambridge: Massachusetts Institute of Technology, Center for International Studies), p. 18.

43. *The Brownfieldite*, October, 15, 1903. "*The Brownfieldite*" is a pseudonym of Brownfield's local newspaper.

44. U. S. Bureau of the Census, *Reports, Vol. 1. Twelfth Census of the United States Population, 1900.* (Washington, D.C.: GPO, 1901), pp. 6–22

45. U. S. Bureau of the Census, *U. S. Census of the Population: 1900*, Vol. 1, *Twelfth Census of the United States* (Washington D. C.: GPO, 1901), p. 610; *Thirteenth Census of the United States*. Brownfield Province, Population Microfilm, 1900; *U. S. Census of the Population: 1910*, Vol. 2, *Thirteenth Census, 1913*. p. 184; U. S. Bureau of the Census. *Thirteenth Census of the United States*. Brownfield Province, Population Microfilms, 1910; *U. S. Census of the Population: 1920*, Vol. 3, *Composition and Characteristics, Fourteenth Census, 1922*, p. 122; U. S. Bureau of the Census. *U. S. Census of the Population: 1930*, Vol. 3, Part 1, *Fifteenth Census 1932*, p. 266; *U. S. Census of the Population: 1940*, Vol. 2, *Sixteenth Census, 1943*, p. 598.

46. Cubberley, Ellwood P. (1914), *Rural Life and Education: A Study of the Rural-School Problem as a Phase of the Rural-Life Problem* (Boston: Houghton Mifflin), pp. 55–56, 70–71.

47. Bogardus, Emory S. (1919), *Essentials of Americanization* (Los Angeles: University of California Press), pp. 223–224.

48. *The Harvard Encyclopedia of American Ethnic Groups* (1980) (Cambridge: Harvard University Press), p. 250.

49. London, Jack (1913), *The Valley of the Moon* (New York: Oxford University Press), pp. 262–266.

50. *The Brownfieldite*, July 17, 1915.

51. Ibid., July 26, 1914.

52. Ibid., February 8, 1912.

53. *The Brownfield City Directory* 1910; *The Brownfieldite*, June 30, 1915.

54. *U. S. Census of the Population: 1900*, Vol. 1, GPO, 1901, p. 610; *Thirteenth Census: 1910;* Vol. 2, *Population, Alabama-Montana*, 1913, p. 184; *Fourteenth Census: 1920*, Vol. 3, *Composition and Characteristics of the Population, 1922*, p. 122; *Fifteenth Census: 1930*, Vol. 3 Part 1, *The Composition and Characteristics of the Population—Alabama—Missouri, 1932*, p. 266; *Sixteenth Census: 1940*, Vol. 2, *Characteristics of the Population, 1943*, p. 598. Note: The racial/ethnic breakdown for the Asian and Black population was as follows: (1900, Asian

74; Black 25) (1910, Asian 184; Black 7) (1920, Asian 414; Black 11) (1930, Asian 978; Black 17) (1940, Asian 806; Black 6).

55. *The Brownfieldite*, February 24, 1926, p. 8.

56. *The Brownfieldite*, January 28, 1928, and January 30, 1928.

57. Ibid., October 1, 1943, p. 6. One way that communities tried to keep Mexican laborers in their communities was to provide Mexican movies.

58. Santa Rita Recorders Office, Santa Rita, California, 1914; Borg, Jane (1977), *A Sampler of Early [Brownfield] Schools* ([Santa Rita]: P & M Business Service); Kock, Margaret (1978), *Going to School in Santa Rita County; A History of [Santa Rita] County Schools* (Santa Rita County Office of Education); Brownfield Historical Association (n.d.). *A Historic Tour of the Brownfield Schools*.

59. [Santa Rita] County Office of Education, *Active Enrollments*, 1944–1965.

60. *The Orchard: Brownfield High School Yearbook*, 1940, 1950, 1960; The County Office of Education, *Active Enrollments*, 1944–1960; *The Brownfieldite*, June 4, 1940, p. 5; *U. S. Bureau of the Census, Sixteen Census of the Population: 1940*, Vol. 2, *Characteristics of the Population*, GPO, 1943. p. 598; *U. S. Census of the Population: 1970*, Volume 1, Part 6, Section 1, 1973. For the 1967 enrollment figures, see the California State Department of Education, *Racial/Ethnic Survey*, 1967.

61. Small Junior High, *The Brownfieldite*, June 4, 1940, p. 6; June 6, 1950, p. 2; Large Junior High, *The Brownfieldite*, June 5, 1954, p. 3; June 17, 1960, p. 7; *The Brownfieldite,* June 4, 1940, p. 5. For Mexican American enrollments at the high school level, see active enrollments from the Santa Rita County Office of Education, 1944–1960. Also, *The Brownfieldite* and high school yearbooks. Evidence suggested that 95 percent of Mexican American students enrolled in school between 1940 and 1960 attended Corridor Jr. High, Brownfield, K-8, and Brownfield High. Mexican American graduation rates were taken from the local newspaper: June 4, 1940, p. 6; June 12, 1945, p. 7; June 6, 1950, p. 2; Corridor Jr. High, June 5, 1954, p. 3; June 17, 1960, p. 7. The number of Mexican Americans graduating from high school from 1940 to 1960 were as follows: 1940, total graduating class, 295, Mexican American, 3; 1945, total graduating class, 150, Mexican American, 3; 1950, total graduating class, 309, Mexican American, 4; 1960, total graduating class, 316, Mexican American 16.

62. Spencer, Maxy J. (1977), "The Idea of Consolidation in Southern Education During the Early Decades of the Twentieth Century," *Peabody Journal of Education* 53: 216; Sher, Jonathan P. (1977), "Rethinking School District Reorganization," *Compact* 11: 13–15.

63. Tyack, David (1974), *The One Best System: A History of American Urban Education* (Cambridge: Harvard University Press), p. 28.

64. Mulins, Carolyn (1973), "School District Consolidation: Odds Are 2 to 1 It'll Get You," *American School Board Journal* 160: 23; also see Rubin, Lillian (1972), *Busing and Backlash: Whites against Whites in a California School District.* (Berkeley: University of California Press), p. 22.

65. Sher, J. P. and Tomkins, R. "The Myths of Rural School District Consolidation," p. 96. Also, see Norlin, George (1929), "The Teacher Again," *School and Society* 30: 364. Horace Mann was supporting consolidation as early as 1838. The reform did not become a major issue until the early twentieth century.

66. Anrig, Gregory R. (1963), "Sociological Factors Which Resist School Consolidation," *Clearing House* 38: 162.

67. Blumer, Herbert (1951), "Collective Behavior," in Lee Alfred (ed.), *Principles of Sociology* (New York: Barnes and Noble, Inc.), p. 190; Moehlman, Arthur H. (1950–51), "Social Change and District Reorganization," *The Phi Delta Kappan* 32: 301–302; Thaden, J. F. (1952), "Compatibility of Educational and Sociological Criteria in Formation of Community School Districts," *Rural Sociology* 17: 174.

68. The philosophy that rural schools were inadequate was reflected in Cubberley's *Rural Life and Education*.

69. *The Evening Brownfieldite*, July 26, 1926, p. 12.

70. Ibid., November 15, 1921, and March 1, 1926, p. 8.

71. *The Brownfieldite*, January 23, 1931, p. 6.

72. Ibid., January 25, 1931, p. 2.

73. Ibid., December 24, 1940, December 27, 1940. When these two small schools were unified with the Brownfield Joint Union, fifty to sixty students were added to the district.

74. Ibid., December 28, 1945, No. 226.

75. Some small rural school districts opposed unification. Some school districts did not participate in the process at all. Most communities feared they would lose control of their schools.

76. *The Brownfieldite*, August 19, 1948.

77. Ibid., November 30, 1948.

78. Ibid., October 19, 1948, p. 3.

79. Cushman, M. C. (1950–51), "The Ideal School District," *The Phi Delta Kappan* 32: 331.

80. Sher, Jonathan (1977), *Education in Rural America* (Boulder: Westview Press), p. 40.

81. U. S. Department of Commerce, Bureau of the Census (1980), *Census of the Population Characteristics* (July 1982), California. PC 80–1–B6, Table 16, 6–30.

82. Oral interview, Phyllis Peninsular, August 20, 1991.

83. Oral interview, Butch Tabasco, February 1992.

84. *The Santa Rita Guard*, June 14, 1957.

85. Ibid., June 28, 1957.

86. Ibid.

87. Ibid., September 6, 1957.

88. The Brownfield Union School District, *Board Minutes*, November 12, 1958, p. 395.

89. *The Brownfieldite*, May, 18, 1960, p. 12. On August 16, 1961, an article noted that "unification itself is not mandatory but the studies are."

90. Oral interview, Phyllis Peninsular, August 20, 1991. Phyllis Peninsular moved into the Brownfield area in late 1930s. She was also a school board candidate in 1964–1965. *The Brownfieldite*, August 15, 1961, p. 7.

91. *The Brownfieldite*, August 16, 1961, p. 7

92. Ibid., August 16, 1961, p. 18.

93. The Brownfield Joint Union High School District, *Board Minutes*, December 13, 1961, p. 118.

94. *The Brownfieldite*, September 17, 1964, p. 9.

95. Ibid., October 30, 1964, p. 16.

96. Oral interview, Phyllis Peninsular, August 20, 1991.

97. *The Brownfieldite*, August 15, 1961, p. 7.

98. Ibid., January 15, 1970.

99. The Brownfield Unified School District, *School Board Election Documents*, 1965. New Board Members: Virginia Barns, Richard Del Sol, Dr. Jan Bello, Ernest Scalia, A. E. Michaels.

100. California State Department of Education, *Racial/Ethnic Survey*, 1967.

101. *The Brownfieldite*, April 19, 1965, p. 16.

102. Ravitch, Diane (1983), *The Troubled Crusade: American Education, 1945–1980* (New York: Basic Books), p. 148.

103. *The Brownfieldite*, April 19, 1965, p. 16.

104. Tyack, *The One Best System*, p. 25.

105. California State Department of Education, *Racial/Ethnic Survey*, 1967 and 1971.

CHAPTER 3. EMERGENCE OF GRASSROOTS ACTIVISM

1. Gomez-Quiñones, Juan (1990), *Chicano Politics: Reality and Promise, 1940–1990* (Albuquerque: University of New Mexico Press), p. 103.

2. *El Grito* was the first scholarly journal, published in 1968; *Aztlan* followed in 1970, coming out of the University of California at Los Angeles; The National Caucus of Chicano Social Scientists was started in New Mexico Highlands University in 1973. The gathering at the University of California, Santa Barbara, was held in 1969 (i.e., El Plan de Aztlan), and the Chicano Youth Liberation Conference was held in Denver, Colorado, during the same year.

3. The Spiritual Plan of Aztlan (March, 31, 1969). Reprinted in Johnson, Henry. S., and Hernandez, William. J (1970), *Educating the Mexican American* (Valley Forge: Judson Press), pp. 20–23.

4. Rendon, Armando (1971), *Chicano Manifesto* (New York: Collier Books), pp. 9–10, 16, 178.

5. Gonzalez, Rodolfo (1972), *I Am Joaquin* (New York: Bantam Pathfinders), pp. 6–9.

6. Fantini, Mario, and Gittell, Marilyn (1973), *Decentralization: Achieving Reform* (New York: Praeger), p. 41.

7. Wirt, Frederick, and Kirst, Michael (1972), *The Political Web of American Schools* (Boston: Little, Brown and Co.).

8. Ibid., p. x.

9. McCarty, Donald, and Ramsey, Charles (1971), *The School Managers: Power and Conflict in American Public Education* (Westport: Greenwood Publishing Corporation). The power structures, types of school boards, and superintendent styles were categorized as follows:

Community power structure	Types of school boards	Superintendent styles
Dominated	Dominated	Functionary
Factional	Factional	Political
Pluralistic	Pluralistic	Advisor
Inert	Sanctioning	Decision Maker

10. Boyd, William (1976), "The Public, The Professionals, and Educational Policy Making: Who Governs?" *Teachers College Record* 77, 4: 539–577.

11. Zeigler, Harmon, and Tucker, Harvey (1981), "Who Governs American Education: One More Time," in Davis, Don (ed.), *Communities and Their Schools* (New York: McGraw-Hill Book Co.), p. 38.

12. McGivney, Joseph, and Haught, James (1972), "The Politics of Education: A View from the Perspective of the Central Office Staff," *Educational Administration Quarterly* 8, 3: 18–38.

13. Fantini and Gittell, *Decentralization,* p. 42.

14. Davies, Don (1981), *Communities and Their Schools* (New York: McGraw Hill).

15. Rowan, Helen (1967), "A Minority Nobody Knows," *The Atlantic* 219: p. 47.

16. Ibid.

17. Castaneda, Alfredo, *et al.* (1974), *Mexican Americans and Educational Change* (New York: Arno Press); Foley, Douglas (1990), *Learning Capitalist Culture: Deep in the Heart of Tejas* (Philadelphia: University of Pennsylvania Press); Post, Don E. (1977), "Ethnic Conflict in Two South Texas Towns," *Integrated Education* 15, 5: 10–14; Shockley, John S. (1974), *Chicano Revolt in a Texas Town* (Notre Dame: University of Notre Dame Press).

18. Mexican American Education Committee (1963), *Mexican American Education Committee of Metropolitan Los Angeles,* ERIC No. ED001497, pp. 2–3.

19. Rowan, "A Minority Nobody Knows," p. 47.

20. Ibid.

21. Brace, Clayton (1967), *Federal Programs to Improve Mexican-American Education,* U. S. Office of Education, Mexican-American Affairs Unit, Washington, D. C., ERIC Document. No. ED014338, p. 1. Members of the advisory committee included Clayton Brace, Robert Esparza, Ernestine Evans, Nick Garza, Ralph Guzman, Alfred Hernandez, Leonard Lane, Miguel Montes, Maria Urquides, Bernard Valdez, Jack Crowther, Frank Hubert, and Jesse Stratton.

22. Report by the National Advisory Committee on Mexican American Education (1968), *The Mexican American: Quest for Equality,* U. S. Department of Health, Education and Welfare, ERIC No. ED049841, p. 5.

23. Memo from John Plakos, Coordinator, Mexican-American Education Research Project. Mexican-American Education Research Project Progress Report to Educational Programs Committee of the State Board of Education (July, 13, 1967) (Los Angeles: State Department of Education), ERIC No. ED018281.

24. Ibid, pp. 10–11.

25. Rowan, "A Minority Nobody Knows," p. 52.

26. California State Department of Education and the Office of Education, Department of Health Education and Welfare, Washington, D. C. (1969), *The Education of the Mexican American: A Summary of the Proceedings of the Lake Arrowhead and Anaheim conferences* (California State Department of Education, Sacramento, California), ERIC No. ED050844.

27. Ibid., p. 1.

28. Ibid., p. 2.

29. Ibid., p. 3.

30. Report of an Open Meeting by the California State Advisory Committee to the U. S. Commission on Civil Rights (April 1968), *Education and the Mexican American Community In Los Angeles*, U. S. Department of Health, Education and Welfare, ERIC No. ED025355, p. 3. The two-day meeting was held in June 1967.

31. Ibid., p. 5.

32. Ibid., p. 7.

33. Ibid.

34. Ibid., p. 15.

35. *The National Elementary Principal* (November 5, 1970), p. 31.

36. Hittenger, Martha S. (1969), "Bilingualism and Self-Identity," *Educational Leadership* 27, 3: 248.

37. Rowan, "A Minority Nobody Knows," p. 52.

38. Report of an Open Meeting by the California State Advisory Committee to the U. S. Commission on Civil Rights (April 1968), *Education and the Mexican American Community In Los Angeles*, U. S. Department of Health, Education and Welfare, ERIC No. ED025355, p. 3.

39. Ibid., p. 21.

40. California State Department of Education (1968), *Development of a Bilingual Task Force to Improve Education of Mexican American Students* (Sacramento: California State Department of Education), ERIC No. ED024493, pp. 2–3.

41. Carter, Thomas (1969), *Preparing Teachers for Mexican American Children* (Washington, D.C.: National Education Association), ERIC No. ED025367, p. 4.

42. Ibid., p. 5. Although various empirical studies have noted that Head Start and remedial programs have not been very effective, ESL and other "cultural enrichment" programs have produced Mexican American school success. Two major studies of programs that produce Mexican American school success were published almost two decades later. See: (1) Carter, Thomas, and Chatfield, M. (1986), "Effective Bilingual Schools: Implications for Policy and Practice," *American Journal of Education* 95: 200–232; and (2); Lucas, T., Henze, R., and Donato, R. (1990), "Promoting the Success of Latino Language-Minority Students: An Exploratory Study of Six High Schools," *Harvard Educational Review* 60: 313–340.

43. Carter, *Preparing Teachers*, p. 6.

44. Ibid.

45. Ibid., pp. 6–7.

46. Association of Mexican-American Educators (1967–1970), *Education of Mexican-American Children*, U. S. Department of Health, Education and Welfare, National Institute of Education, ERIC No. ED104240.

47. U. S. Commission on Civil Rights (1971), *Equal Educational Opportunities for the Spanish-Speaking Child: Bilingual and Bicultural Educational Programs* (Washington, D.C.: U. S. Department of Health, Education and Welfare), ERIC No. ED073866.

48. Lewis, Oscar (1959), *Five Families: Mexican Case Studies in the Culture of Poverty* (New York: Basic Books). For the cultural deprivation theory, see Riessman, Frank (1962), *The Culturally Deprived Child* (New York: Harper); Roseham, David (1967), "Cultural Deprivation and Learning: An Examination of

Method and Theory," in Harry Miller (ed.), *Education for the Disadvantaged* (New York: The Free Press).

49. *The Brownfieldite*, April 19, 1965, p. 16.

50. Ibid., September 14, 1967, p. 13.

51. Ibid., California State Department of Education, *Racial/Ethnic Survey*, 1967.

52. *The Brownfieldite*, May 16, 1968, No. 63. Another way of looking at the problem was that although they represented 22 percent of high school enrollments, they made up only 13 percent of the graduating class.

53. Brownfield High School Yearbook, *The Orchard* (1950–1966).

54. Ibid.

55. Grant, Gerald (1988), *The Wonderful World We Created at Hamilton High* (Cambridge: Harvard University Press), p. 31. Also see Hammpel, Robert (1986), *The Last Little Citadel: American High Schools Since 1940* (Boston: Houghton Mifflin Co.).

56. *The Brownfieldite*, May 16, 1968, No. 63.

57. Ibid.

58. Ibid., May 25, 1968, No. 71.

59. Ibid.

60. Ibid., June 4, 1969.

61. Kelly, Richard K. (1968), "An Experimental Work-Study Program for Disadvantaged Youth," *Educational Record* 49: 214–220.

62. Carter, T. (1970), *Mexican Americans in Schools: A History of Educational Neglect* (New York: College Entrance Examination Board), p. 180.

63. *The Brownfieldite*, May 18, 1968. Principal Bowing argued that Mexican American and Anglo students' problems were the same because all poor students came from culturally or financially deprived backgrounds. Bowman noted: "A lot of our Mexican Americans students are integrating very well in school." Ibid., May 25, 1968. Oral interview, Superintendent, July 25, 1985. Joe Banks noted that he had no problems with vocational education. However, the "tracking system should have been abolished first." He observed that Mexican American students had virtually no opportunities of being prepared for college. The "XYZ" tracking system was allegedly dropped in June 1969; but beneath the surface, tracking continued.

64. *The Brownfieldite*, August 10, 1968, No. 137.

65. Ibid.

66. Ibid., p. 2.

67. Ibid., August 29, 1968, p. 9. Also oral interview, Superintendent, July 1985. Asked if the Mexican American parents had a legitimate complaint regarding the school teachers' negative attitudes toward their children, Banks, who worked his way up from a classroom teacher to superintendent, gestured "yes." One had to understand, he noted, the history of the high school. He claimed Brownfield High School "had a long history in the town of being an Anglo high school, well financed, and college prep. . . . The school was inbred where one-third of the school's teachers were Brownfield high school graduates." These teachers expected Mexican Americans to assimilate into the mainstream.

68. Parsons, Theodore (1965), "Ethnic Cleavage in a California School." Doctoral dissertation, Stanford University, pp. 296–297.

69. Parsons, "Ethnic Cleavage," pp. 207, 264, 271, 281.

70. Foley, *Learning Capitalist Culture: Deep Down in the Heart of Tejas* (Philadelphia: University of Pennsylvania Press), p. 106.

71. *The Brownfieldite*, September 13, 1968, p. 12.

72. Ibid.

73. Levin, Henry (ed.) (1970), *Community Control of Schools* (New York: Simon and Schuster). Oral interview, ex-COPE members, July 1985.

74. Guerra, Manuel (1972), "Educating Chicano Children and Youths," *Phi Delta Kappan* 3, 5: 313–314.

75. Grant, Carl (1979), *Community Participation in Education* (Boston: Allyn and Bacon), p. 119.

76. Reed, D. B, and Mitchell, D. E. (1975), The Structure of Citizen Participation: Public Decisions for Public Schools, in *Public Testimony of Public Schools*, National Committee for Citizens in Education, Commission on Educational Governance (Berkeley: McCutchan Publishing Corporation), p. 190.

77. Oral interview, ex-COPE members, July 1985.

78. Brownfield Unified School District, *Board Minutes,* November 4, 1969, p. 312; oral interview, middle-school teacher, August 1985. This teacher recalled using school equipment in his class purchased from Title 1 money but had no "Title 1 students."

79. *The Brownfieldite*, November 26, 1969, No. 246.

80. The Brownfield School District, *Board Minutes,* November 25, 1969, p. 328. The COPE agenda also appeared in *The Brownfieldite* the following day.

81. *The Brownfieldite*, November 26, 1969, p. 2.

82. Ibid., December 18, 1969.

83. California State Department of Education, *Racial/Ethnic Survey*, 1967; California State Department of Education, *Teacher Racial/Ethnic survey,* 1971.

84. U. S. Commission on Civil Rights (1971), *Ethnic Isolation of Mexican Americans in the Public Schools of the Southwest,* Report 1, Mexican American Education Study (Washington, D.C.: U. S. GPO). In addition to teacher and administrative data, 5.4 percent of school boards had Mexican American representation.

85. Oral interview, Rudolfo Orellano, August 1991; oral interview, Superintendent, July 1985.

86. Grant, G. (1988), *The Wonderful World We Created at Hamilton High*, p. 18.

87. Oral interview, Rodolfo Orellano, August 1991.

88. Ibid.

89. Weinberg, Meyer (1977), *A Chance to Learn: A History of Race and Education in the United States* (New York: Cambridge University Press), p. 149.

90. Ibid., pp. 149–150. Weinberg quoted from testimony of Senator Joe Bernal, at U. S. Commission on Civil Rights hearing held in San Antonio, December 9–14, 1968, p. 257.

91. Ibid., p. 171.

92. Muñoz, Carlos, *The Politics of Educational Change in East Los Angeles*, pp. 85–87. Also see Meyer Weinberg (1977), *A Chance to Learn*, pp. 171–172, for a list of Chicano student demands.

93. Heussenstamm, F. K. (1972), "Student Strikes in East Los Angeles High Schools," *School & Society* 100: 182–185.

94. Muñoz, Carlos, *The Politics of Educational Change*, pp. 85–87. Mexican-American enrollments in the protesting high schools ranged from 64 to 93.6 percent in 1970. Also see Harrington, John H. (1968), "LA's Student Blowout," *Phi Delta Kappan* 50, 2: 74–79.

95. Weinberg, M. (1977), *A Chance to Learn*, p. 150; U. S. Commission on Civil Rights (1974), *The Unfinished Education: Outcomes for Minorities in the Five Southwestern States*, Report II: Mexican-American Education Study (Washington, D.C.: GPO), pp. 14–20; Carter, Thomas, and Segura, Roberto (1979), *Mexican Americans in Schools. A Decade of Change* (New York: College Entrance Examination Board), pp. 48, 59, 65.

96. Foley, *Learning Capitalist Culture*, p. 102.

97. Oral interview, COPE member, July 1985.

98. The Brownfield Unified School District, *Board Minutes*, July 21, 1970, p. 156; oral interview, ex-COPE members, July 1985; also *The Brownfieldite*, September 2, 1970.

99. The Brownfield Unified School District, *Board Minutes*, September 1, 1970, p. 49; *The Brownfieldite*, September 2, 1970.

100. *The Brownfieldite*, November 5, 1970, No. 211.

101. Uranga, Susana N., *The Study of Mexican American Education in the Southwest*, p. 13. It was in the Lake Arrowhead and Anaheim conferences, for example, that Mexican American educators began to advocate the use of community relations specialists. They cautioned, however, that those "charged with school-community relations in Mexican-American neighborhoods should be knowledgeable about the Mexican American culture and the Spanish language if they are to carry out their assignments effectively" (California State Department of Education and the Office of Education, Department of Health Education and Welfare [1969], *The Education of the Mexican American: A Summary of the Proceedings of the Lake Arrowhead and Anaheim Conferences*, ERIC No. ED050844).

102. U. S. Commission on Civil Rights (1972), *The Excluded Student: Educational Practices Affecting Mexican Americans in the Southwest*, Report No. 3: Mexican American Education Study (Washington, D.C.: U. S. GPO), pp. 37–38.

103. Uranga, *The Study of Mexican American Education*, p. 14.

104. U. S. Commission on Civil Rights (1972), Report No. 3: Mexican American Education Study, *The Excluded Student: Educational Practices Affecting Mexican Americans in the Southwest* (Washington, D.C.: U. S. GPO), p. 37–38.

105. *The Brownfieldite*, July 19, 1971.

106. Ibid. Of the 3,376 signatures, 1,952 were from residents within the school district. The rest were from outside the district. Ibid., July 21, 1971, No. 19.

107. *The Brownfieldite*, July 19, 1971 and July 21, 1971.

108. Guerra, Manuel H. (1972), "Educating Chicano Children and Youth," *Phi Delta Kappan* 53, 5: 313–314.

109. *The Brownfieldite*, July 22, 1971; oral interview, ex-COPE members, July 1985.

110. Ibid., July 23, 1971, p. 2.

111. Ibid., oral interview, Superintendent, July 1985; oral interview, Mary Guerra, July 1985. The superintendent noted that the community advocate position was eliminated because "it never had a clear definition." Mary Guerra argued that the position was eliminated because she was able to garner the support of the Mexican American community on local reform issues; Ibid., July 30, 1971, No. 127. On July 30, *The Brownfieldite* reported that the community advocate position had been eliminated, and that there were some verbal attacks on the school board from the Mexican American community.

112. *The Brownfieldite*, July 30, 1971.

113. Ibid., July 26, 1971, p. 12.

114. Ibid., oral interview, ex-COPE members, July 1985. COPE members said that there had always been such divisive sentiments between Mexicans and Anglos in Brownfield. Tension was merely exacerbated after the Gensen letter.

115. *The Brownfieldite*, July 29, 1971, p. 14. In a letter to the editor on August 4, 1971, p. 4, one Mexican American wrote a response to the Gensen letter, arguing that the letter was an attack on the entire Mexican American community.

116. Ibid., July 28, 1971.

117. Ibid., August 11, 1971.

118. Ibid., July 13, 1971.

119. Ibid., July 28, 1971.

120. Ibid., August 2, 1971.

121. Ibid., August 4, 1971. A letter in *The Brownfieldite* on August 6, 1971, p. 6, suggested that other Japanese Americans did not side with the Mexican American community.

122. Spring, Joel (1991), *American Education: An Introduction to Social and Political Aspects* (New York: Longman), p. 7.

123. Ibid.

124. *The Brownfieldite*, August 4, 1971.

125. Ibid., August 6, 1971, p. 6.

126. See Post, Don E. (1977), "Ethnic Conflict in Two South Texas Towns," *Integrated Education* 15, 5: 10–14; see Foley, *Learning Capitalist Culture*; Shockley, *Chicano Revolt in a Texas Town*; San Miguel, *Let All of Them Take Heed: Mexican Americans and the Campaign for Educational Equality in Texas, 1910–1981* (Austin: University of Texas Press); Bilingual Education Act of 1968, Title VII of the Elementary and Secondary Education Act of 1965 (P. L. 90–247), For the May 25, 1970, memo, see U. S. Commission on Civil Rights (1971), *Mexican American Education Study*, Report 3, p. 83.

127. *The Brownfieldite*, August 13, 1971.

128. Ibid.

129. Ibid., August 24, 1971.

130. Oral interview, Superintendent, July 1985; oral interview, ex-COPE members, July 1985. The pilot bilingual-bicultural school was established in 1972. However, as we shall see in Chapter 8, very little desegregation took place.

CHAPTER 4. THE IRONY OF YEAR-ROUND SCHOOLS

1. Ravitch, Diane (1983), *The Troubled Crusade: American Education, 1945–1980* (New York: Basic Books). See, for example, Chapter 8, "The New Politics of Education"; Glazer, Nathan (1983), *Ethnic Dilemmas: 1964–1982* (Cambridge: Harvard University Press). See Part 2, "Cultural Pluralism and Bilingualism."

2. See Castaneda, Alfredo, *et al.* (eds.) (1974), *Mexican Americans and Educational Change* (New York: Arno Press); Ramirez, Manuel, and Castaneda, Alfredo (1974), *Cultural Democracy, Bicognitive Development, and Education* (New York: Academic Press); Poblano, Ralph (1973), *Ghosts in the Barrio: Issues in Bilingual-Bicultural Education* (San Rafael.: Leswing Press).

3. Glines, D. (1994), *YRE Basics: History, Methods, Concerns, Future.* Paper presented at the Annual Meeting of the National Association for Year-Round Education, San Diego. ERIC No. ED369144; Moon, J. (1964), "The Extended School Year," *The Education Digest* 30: 35–38.

4. Tyack, David, Lowe, Robert, and Hansot, Elizabeth (1984), *Public Schools in Hard Times: The Great Depression and Recent Years* (Cambridge: Harvard University Press), p. 189.

5. "The Extended School Year: What's Being Done" (July 1968), *Education Summary* 21, p. 4; Howard, S. (1966), "Traditional and Newly Emerging Approaches to Year-Round Operations," *Liberal Education* 52: 218–228; Moon, "The Extended School Year."

6. McGraw, Pat (1973), "Junior Doesn't Have to Bale Hay Anymore," *Compact* 4: 10.

7. Moon, "The Extended School Year," p. 35.

8. Ellena, William (1969), "Extending the School Year," *Today's Education* 58: 48.

9. Letson, John (1970), "Atlanta Has Begun," *Compact* 4: 15.

10. Jensen, George (1970), "Does Year-Round School Make Sense?" *Compact* 4: 4–6.

11. "The Extended School Year: What's Being Done," p. 5.

12. Farnsworth, J. (1970), "Legal Action in Michigan," *Compact* 4: 18–19.

13. Ibid., p. 20.

14. Jensen, George (1973a, May 8–11), "The Many Faces of Year-Round Education." Speech given before the year-round education national seminar, Virginia Beach, Va. ERIC No. ED081084, pp. 11–12.

15. McGraw, "Junior Doesn't Have to Bale Hay Anymore," p. 10; McLain, J. D. (1970), "Emerging Plans for Year-Round Education," *Compact* 4: 7–8; Richmond, M., and Riegle, J. (1974), "Current Status of the Extended School Year Movement," *Phi Delta Kappan* 55: 490; Thomas, G.I. (1970), "The Legal and Financial Questions," *Compact* 4: 9–14.

16. Adams, A. (1968), "Look Hard at This Year-Round School Plan," *American School Board Journal* 156: 11–15; Jensen, George, "Does Year-Round School Make Sense?"; Richmond, M. (1977), *Issues in Year-Round Schools* (North Quincy: The Christopher Publishing House); Tsitrian, J. (1973), "The Furguson Plan for All-Year School," *Phi Delta Kappan* 54: 314–315; White, D. W. (1973), "Year-Round

Education for K–12 Districts," *Phi Delta Kappan* 54: 312–313; Heller, M. R, and Bailey, M. A. (1976), "Year-Round School: Problems and Opportunities," *The Clearing House* 49: 363–364.

17. A review of the local newspaper shows that between 1936 and 1964, the community never rejected a bond issue or a special tax increase (*The Brownfieldite*, September 21, 1936; April 12, 1946; July 11, 1946; March 8, 1947; May 1, 1947; August 26, 1949; August 17, 1954; June 14, 1956; August 14, 1958; October 19, 1961; April 13, 1963; January 15, 1963; May 28, 1964; and July 15, 1964), Bond and tax proposals were not turned down until after 1965.

18. District superintendent, personal communication, August 1985; *The Brownfieldite*, January 19, 1972.

19. McCarty, D., and Ramsey, C. (1971), *The School Managers: Power and Conflict in American Public Education* (Westport: Greenwood), p 136.

20. "Year-Round Education for the Third Century of America," a report of the 8th national seminar on year-round education, sponsored by the California State Department of Education, Wilson Riles, Superintendent of Public Instruction, Long Beach, Cal. (January 25–28, 1976). ERIC No. ED135084, p. 44.

21. Shepard, M., and Baker, K. (1977), *Year-Round Schools* (Lexington, Mass: D. C. Heath), p. 28.

22. *The Brownfieldite*, November 16, 1971.

23. Thomas, "The Legal and Financial Questions," p. 9.

24. McLain, J. D. (1970), "Emerging Plans for Year-Round Education"; Parks, D. (April 15–19, 1974), "Research on Year-Round Education" (ED090662), paper presented at the American Educational Research Association Annual Meeting, Chicago.

25. Jensen, G. (1973b, April 7–10), *Year-Round School: Here's What's Happening*. Speech given before the National School Boards Association Annual Convention, Anaheim, Cal. ERIC No. ED081085, p. 4.

26. McLain, "Emerging Plans for Year-Round Education," p. 8.

27. *The Brownfieldite*, January 19,1972.

28. McGraw, "Junior Doesn't Have to Bale Hay Anymore," p. 12.

29. *The Brownfieldite*, January 21, 1972.

30. Holt, H. (January, 1973), "Year-Round Schools and System Shock," *Phi Delta Kappan* 54: 311.

31. Gillis, R. (1968), "The 12-Month School Year: Plans and Strategy," *Education Summary* 21: 8.

32. Ibid.

33. Driscoll, T. F. (1971), "School Around the Calendar," *American Education* 7: 23.

34. *The Brownfieldite*, January 24, 1972.

35. Jensen, George, "The Many Faces of Year-Round Education," p. 4.

36. Hill, B. (1980), "The Attitude of Patrons Toward Year-Round School in the Hillsboro, Oregon, Union High-School District." Doctoral dissertation, Brigham Young University; McDaniel, W. (1976), "A Study of the Attitudes of Selected Groups of Citizens in Onondaga County Toward the Year-Round School Concept." Doctoral dissertation, Syracuse University; Russell, C. (1976), "Split-Shift and Year-Round Schools: Two Nontraditional Methods of Organizing School Time." Doctoral dissertation, University of Arkansas.

37. Carpenter, S. (1977), "A Survey of the Attitudes of Parents of North Carolina Public Schools Toward Extended School Year Programs." Doctoral dissertation, Duke University.

38. *The Brownfieldite*, January 24, 1972.

39. Jensen, "Year-Round School: Here's What's Happening," p. 5.

40. Carter, T., and Segura, R. (1979), *Mexican American in Schools: A Decade of Change* (New York: College Entrance Examination Board), p. 303.

41. Campbell, R. E., Cunningham, L. L., Nystrand, R, O., and Usdan, M. D. (1985), *The Organization and Control of American Schools* (Columbus: Charles E. Merrill), pp. 181–182; see also Tyack, D., and Hansot, E. (1982), *Managers of Virtue: Public School Leadership in America, 1820-1980* (New York: Basic Books).

42. *The Brownfieldite*, February 29, 1972.

43. *Las Noticias*, 1972, n.d.

44. Ibid.

45. Ibid.

46. *The Brownfieldite*, February 29, 1972.

47. Ibid., March 1, 1972.

48. Ibid., COPE member, personal communication, August 1985.

49. *Las Noticias*, March 1971.

50. *The Brownfieldite*, March 1, 1972.

51. Ibid., March 2, 1972.

52. Ibid.

53. *Las Noticias*, March 20, 1972.

54. Ibid., March 1972.

55. *The Brownfieldite*, March 20, 1972.

56. Ibid., March 23, 1972.

57. Ibid., April 4, 1972; April 13, 1972; April 14, 1972.

58. Jensen, "Year-Round School: Here's What's Happening," p. 8.

59. Brownfield School District, *School Board Minutes*, May 22, 1972.

60. Ibid.

61. Ibid., June 27, 1972.

62. Oral interview, ex-COPE member, July 1985.

63. Brownfield School District, *School Board Minutes*, July 18, 1972.

64. Ibid., *Racial/ Ethnic Survey,* October 1972; Brownfield School District, *School Board Minutes*, July 18, 1972.

65. COPE members, personal communication, November 1985.

66. Baker, J. (January 22, 1976), "Migrant Education in Year-Round Schools of the [Brownfield] Unified School District." Unpublished manuscript.

67. *Las Noticias*, 1972, n.d..

68. Baker, J., and Johnson, V. (March, 1973), "Another Experiment with a 45–15 Plan. *School Management* 10: 21–24. The 45–15 plan could not have been as successful as school officials characterized it because it was later reduced from five schools to one. More important, the district's only operating year-round plan was modified from the 45–15 plan to another design. Moreover, Barbara Merino (1983), "The Impact of Year-Round Schooling: A Review," *Urban Education* 18: 289–316, challenged Baker and Johnson's conclusions, noting that "[The] weakness of this

interview approach to the study of attitude is that segments of the population, especially ethnic minority groups, may not favor an educational change but see no place where this dissatisfaction can be articulated except through extreme means such as boycotts, which may fail for other reasons than a change in attitude" (p. 306). Merino did not push this issue but was merely trying to point out that Mexican parents were only able to express their concerns through protest and boycotts because their voices are rarely heard.

69. Boyd, W. (1976), "The Public, The Professionals, and Educational Policy Making: Who Governs," *Teachers College Record* 77 (4): 539–577; Fantini, M., and Gittell, M. (1973), *Decentralization: Achieving Reform* (New York: Praeger); McCarty and Ramsey, *The School Managers*; Zeigler, H., and Tucker, H. (1981), "Who Governs American Education: One More Time," in Davis, D. (ed.), *Communities and Their Schools* (New York: McGraw-Hill).

CHAPTER 5. MANDATED BILINGUAL EDUCATION COMES TO TOWN

1. San Miguel, Guadalupe (1985), "Conflict and Controversy in the Evolution of Bilingual Education in the United States—An Interpretation," in Rodolfo de la Garza *et al.* (eds.), *The Mexican American Experience: An Interdisciplinary Anthology* (Austin: University of Texas Press).

2. Tyack, David (1974), *The One Best System: A History of American Urban Education* (Cambridge: Harvard University Press), p. 106. According to Tyack, St. Louis, Milwaukee, Baltimore, Louisville, St. Paul, and Indianapolis were places where the high status of the German populations gave them political power.

3. Quoted from Tyack (1974), *The One Best System*, p. 107.

4. Gann, L. H., and Duignan, Peter, J. (1986), *The Hispanic in the United States: A History* (Boulder: Westview Press), p. 233.

5. San Miguel, Guadalupe (1987), *Let All of Them Take Heed: Mexican Americans and the Campaign for Educational Equality in Texas, 1910–1981* (Austin: University of Texas Press). Also see Marquez, Benjamin (1993), *LULAC: The Evolution of a Mexican American Political Organization* (Austin: University of Texas Press).

6. Poblano, Ralph (1973), *Ghosts in the Barrio: Issues in Bilingual-Bicultural Education* (San Rafael: Leswing Press).

7. Ovando, Carlos, and Collier, Virginia (1985), *Bilingual and ESL Classrooms: Teaching in Multicultural Contexts* (New York: McGraw Hill).

8. See Tyack, *The One Best System*, pp. 106–109; Crawford, James (1991), *Bilingual Education: History, Politics, Theory, and Practice* (Los Angeles: Bilingual Educational Services), p. 12.

9. *U. S. Statutes at Large, 1968*, 81: 816 (January 2, 1968); 880 (b).

10. Pottinger, J. Stanley (1970), Memorandum of May 25, 1970, with More Than Five Percent National Origin Minority Group Children (Washington, D.C.: Department of Health, Education, and Welfare, Office for Civil Rights), p. 2. In addition, the commission made an important statement about prohibiting public schools from assigning LEP students to special education or low-ability classes.

11. *Lau v. Nichols*, 1974. 414 U. S. 563, 94 S. Ct. 786.

12. Teitelbaum, H., and Hiller, R. (1979), "Bilingual Education: The Legal Mandate," in Trueba, Henry T., and Barnet-Mazrachi, Carol (eds.), *Bilingual Multicultural Education and the Professional: From Theory to Practice* (Rawley, Mass.: Newbury House), p. 48; Zerkel, P. (1978), "The Legal Vicissitudes of Bilingual Education," in LaFontaine, Hernan *et al.* (eds.), *Bilingual Education* (Wayne, N. J.: Avey Publishing Group), p. 50.

13. California State Department of Education, Department of Bilingual Education, AB–1329, 1976. This bill required each school district to count the limited-English-proficient (LEP) students in the district and report its findings to the Department of Education. The bill required each LEP pupil, as defined, enrolled in the California public school system in kindergarten through twelfth grade to receive instruction in a language understandable to the student. The bill recognizes the pupil's primary language in addition to teaching the pupil English.

14. Bilingual education had always been a sensitive issue in the Brownfield schools. Bilingual education was uncommon in California in 1972. *The Annual Reports of Financial Transactions Concerning School Districts*, 1972–73 (Sacramento: Houston I. Flournoy, State Controller Office), The reports pointed out (p. xi) that out of the 1,336 school districts in California in 1972, only 48 experimented with federal funds for bilingual education purposes. The Brownfield Unified School District (BUSD) was one of those districts.

15. Gann and Duignan, *Hispanics in the United States*, p. 238.

16. U. S. Bureau of the Census. *U. S. Census of Population: 1980*, Characteristics of the Population, Vol. 1, Chapter A, Part 6 (U. S. GPO, 1982), pp. 6–17, 6–39; *U. S. Census of Population: 1970*, Vol. 1, Part 6, Section 1 (1973), pp. 6–15, 6–85, 6–933. The actual Mexican American population was 10,800. The "other" 259 Hispanics (that is, Cuban, Puerto Rican, etc.) were included in the data. About 16.5 percent of Brownfield's population were Asians.

17. The Brownfield Unified School District, *Racial/Ethnic Survey*, 1971-1979. Brownfield, California.

18. Although the BUSD claimed it was offering bilingual education in six elementary schools and at Brownfield High in 1976, several teachers, who wanted to remain anonymous, said the programs were nothing more than ESL classes. In an oral interview the district superintendent said that besides the pilot bilingual-bicultural school, only some classes in a small elementary school across the river in the other county offered bilingual education to LEP Mexican American students.

19. The Brownfield Unified School District, *Board Minutes*, March 19, 1974, p. 181.

20. Except for La Coalición, there were no strong groups reminiscent of the early 1970s in the local Mexican American community that placed demands on the BUSD with respect to bilingual education.

21. *The Brownfieldite*, April 2, 1977, p. 16. Toward the end of Crawlings' letter to the editor, he expressed fear about walking around in town on Thursday nights and Sunday afternoons because those were the days Mexican Americans socialized around the town plaza and on Main Street.

22. *The Brownfieldite*, April 7, 1977, p. 24.

23. Ibid., July 7, 1977, No. 108.

24. Ibid. Mexican American school board member, oral interview, February 1992. Part of one Mexican American board member's platform was his support for bilingual education. He remembered that in 1941, when he was in elementary school, he was not allowed to speak Spanish. "We were punished," he said; " I resented not being able to speak Spanish."

25. Ibid.

26. Crawford, James (1991), *Bilingual Education: History, Politics, Theory, and Practice* (Los Angeles: Bilingual Educational Services, Inc.) California State Department of Education, *Assembly Bill 1329*, 1976; also see Fishman, Joshua A., and Keller, Gary D. (1982), *Bilingual Education for Hispanic Students in the United States* (New York: Teachers College, Columbia University), p. 13.

27. *The Brownfieldite*, September 6, 1977.

28. Ibid.

29. Ibid., September 8, 1977.

30. The Brownfield Unified School District, *Office of Compensatory Education and Research Services*, 1975. It must be noted that during this time period the state was distinguishing between limited-English-speaking (LES) and non–English-speaking (NES) students. These terms were later combined as limited English proficient (LEP) students.

31. *The Brownfieldite*, September 16, 1977, p. 24.

32. Ibid., November 23, 1977.

33. Ibid.

34. Ibid.

35. Ibid., December 3, 1977.

36. Foote, Tom H., Espinosa, Ruben W., and Garcia, Joseph O., *Ethnic Groups and Public Education in California A Joint Publication of the California School Finance Report Project and the California: Association for Bilingual Education* (San Diego: 1978), pp. 42–43. According to Foote, Espinosa, and Garcia, in 1975 California had 234,000 LEP students, in 1976 290,000, and in 1977 233,000. At the same time, there were only 4,071 credentialed bilingual teachers in the state; Also see *The Condition of Education, A Statistical Report on the Condition of Education in the United States*, National Center for Educational Statistics, U. S. Department of Health, Education and Welfare, 1975, p. 71; and *The Condition of Education* for years 1977, Vol. 3, Part 1, p. 39, and 1978, p. 173.

37. *The Brownfieldite*, December 3, 1977.

38. Ibid. Oral interview, parent and member of Concerned Citizens for Education, August 1991.

39. *The Brownfieldite*, December 8, 1977.

40. Ibid.

41. Oral interview, parent and member of Concerned Citizens For Education, August 1991.

42. *The Brownfieldite*, December 8, 1977.

43. Ibid.

44. Ibid. The group of parents and teachers that responded to Concerned Citizens for Education were six whites and four Mexican Americans.

45. Ibid., January 5, 1978. Also personal interview, Superintendent of Schools, November 1985. In this interview, the superintendent said that he and others were on their way to Sacramento to meet with state officials and Concerned Citizens for Education. He missed the meeting due to a serious accident on Highway 17. Oral interview, Concerned Citizen for Education, August 1991. This parent said that "there was a few of us who went up to Sacramento to talk to state legislators and the State Board of Education to get them to understand how we felt."

46. *The Brownfieldite*, January 13, 1978.

47. Ibid.

48. Oral interview, parent and member of Concerned Citizens for Education. August 1991. This parent stated that the group "rented a community room over by the savings and loan" to discuss the bilingual education issue. "We could not get all the people in the place. Most of the people that came were Anglo. They were angry. It was not a good time."

49. Oral interview, Guillermo Lopez, February 1992.

50. *The Brownfieldite*, December 31, 1977, p. 11; also in The Brownfield Unified School District, *Board Minutes*, January 13, 1978, p. 152.

51. *The Brownfieldite*, January 13, 1978.

52. Ibid., January 28, 1978, p. 20.

53. Ibid.

54. Ibid., February 1, 1978, p. 2.

55. Ibid., February 22, 1978.

56. Ibid., February 22, 1978, p. 2.

57. Ibid., April 13, 1978, No. 34.

58. Ibid.

59. Ibid., April 20, 1978.

60. Ibid., May 5, 1978.

61. Oral interview, Concerned Citizen for Education, August 1991.

CHAPTER 6. SELF-INTEREST AND COMPLIANCE IN THE DESEGREGATION PROCESS

1. Kluger, Richard (1975), *Simple Justice: The History of Brown v. Board of Education and Black America's Struggle for Equality* (New York: Vintage Books).

2. Rossell, Christine (1990), *The Carrot or the Stick for School Desegregation Policy: Magnet Schools or Forced Busing* (Philadelphia: Temple University Press), p. 5

3. Rist, Ray (1979), *Desegregated Schools: An Appraisal of an American Experiment* (New York: Academic Press).

4. *Green v. County School Board of New Kent County* (Virginia), 391 U. S. 430 (1968).

5. Orfield, Gary (1978), *Must We Bus? Segregated Schools and National Policy* (Washington, D.C.: The Brookings Institution).

6. *Swann v. Charlotte-Mecklenburg Board of Education* (North Carolina) 402 U. S. 1 (1971).

7. Hochschild, Jennifer (1984), *The New American Dilemma: Liberal Democracy and School Desegregation* (New Haven: Yale University Press), p. 28.

8. Edwards, Bentley T., and Wirt, Frederick (1967), *School Desegregation in the North: The Challenge and the Experience* (San Francisco: Chandler Publishing Co.); Monti, Daniel (1985), *A Semblance of Justice: St. Louis School Desegregation and Order in Urban America*. (Columbia: University of Missouri Press); Crain, Robert (1968), *The Politics of School Desegregation* (Chicago: Aldine Publishing Co.)

9. *Keys v. School District No. 1* (Colorado), 413 U. S. 189. (1973).

10. Orfield, *Must We Bus?* See Chapter 2, "Segregated Cities, Segregated Schools," pp. 40–76.

11. *Milliken v. Bradley* (Michigan), 418 U. S. 717 (1974).

12. Hochschild, *The New American Dilemma*, pp. 31–32. Also see Oakes, Jeannie (1985), *Keeping Track: How Schools Structure Inequality* (New Haven: Yale University Press).

13. Gary Orfield was one of the few social scientists in the nation who was giving attention to the school segregation of Hispanics in the United States.

14. Arias, Beatrice M. (1979), *Hispanics and School Desegregation: Issues for the 1980's* (Los Angeles: Graduate School of Education, University of California); Haro, Carlos Manuel (1977), *Mexican/Chicano Concerns and School Desegregation in Los Angeles* (Los Angeles: Chicano Studies Center Publications, University of California); Castellanos, Diego (1979), *Desegregation of Hispanics and its Implications: A Critical Issue for the 1980s* (Trenton, N.J.: Department of Education), ERIC Number: ED206786.

15. Valencia, Richard (1991), *Chicano School Failure and Success: Policy Agendas for the 1990s* (New York: Falmer Press). See Chapter 2, "Segregation, Desegregation, and Integration of Chicano Students: Problems and Prospects," pp. 27–63.

16. *Keys v. School District No. 1* (Colorado), 413 U. S. 189 (1973).

17. Orfield, Gary (1978), *Must We Bus?* p. 202.

18. Valencia, Richard (1991), *Chicano School Failure and Success: Research and Policy Agendas for the 1990s* (New York: Falmer Press).

19. Gonzalez, Gilbert (1990), *Chicano Education in the Era of Segregation*, (Philadelphia: The Balch Institute Press), pp. 21–22.

20. Orfield, *Must We Bus?* p. 205.

21. Ibid., pp. 205–206.

22. Orfield, Gary (1988), "School Desegregation in the 1980s," *Equity and Choice* 4.

23. Gonzalez, *Chicano Education*, p. 22.

24. Oakes, *Keeping Track*, p. 3.

25. Valverde, Leonard (1976), *Segregation, Desegregation, and Resegregation of the Spanish-Surname Student in the United States* (Washington, D.C.: National Institute of Education, Department of Health, Education and Welfare), ERIC No. ED131963.

26. Carter, Thomas, and Segura, Roberto (1979), *Mexican Americans in Schools: A Decade of Change* (New York: College Entrance Examination Board).

27. Zerkel, Perry (1977), "Bilingual Education and Desegregation: A Case of Uncoordinated Remedies," *The Bilingual Review* 4: 181.

28. Ibid.

29. Cardenas, Jose (1975), "Bilingual Education, Desegregation, and a Third Alternative," *Inequality in Education* 14: 20.

30. Stephan, Walter, and Feagin, Joe (1980), *School Desegregation: Past, Present, and Future* (New York: Plenum Press), p. 323.

31. California State Department of Education (1983), *Desegregation and Bilingual Education: Partners in Quality Education*, Sacramento, Conference Proceedings, p. 7.

32. Ibid., p. 15.

33. Arias, Beatriz, and Bray, J. L. (1983), *Equal Educational Opportunity and School Desegregation in Triethnic Districts* (Report submitted to National Institute of Education), LEC–83–14.

34. Roos, Peter (1978), "Bilingual Education: The Hispanic Response to Unequal Educational Opportunity," *Law and Contemporary Problems* 43: 135.

35. Ibid., p. 136.

36. The Brownfield Unified School District, *Board Minutes,* February 15, 1971, p. 282. According to the California racial/ethnic survey in 1966, the BUSD already had several racially isolated schools. "Other" refers to Asian, Native American, and black students. Native American and black children made up a very small percentage of this student population. "Other minority" generally referred to Asian children.

37. Colley, Nathaniel S. Jr. (1971), *Public School Desegregation in California Historical Background*, School Desegregation Series. Western Regional School Desegregation Projects, ERIC No. ED056408, p. 20.

38. The Brownfield Unified School District, *Board Minutes*, December 14, 1971, p. 254.

39. Ibid., October 19, 1971. p. 234. The California State Department of Education gave the BVUSD a copy of a letter dated September 15, 1971, and reported that "eleven of the district's schools [were] imbalanced."

40. *The Brownfieldite*, March 3, 1971, p. 16.

41. Ibid., April 19, 1972, p. 3.

42. Ibid.; The Brownfield Unified School District, *Racial and Ethnic Balance, Policy Range: 6260–6269*, May 2, 1972. This latter document demonstrates that the superintendent and most school board members were nervous about integrating Mexican Americans from Brownfield and whites from Atherton. For example, policy section 6262 read: "The unique geographical arrangement of population within the District is recognized. This fact produces two significant population centers separated by approximately 10 to 12 miles of sparsely populated coastal and forest land. For purposes of racial and ethnic student balance with the schools of the district, imbalance will be determined by utilizing a Northern/Southern zone concept. Percentage definitions of balance or imbalance will be determined within each defined zone." Policy section 6262.1 stated that "The Northern Zone is defined as an area including those students attending [Atherton] High School and all junior high and elementary schools progressing to [Atherton] High School." Section 6262.2 stated that "the Southern Zone is defined as an area including those students attending [Brownfield] High School and all junior high and elementary schools progressing to [Brownfield] High School."

43. *The Brownfieldite*, April 19, 1972, p. 3.

44. The California State Department of Education, *State Board Desegregation Guidelines, 1978* (Sacramento: The California State Board of Education, 1978); *Plans to Alleviate Racial and Ethnic Segregation of Minority Students* (California Administrative Code, Title 5, Section 90–101), April 12, 1978, p. 22; also *The Brownfieldite*, May 26, 1978.

45. The California State Board of Education, *State Board Desegregation Guidelines, 1978*, p. 9. In addition to the five recommendations, other suggestions were considered important for school boards to follow: "1. The skill, education and experience of certificated staff. 2. The scope, variety criteria and quality of the educational program as indicated by student performance, achievement and/or other indicators of educational progress. 3. The teacher/pupil ratio exclusive of special (categorical) funding support. 4. Such other factors or criteria that may be relevant to the local circumstances. 5. Demographic and other data or factors on an area or regional basis which have an effect on the stability and/or mobility of various groups or the rate of change in the racial and ethnic composition of various schools and of the district."

46. *The Brownfieldite*, May 9, 1977, p. 13.

47. The California State Department of Education, *State Board Desegregation Guidelines*, p. 22.

48. *The Brownfieldite*, October 25, 1978.

49. Ibid., May 26, 1978.

50. Ibid.

51. The California State Department of Education, *State Board Desegregation Guidelines*, p. 13; *The Brownfieldite*, October 25, 1978.

52. The Brownfield Unified School District, *Board Minutes*, November 1, 1978, p. 328; oral interview, Butch Tabasco, February 1992.

53. Pluralists included both Mexican Americans and white members

54. *The Santa Rita Guard*, November 2, 1978.

55. *The Brownfieldite*, January 10, 1979, p. 15.

56. Ibid., March 7, 1979, p. 13.

57. Ibid., March 21, 1979, p. 15, and March 24, 1979.

58. Ibid., March 27, 1979, p. 11.

59. Ibid., April 3, 1979, p. 10. *The Brownfieldite* indicated the following schools were racially imbalanced: Lynn 99 percent minority, Harvard 93, Libre 78, Bird 77, Corridor 76, Blanca 76, Esconde 70, Corridor Elementary 65, and McDonald 63 percent.

60. *The Brownfieldite*, March 24, 1979; oral interview, Mexican American school board member, February 1992.

61. Ibid.

62. *The Brownfieldite*, April 11, 1979, p. 13; also The California State Department of Education, *State Board Guidelines,* p. 13. According to the desegregation guidelines, school districts were allowed to use the following methods and techniques to avoid and alleviate racial isolation: "1. Geographic Attendance Zones: Zone boundaries can be drawn or redrawn in a manner promoting maximum racial and ethnic balance in each school. 2. School Pairing: Where two or more comparable schools are situated within a relatively short distance and are imbalanced with

respect to each other, their attendance areas can be merged to form one larger attendance area, and the assignment or grand pattern modified so that each facility is shared by a balance group of students. 3. Reorganization of Grade Structure: In some school systems a change in the basic grade organization will eliminate imbalance. For example, a change to a uniform 7–3–3, 7–2–4, 5–4–4, 4–3–3–3, or other grade pattern may maximize balance within an entire district or within each several complexes or subdistricts. (It also may maximize utilization of space in all facilities. 4. Central Schools: One or more schools may be converted into central facilities for one or more grades, to serve all or part of a school district. 5. School Closing and Consolidation: Small, inadequate schools, or others in locations that have become impractical to operate and maintain, can be closed and their students reassigned. In some cases, alternative use can be made of the facility; in others, the building and/ or the site can be sold. In considering this technique in particular, the fairness of the plan to the minority community should be considered of great importance."

63. *The Santa Rita Guard*, May 8, 1979.

64. *The Brownfieldite*, May 9, 1979, p. 13.

65. The California Department of Education, *State Board Guidelines*, pp. 12–13. *The Brownfieldite*, May 9, 1979, p. 13.

66. *The Brownfieldite*, May 23, 1979, p. 15. Unlike the ad hoc Mexican American community organizations in the past, La Coalición challenged more than educational issues. By the late 1970s they were providing legal services for low-income people in general. Instead of providing only for the Mexican American community, they were also serving other ethnic groups. Their clientele was 70 percent Mexican American, 20 percent Anglo, and 10 percent black, Asian, and Native Americans. Of the organization's 35 members, 70 percent were Mexican American, 25 percent Anglo, and 5 percent black, Asian, and Native American.

67. *The Brownfieldite*, June 7, 1979.

68. Ibid., oral Interview, Butch Tabasco, February 1992.

69. *The Santa Rita Guard*, June 8, 1979.

70. T*he Brownfieldite*, July 12, 1979, p. 11.

71. Ibid., July 25, 1979; oral Interview, Butch Tabasco, February 1992.

72. Ibid.

73. Ibid.

74. *The Santa Rita Guard*, August 1, 1979.

75. Oral interview, Anita Jones, February 1992.

76. *The Brownfieldite*, August 14, 1979, p. 2.

77. Oral interview, Anita Jones, February 1992.

78. *The Brownfieldite*, August 14, 1979, p. 2.

79. *The Santa Rita Guard*, August 15, 1979.

80. *The Brownfieldite*, September 5, 1979, p. 2.

81. *The Santa Rita Guard*, October 10, 1979.

82. Ibid., November 25, 1979.

83. Ibid., November 29, 1979.

84. Ibid.

85. Oral interview, Anita Jones, February 1992.

86. *The Brownfieldite*, December 13, 1979.

87. *The Santa Rita Guard*, December 21, 1979; The *Brownfieldite*, December 18, 1979, p. 24.

88. Brownfield School District, *The Desegregation-Integration Plan*, 1985–87, p. 5.

Title -> The _other_ struggle indicates that the book will some how be compareing The mex-Amer struggle to another more focused on group -> seemeingly Af-Amer but I don't see the compareson.

Book Reviews

Bibliography

BOOKS, ARTICLES, AND PAMPHLETS

Acuna, Rodolfo (1972). *Occupied America: The Chicano's Struggle Toward Liberation.* San Francisco: Canfield Press.

Adams, A. (1968). "Look Hard at This Year-Round School Plan." *American School Board Journal* 156: 11–15.

Addams, Jane (1902). *Democracy and Social Ethic.* New York: Macmillan.

Alvarez, Robert (1986). "The Lemon Grove Incident: The Nation's First Successful Desegregation Court Case." *Journal of San Diego History* (Spring): 116–135.

Anrig, Gregory R. (1963). "Sociological Factors Which Resist School Consolidation." *Clearing House* 38: 13–19.

Arias, Beatriz, and Bray, J. L. (1983). *Equal Educational Opportunity and School Desegregation in Triethnic Districts* (Report submitted to National Institute of Education). LEC–83–14.

Armour, Basil (1932). "Problems in the Education of the Mexican Child." *Texas Outlook* 16: 29–31.

Baker, James, and Johnson, Viola (1973, March). "Another Experiment with a 45–15 Plan." *School Management* 10: 21–24.

Barerra, Mario (1979). *Race and Class in the Southwest.* Notre Dame: University of Notre Dame Press.

Binet, Alfred, and Simon, Thomas (1911). *A Method of Measuring the Development of the Intelligence of Young Children.* Lincoln, Ill.: Courier Company.

Blumer, Herbert (1951). "Collective Behavior." In Lee Alfred (ed.), *Principles of Sociology.* New York: Barnes and Noble, Inc.

Bogardus, Emory S. (1919). *Essentials of Americanization.* Los Angeles: University of Southern California Press.

Bond, Horace Mann (1934). *The Education of the Negro in the American Social Order*. New York: Octagon Books.

Bourdieu, P., and Passrow, J. C. (1977). *Reproduction*. Beverly Hills, Cal.: Sage Publications.

Bowles, Samuel, and Gintis, Herbert (1976). *Schooling in Capitalist American: Educational Reform and the Contradictions of Economic Life*. New York: Basic Books.

Boyd, William (1976). "The Public, The Professionals, and Educational Policy Making: Who Governs." *Teachers College Record* 77 (4): 539–577.

Brigham, Carl (1923). *A Study of American Intelligence*. Princeton: Princton University Press.

Bullock, Henry Allen (1967). *A History of Negro Education in the South, From 1619 to the Present*. New York: Praeger.

Burma, John (1954). *Spanish-Speaking Groups in the United States*. Durham: Duke University Press.

Camarillo, Albert (1984). *Chicanos in a Changing Society: From Mexican Pueblos to American Barrios in Santa Barbara and Southern California*. Cambridge: Harvard University Press.

———. (1984). *Chicanos in California: A History of Mexican Americans in California*. San Francisco: Boyd and Fraser.

Campbell, R. E., Cunningham, L. L., Nystrand, R, O., and Usdan, M. D. (1985). *The Organization and Control of American Schools*. Columbus: Charles E. Merrill.

Cardenas, Jose (1975). "Bilingual Education, Desegregation, and a Third Alternative." *Inequality in Education* 14: 19–22.

Carter, Thomas, (1969). *Preparing Teachers for Mexican American Children*. Washington, D.C.: National Education Association, ERIC No. ED025367.

———. (1970). *Mexican Americans in Schools: A History of Educational Neglect*. New York: College Entrance Examination Board.

Carter, Thomas, and Chatfield, M. L. (1986). "Effective Bilingual Schools: Implications for Policy and Practice." *American Journal of Education* 95: 200–232.

Carter, Thomas, and Segura, Roberto (1979). *Mexican Americans in Schools: A Decade of Change*. New York: College Entrance Examination Board.

Castaneda, Alfredo, Ramirez, Manuel, Cortez, Carlos, and Barerra, Mario (1974). *Mexican Americans and Educational Change*. New York: Arno Press.

Colley, Nathaniel S., Jr. (1971). *Public School Desegregation in California Historical Background*. School Desegregation Series. Western Regional School Desegregation Projects. ERIC No. ED056408.

Cooke, Henry W. (1948). "The Segregation of Mexican American Children in Southern California." *School and Society* 67: 417–421.

Cornelius, Wayne A. (1978). *Mexican Migration to the United States: Causes, Consequences and U. S. Responses.* Cambridge: Massachusetts Institute of Technology, Center for International Studies.

Covello, Leonard (1958). *The Heart Is the Teacher.* New York: McGraw Hill.

Crain, Robert (1968). *The Politics of School Desegregation.* Chicago: Aldine Publishing Co.

Crawford, James (1991). *Bilingual Education: History, Politics, Theory, and Practice.* Los Angeles: Bilingual Educational Services, Inc.

Cubberley, Ellwood (1909). *Changing Conceptions of Education.* Boston: Houghton Mifflin.

————. (1914). *Rural Life and Education: A Study of the Rural-School Problem as a Phase of the Rural-Life Problem.* Boston: Houghton Mifflin.

Davies, Don (ed.) (1981). *Communities and Their Schools.* New York: McGraw-Hill.

de la Garza, Rodolfo, Bean, Frank, Bonjean, Charles, Romo, Ricardo, and Alvarez, Rodolfo. *The Mexican American Experience: An Interdisciplinary Anthology.* Austin: University of Texas Press.

"Discrimination: School Bias Toward Mexican-Americans." *School & Society,* November 1966: 94: 378.

Donato, Ruben, Menchaca, Marta, and Valencia, Richard (1991). "Segregation, Desegregation, and Integration of Chicano Students: Problems and Prospects." In Valencia, Richard (ed.). *Chicano School Failure and Success. Research and Policy Agendas for the 1990s.* New York: Falmer Press, 27–63.

Driscoll, T. F. (1971). "School Around the Calendar." *American Education* 7: 21–23.

Edwards, Bentley, and Wirt, Frederick (1967). *School Desegregation in the North: The Challenge and the Experience.* San Francisco: Chandler Publishing Co.

Ellena, William (1969). "Extending the School Year." *Today's Education* 58: 48–49.

Estrada, Leobardo, Garcia, Chris F., Macias, Reynaldo F., and Maldonado, Lionel (1988). "Chicanos in the United States: A History of Exploitation and Resistance." In Garcia, Chris F. (ed.). *Latinos and the Political System.* Notre Dame: University of Notre Dame Press.

"Extended School Year: What's Being Done." (1968, July). *Education Summary* 21: 48.

Fantini, Mario, and Gittell, Marilyn (1973). *Decentralization: Achieving Reform.* New York: Praeger.

Farnsworth, James (1970). "Legal Action in Michigan." *Compact* 4: 18–19.

Fishman, Joshua A., and Keller, Gary D. (1982). *Bilingual Education for Hispanic Students in the United States.* New York: Teachers College, Columbia University.

Foley, Douglas (1990). *Learning Capitalist Culture: Deep in the Heart of Tejas.* Philadelphia: University of Pennsylvania Press.

Foote, Tom H., Espinosa, Ruben W., and Garcia, Joseph O. (1978). *Ethnic Groups and Public Education in California: A Joint Publication of the California School Finance Report Project and the California Association for Bilingual Education.* San Diego.

Gann, L. H., and Duignan, Peter J. (1986). The Hispanics in the United States: A History. Boulder: Westview Press.

Garretson, O. K. (1928). "A Study of Causes of Retardation Among Mexican Children in a Small Public School System in Arizona." *Journal of Educational Psychology* 19: 31–40.

Garth, Thomas (1923). "A Comparison of the Intelligence of Mexican and Mixed and Full Blood Indian Children." *Psychological Review* 30: 388–401.

———. (1928). "The Intelligence of Mexican School Children." *School and Society* 27: 791–794.

Gillis, R. (1968). "The 12-Month School Year: Plans and Strategy." *Education Summary* 21: 5–8.

Glazer, Nathan (1983). *Ethnic Dilemmas: 1964–1982.* Cambridge: Harvard University Press.

Glines, D. (1994). *YRE Basics: History, Methods, Concerns, Future.* Paper presented at the Annual Meeting of the National Association for Year-Round Education, San Diego. ERIC No. ED369144.

Gomez-Quinones, Juan (1990). *Chicano Politics: Reality & Promise, 1940–1990.* Albuquerque: University of New Mexico Press.

Gonzalez, Gilbert (1990). *Chicano Education in the Era of Segregation.* Philadelphia: The Balch Institute Press.

Gonzalez, Rodolfo (1972). *I Am Joaquin.* New York: Bantam Pathfinders.

Goodenough, Florence (1928). "Racial Differences in Intelligence of School Children." *Journal of Experimental Psychology* 9: 395.

Gould, Stephen J. (1981). *The Mismeasure of Man.* New York: W.W. Norton & Company.

Grant, Carl (1979). *Community Participation in Education.* Boston: Allyn and Bacon.

Grant, Gerald (1988). *The Wonderful World We Created at Hamilton High.* Cambridge: Harvard University Press.

Gross, Beatrice, and Gross, Ronald (eds.) (1969). *Radical School Reform.* New York: Simon and Schuster.

Guerra, Manuel (1972). "Educating Chicano Children and Youth." *Phi Delta Kappan* 3, No. 5: 313–314.

Gutierrez, Armando, and Hirsch, Herbert (1974). "The Militant Challenge to the American Ethos: Chicanos and Mexican Americans." In Garcia, F. Chris (ed.). *La Causa Politica: A Chicano Politics Reader.* Notre Dame: University of Notre Dame Press, 86–103.

Hammpel, Robert (1986). *The Last Little Citadel: American High Schools Since 1940.* Boston: Houghton Mifflin Co.

Handlin, Oscar (1951). *The Uprooted: The Epic Story of the Great Migrations that Made the American People.* Boston: Little Brown.

Haro, Carlos Manuel (1977). *Mexican/Chicano Concerns and School Desegregation in Los Angeles.* Los Angeles: Chicano Studies Center Publications, University of California.

Harrington, John H. (1968). "LA's Student Blowout." *Phi Delta Kappan* 50 No. 2: 74–79.

Harvard Educational Review (1969). *Equal Educational Opportunity.* Cambridge: Harvard University Press.

Harvard Encyclopedia of American Ethnic Groups (1980). Cambridge: Harvard University Press.

Haught, B. F. (1931). "The Language Difficulty of Spanish American Children." *Journal of Applied Psychology* 15: 92–95.

Heller, M. P, and Bailey, Max A. (1976). "Year-Round School: Problems and Opportunities." *The Clearing House* 49: 363-364.

Hendrick, Irving (1977). *The Education of Non-Whites in California: 1848–1970.* San Francisco: R & E Associates.

Heussenstamm, F. K (1972). "Student Strikes in East Los Angeles High Schools." *School & Society* 100: 182–185.

Hittenger, Martha S. (1969). "Bilingualism and Self-Identity." *Educational Leadership* 27, No. 3: 247–249.

Hochschild, Jennifer (1984). *The New American Dilemma: Liberal Democracy and School Desegregation.* New Haven: Yale University Press.

Hoffman, Abraham (1974). *Unwanted Mexican Americans in the Great Depression: Repatriation Pressures, 1929–1939.* Tucson: University of Arizona Press.

Holt, Howard (1973, January). "Year-Round Schools and System Shock." *Phi Delta Kappan* 54: 310–311.

Howard, Sumner (1966). "Traditional and Newly Emerging Approaches to Year-Round Operations." *Liberal Education* 52: 218-228.

Jencks, Christopher (1972). *Inequality: A Reassessment of the Effects of Family and Schooling in America.* New York: Harper and Row.

Jensen, George (1970). "Does Year-Round School Make Sense?" *Compact* 4: 4-6.

———. (1973a, May 8-11). *The Many Faces of Year-Round Education.* Speech given before the year-round education national seminar, Virginia Beach, Va. ERIC No. ED081084, pp. 11–12.

———. (1973b, April 7-10). *Year-Round School: Here's What's Happening.* Speech given before the National School Boards Association Annual Convention, Anaheim, Cal. ERIC No. ED081085.

Johnson, Henry. S., and Hernandez, William. J. (1970). *Educating the Mexican American.* Valley Forge: Judson Press.

Kamin, Leaon (1974). *The Science and Politics of IQ.* Potomac: Erlbaum Associates.

Kantor, Harvey (1988). *Learning to Earn: School, Work, and Vocational Reform in California, 1880–1930.* Madison: University of Wisconsin Press.

Karier, Clarence (1975). *Shaping the American Educational State: 1900 to the Present.* New York: The Free Press.

Katz Michael. (1971). *Class, Bureaucracy and Schools: The Illusion of Educational Change in America.* New York: Praeger.

———. (1987). *Restructuring American Education.* Cambridge: Harvard University Press.

Kelly, Richard K. (1968). "An Experimental Work-Study Program for Disadvantaged Youth." *Educational Record* 49: 214–220.

Kibbe, Pauline R. (1946). *Latin Americans in Texas.* Albuquerque: University of New Mexico Press.

Kliebard, Herbert (1986). *The Struggle for the American Curriculum, 1893–1958.* Boston: Routledge & Kegan Paul.

Kluger, Richard (1975). *Simple Justice: The History of Brown v. Board of Education and Black America's Struggle for Equality.* New York: Vantage Books.

Kozol, Jonathan (1967). *Death at an Early Age: The Destruction of the Hearts and Minds of Negro Children in the Boston Public Schools.* Boston: Houghton Mifflin.

Krug, Edward (1964). *The Shaping of the American High School: Vol. 1.* New York: Harper & Row.

———. (1972). *The Shaping of the American High School, Vol 2: 1920–1941.* Madison: University of Wisconsin Press.

Lazerson, Marvin, and Grubb, Norton (1974). *American Education and Vocationalism: A Documentary History, 1870–1970.* New York: Teachers College Press.

Letson, John (1970). "Atlanta Has Begun." *Compact* 4: 15–17.

Levin, Henry (ed.) (1970). *Community Control of Schools.* New York: Simon and Schuster.

Levine, David. M., and Bane, Mary Jo (eds.) (1975). *The "Inequality" Controversy: Schooling and Distributive Justice.* New York: Basic Books.

Lewis, Oscar (1959). *Five Families: Mexican Case Studies in the Culture of Poverty.* New York: Basic Books.

London, Jack (1913). *The Valley of the Moon.* New York: Oxford University Press.

Lucas, Tamara, Henze, Rosemary, and Donato, Ruben (1990). "Promoting the Success of Latino Language-Minority Students: An Exploratory Study of Six High Schools." *Harvard Educational Review* 60: 315–340.

Manuel, Hershel T. (1934). "The Educational Problem Presented by the Spanish-Speaking Child of the Southwest." *School and Society* 40: 692–695.

––––––. (1965). *Spanish-Speaking Children in the Southwest: Their Education and the Public Welfare.* Austin: University of Texas Press.

McCarty, Donald, and Ramsey, Charles (1971). *The School Managers: Power and Conflict in American Public Education.* Westport: Greenwood Publishing Corporation.

McClellan, Edward, and Reese, William (1988). *The Social History of American Education.* Urbana: University of Illinois Press.

McDonaugh, Edward, C. (1949). "Status Levels of Mexicans." *Sociology and Social Research* 33: 449–459.

McGivney, Joseph, and Haught, James (1972). "The Politics of Education: A View from the Central Office Staff." *Educational Administration Quarterly* 8: 18–38.

McGorray, William E. (1943). "The Needs of a Mexican Community." *California Journal of Secondary Education* 18: 349–350.

McGraw, Pat (1973). "Junior Doesn't Have to Bale Hay Anymore." *Compact* 4: 10–12.

McLain, J. D. (1970). "Emerging Plans for Year-Round Education." *Compact* 4: 7–8.

McLemore, Dale, and Romo, Ricardo (1985). "The Origins and Development of the Mexican American People." In de la Garza, Rodolfo, Bean, Frank, Bonjean, Charles, Romo, Ricardo, and Alvarez, Rodolfo (eds.) *The Mexican American Experience: An Interdisciplinary Anthology.* Austin: University of Texas Press, 3–32.

McWilliams, Carey (1942). *Ill Fares the Land.* New York: Barnes & Noble.

––––––. (1943). "The Forgotten Mexicans." *Common Ground* 3: 65–78.

Merino, Barbara (1983). "The Impact of Year-Round Schooling: A Review." *Urban Education* 18: 289-316.

Mexican American Education Committee (1963). *Mexican American Education Committee of Metropolitan Los Angeles.* ERIC No. ED001497, pp. 2–3.

Moehlman, Arthur H. (1950-51). "Social Change and District Reorganization." *The Phi Delta Kappan* 32: 301.

Monti, Daniel (1985). *A Semblance of Justice: St. Louis School Desegregation and Order in Urban America.* Columbia: University of Missouri Press.

Moon, J. (1964). "The Extended School Year." *The Education Digest* 30: 35-38.

Mosteller, Frederick, and Moynihan, Daniel P. (1972). *On Equality of Educational Opportunity.* New York: Random House.

Muñoz, Carlos. "The Politics of Educational Change in East Los Angeles." In Castaneda, Alfredo, et al. (eds.) (1974). *Mexican Americans and Educational Change.* New York: Arno Press.

Munsterberg, Hugo (1913). *Psychology and Industrial Efficiency.* New York: Houghton Mifflin.

Navarro, Armando. "Educational Change Through Political Action." In Castaneda, Alfredo, et al. (1974) (eds.). *Mexican Americans and Educational Change.* New York: Arno Press, 105–139.

Norlin, George (1929). "The Teacher Again." *School and Society* 30: 351–363.

Oakes, Jeannie (1985). *Keeping Track: How Schools Generate Inequality.* New Haven: Yale University Press.

O'Brien, Sara (1909). *English for Foreigners.* Boston: Houghton Mifflin.

Olneck, Michael, and Lazerson, Marvin (1988). "The School Achievement of Immigrant Children: 1900–1930." In McClellan, B. Edward, and Reese, William (eds.). *The Social History of American Education.* Urbana: University of Illinois Press.

Orfield, Gary (1978). *Must We Bus? Segregated Schools and National Policy.* Washington, D.C.: The Brookings Institution.

Ovando, Carlos, and Collier, Virginia (1985). *Bilingual and ESL Classrooms: Teaching in Multicultural Contexts.* New York: McGraw Hill.

Parks, D. (1974, April 15-19). *Research on Year-Round Education.* Paper presented at the American Educational Research Association Annual Meeting, Chicago. ERIC No. ED090662.

Paschal, Franklin, and Sullivan, Louis (1925). "Racial Differences in the Mental and Physical Development of Mexican Children." *Comparative Psychology Monograph* 3: 1–76.

Peterson, Paul E. (1976). *School Politics, Chicago Style.* Chicago: University of Chicago Press.

Pitt, Leonard (1966). *The Decline of the Californios: A Social History of the Spanish-Speaking Californians, 1846-1890.* Berkeley and Los Angeles: University of California Press.

Poblano, Ralph (1973). *Ghosts in the Barrio: Issues in Bilingual-Bicultural Education.* San Rafael, Cal.: Leswing Press.

Post, Don E. (1977). "Ethnic Conflict in Two South Texas Towns." *Integrated Education* 15, No. 5: 10–14.

Ramirez, Manuel, and Castaneda, Alfredo (1974). *Cultural Democracy, Bicognitive Development, and Education.* New York: Academic Press.

Ravitch, Diane (1983). *The Troubled Crusade: American Education, 1945–1980.* New York: Basic Books.

Reed, Donald, and Mitchell, Douglas (1975). "The Structure of Citizen Participation: Public Decisions for Public Schools." In *Public Testimony of Public Schools.* National Committee for Citizens in Education. Commission on Educational Governance. Berkeley: McCutchan Publishing Corporation, 183–217.

Reese, William (1995). *The Origins of the American High School.* New Haven: Yale University Press.

Rendon, Armando (1971). *Chicano Manifesto.* New York: Collier Books.

Richmond, M. (1977). *Issues in Year-Round Schools.* North Quincy, Mass.: The Christopher Publishing House.

Richmond, M., and Riegle, J. (1974). "Current Status of the Extended School Year Movement." *Phi Delta Kappan* 55: 490–492.

Riessman, Frank (1962). *The Culturally Deprived Child.* New York: Harper and Row.

Rist, Ray (1979). *Desegregated Schools: An Appraisal of an American Experiment.* New York: Academic Press.

Roberts, Kenneth (1928). "The Docile Mexican." *Saturday Evening Post,* February 18.

Roos, Peter (1978). "Bilingual Education: The Hispanic Response to Unequal Educational Opportunity." *Law and Contemporary Problems* 42: 111–140.

Roseham, David (1967). "Cultural Deprivation and Learning: An Examination of Method and Theory." In Miller, Harry (ed.). *Education for the Disadvantaged.* New York: The Free Press.

Rossell, Christine (1990). *The Carrot or the Stick for School Desegregation Policy: Magnet Schools or Forced Busing.* Philadelphia: Temple University Press.

Rowan, Helen (1967). "A Minority Nobody Knows." *The Atlantic* 219: 47–52.

Rubin, Lillian (1972). *Busing and Backlash: Whites against Whites in a California School District.* Berkeley: University of California Press.

Samora, Julian (1971). *Los Mojados: The Wetback Story.* Notre Dame: University of Notre Dame Press.

San Miguel, Guadalupe (1985). "Conflict and Controversy in the Evolution of Bilingual Education in the United States—An Interpretation." In de la Garza, Rodolfo, et al. (eds.). *The Mexican American Experience: An Interdisciplinary Anthology.* Austin: University of Texas Press, 267–280.

———. (1986). "Status of the Historiography of Chicano Education: A Preliminary Analysis." *History of Education Quarterly* 26: 553–554.

———. (1987). *Let Them All Take Heed: Mexican Americans and the Campaign for Educational Equality in Texas, 1910–1981.* Austin: University of Texas Press.

Sanchez, George I. (1932). Group Differences and Spanish-Speaking Children—A Critical Review. *Journal of Applied Psychology* 16: 549–558.

———. (1940). *Forgotten People.* Albuquerque: University of New Mexico Press.

Saxe, Richard W. (1975). *School-Community Interaction.* Berkeley: McCutchan.

Sheldon, William H. (1924). "The Intelligence of Mexican Children." *School and Society* 19: 139–142.

Shepard, Morris, and Baker, Keith (1977). *Year-Round Schools.* Lexington, Mass.: D. C. Heath.

Sher, Jonathan P. (1977a). *Education in Rural America.* Boulder: Westview Press.

———. (1977b). "Rethinking School District Reorganization." *Compact* 11: 13–15.

Shockley, John S. (1974). *Chicano Revolt in a Texas Town.* Notre Dame: University of Notre Dame Press.

Sowell, Thomas (1981). *Ethnic America: A History.* New York: Basic Books.

Spencer, Maxy J. (1977). "The Idea of Consolidation in Southern Education During the Early Decades of the Twentieth Century." *Peabody Journal of Education* 53: 216–222.

Spring, Joel (1972a). "Psychologists and the War: The Meaning of Intelligence in the Alpha and Beta Tests." *History of Education Quarterly* 12: 3–15.

———. (1972b). *Education and the Rise of the Corporate State.* Boston: Beacon Press.

———. (1991). *American Education: An Introduction to Social and Political Aspects.* New York: Longman.

Stanley, Grace (1920). "Special Schools for Mexicans." *The Survey* 45: 714–715.

Stephan, Walter, and Feagin, Joe (1980). *School Desegregation: Past, Present, and Future.* New York: Plenum Press.

Taylor, Paul (1929). *Mexican Labor in the United States: Valley of South Platte, Colorado.* Berkeley: University of California Press.

———. (1934). *An American-Mexican Frontier: Nueces County, Texas.* Chapel Hill: University of North Carolina Press.

Teitelbaum, Herbert, and Hiller, Richard, (1979). "Bilingual Education: The Legal Mandate." In Trueba, Henry T., and Barnet-Mazrachi, Carol (eds.), *Bilingual Multicultural Education and the Professional: From Theory to Practice.* Rawley, Mass: Newbury House, 20–53.

Terman, Lewis (1916). *The Measure of Intelligence.* Boston: Riverside.

Thaden, J. F. (1952). "Compatibility of Educational and Sociological Criteria in Formation of Community School Districts." *Rural Sociology* 17: 172–175.

Theobald, Paul, and Donato, Ruben (1992). "Children of the Harvest: The Schooling of Dust Bowl and Mexican Migrants During the Depression Era." *Peabody Journal of Education* 67: 29–45.

Thomas, G. I. (1970). "The Legal and Financial Questions." *Compact* 4: 9-14.

Trueba, Henry, Rodriguez, Cirenio, Zou, Yali, and Cintron, Jose (1993). *Healing Multicultural America: Mexican Immigrants Rise to Power in Rural California.* New York: The Falmer Press.

Tsitrian, John (1973). "The Furgeson Plan for All-Year School." *Phi Delta Kappan* 54: 314–315.

Tyack, David (1974). *The One Best System. The History of Urban Education in the United States.* Cambridge: Harvard University Press.

Tyack, David, and Hansot, Elizabeth (1982). *Managers of Virtue: Public School Leadership in America, 1820-1980.* New York: Basic Books.

Tyack, David, Lowe, Robert, and Hansot, Elizabeth (1984). *Public Schools in Hard Times: The Great Depression and Recent Years.* Cambridge: Harvard University Press.

Tyack, David (ed.) (1967). *Turning Points in American Educational History.* Walthham, Mass.: Blaisdell.

Valencia, Richard (ed.) (1991). *Chicano School Failure and Success: Research and Policy Agendas for the 1990s.* New York: Falmer Press.

Violas, Paul (1973). *Roots of Crisis.* Chicago: University of Illinois Press.

Weinberg, Meyer (1977). *A Chance to Learn: A History of Race and Education in the United States.* New York: Cambridge University Press.

White, D. W. (1973). "Year-Round Education for K-12 Districts." *Phi Delta Kappan* 54: 312–313.

Willie, Charles, and Greenblatt, Sharon (eds.) (1981). *Community Politics and Educational Change: Ten School Systems Under Court Order.* New York: Longman.

Willis, Paul (1981). *Learning to Labor.* New York: Columbia University Press.

Wirt, Frederick M., and Kirst, Michael (1972). *The Political Web of American Schools.* Boston: Little, Brown.

Yerkes, Robert (1917b). "How May We Discover the Children Who Need Special Care." *Mental Hygiene* 1: 252–259.

Zeigler, Harmon, and Tucker, Harvey (1981). "Who Governs American Education: One More Time." In Davis, D. (ed.). *Communities and Their Schools.* New York: McGraw-Hill.

Zerkel, Perry (1977). "Bilingual Education and Desegregation: A Case of Uncoordinated Remedies." *The Bilingual Review* 4: 180–188.

Zerkel, Perry (1978). "The Legal Vicissitudes of Bilingual Education." In LaFontaine, Hernan, *et al.* (eds.). *Bilingual Education.* Wayne, N.J.: Avey Publishing Group.

UNPUBLISHED MATERIAL

Arias, Beatriz (1979). *Hispanics and School Desegregation: Issues for the 1980s.* Los Angeles: Graduate School of Education, University of California.

Bishop, Hazel Peck (1937). A Case Study of the Improvement of Mexican Homes Through Instruction in Homemaking. Master's thesis. University of Southern California.

Carpenter, Charles (1935). A Study of Segregation Versus Non-Segregation of Mexican Children. Master's thesis. University of Southern California.

Carpenter, S. (1977). A Survey of the Attitudes of Parents of North Carolina Public Schools Toward Extended School Year Programs. Doctoral dissertation. Duke University.

Cobb, Wilbur K. (1932). Retardation in Elementary Schools of Children of Migratory Laborers in Ventura County, California. Master's thesis. University of Southern California.

Drake, Rollen H. (1927). A Comparative Study of the Mentality and Achievement of Mexican and White Children. Master's thesis. University of Southern California.

Gonzalez, Gilbert (1974). System of Public Education and Its Function Within the Chicano Communities. Doctoral dissertation. University of California, Los Angeles.

Hayden, Jessie (1934). The La Hambra Experiment in Mexican Social Education. Master's thesis. Claremont College.

Hill, B. (1980). The Attitude of Patrons Toward Year-Round School in the Hillsboro, Oregon, Union High-School District. Doctoral dissertation. Brigham Young University.

Hill, Merton (1928). The Development of an Americanization Program. Master's thesis. University of California, Los Angeles.

Kaderli, Albert (1940). The Educational Problem in the Americanization of the Spanish-Speaking Pupils of Sugarland, Texas. Master's thesis. University of Texas.

McDaniel, W. (1976). A Study of the Attitudes of Selected Groups of Citizens in Onondaga County Toward the Year-Round School Concept. Doctoral dissertation. Syracuse University.

Meguire, Katherine H. (1938). Educating the Mexican Child in the Elementary School. Master's thesis. University of Southern California.

Parsons, Theodore. W., Jr. (1965). Ethnic Cleavage in a California School. Doctoral dissertation. Stanford University.

Penrod, Vesta (1948). Civil Rights Problems of Mexican-Americans in Southern California. Master's thesis. Claremont Graduate School.

Pratt, Philip S. (1938). A Comparison of the School Achievement and Socio-economic Background of Mexican and White Children in a Delta Colorado Elementary School. Master's thesis. University of Southern California.

Russell, C. (1976). Split-Shift and Year-Round Schools: Two Nontraditional Methods of Organizing School Time. Doctoral dissertation. University of Arkansas.

Treff, Simon (1934). The Education of Mexican Children in Orange County. Master's thesis. University of Southern California.

Van Norman Hogan, Milo (1934). Study of the School Progress of Mexican Children in Imperial Valley. Master's thesis. University of Southern California.

Ward, William L. (1931). The Status of Education for Mexican Children in Four Border States. Master's thesis. University of Southern California.

Whitewell, Inez, M. (1937). A Homemaking Course for Mexican Girls Who Will Be Unable to Attend High School. Master's thesis. University of Southern California.

GOVERNMENT DOCUMENTS

Annual Reports of Financial Transactions Concerning School Districts, 1972–73. Sacramento: Houston I. Flournoy, State Controller Office.

Association of Mexican-American Educators (1967–1970). *Education of Mexican-American Children.* U. S. Department of Health, Education and Welfare. National Institute of Education. ERIC No. ED104240.

Brace, Clayton (1967). *Federal Programs to Improve Mexican-American Education.* U. S. Office of Education. Mexican-American Affairs Unit. Washington, D. C. ERIC No. ED014338.

California State Advisory Committee to the U. S. Commission on Civil Rights (April 1968). *Education and the Mexican American Community In Los Angeles.* U. S. Department of Health, Education and Welfare. ERIC No. ED025355.

California State Department of Education. *Racial/Ethnic Survey,* 1967–1979. Sacramento.

————. (1968). *Development of a Bilingual Task Force to Improve Education of Mexican American Students.* Sacramento: California State Department of Education. ERIC No. ED024493.

————. *Teacher Racial/Ethnic Survey,* 1971. Sacramento.

————. *Assembly Bill 1329,* 1976. Sacramento.

————. (1978). *Plans to Alleviate Racial and Ethnic Segregation of Minority Students.* (California Administrative Code, Title 5, Section 90–101). Sacramento.

————. *State Board Desegregation Guidelines,* 1978. Sacramento.

————. (1983). *Desegregation and Bilingual Education: Partners in Quality Education.* Sacramento. Conference Proceedings.

———— and the Office of Education, Department of Health Education and Welfare (1969). *The Education of the Mexican American: A Summary of the Proceedings of the Lake Arrowhead and Anaheim Conferences.* California State Department of Education, Sacramento. ERIC No. ED050844.

Castellanos, Diego (1979). *Desegregation of Hispanics and its Implications: A Critical Issue for the 1980s.* Trenton, N. J.: Department of Education. ERIC ED206786.

Colorado White House Conference on Child Health and Protection. (1932). Report on the conference called by the Hon. William H. Adams, Governor of Colorado, January 14–16.

Condition of Education, A Statistical Report on the Condition of Education in the United States. National Center for Educational Statistics. U. S. Department of Health, Education and Welfare.

Gibbons, Charles, and Bell, Howard (1925). *Children Working on Farms in Certain Sections of the Western Slope of Colorado.* New York: National Child Labor Committee. National Information Bureau, Inc.

Mexican-American Education Research Project Progress Report to Educational Programs Committee of the State Board of Education (July, 13, 1967). Los Angeles: State Department of Education. ERIC No. ED018281.

National Advisory Committee on Mexican American Education (1968). *The Mexican American: Quest for Equality*. U. S. Department of Health, Education and Welfare. ERIC No. ED049841.

Pottinger, J. Stanley (1970). *Memorandum of May 25, 1970, with More Than Five Percent National Origin Minority Group Children*. Washington, D.C.: Department of Health, Education and Welfare, Office for Civil Rights.

Report of an Open Meeting by the California State Advisory Committee to the U. S. Commission on Civil Rights (April, 1968). *Education and the Mexican American Community in Los Angeles*. U. S. Department of Health, Education and Welfare. ERIC No. ED025355.

Reynolds, Annie (1933). *The Education of Mexican and Spanish-Speaking Children in Five Southwestern States*. United States Department of the Interior. Washington, D.C.: GPO.

U.S. Bureau of the Census. *Thirteenth Census of the United States*. [Brownfield] Province, Population Microfilm, 1900. Washington, D.C.: GPO.

———. *Reports, Vol. 1. Twelfth Census of the United States Population, 1900*. Washington, D.C.: GPO, 1901.

———. *U. S. Census of the Population: 1910*, Vol. 2, *Thirteenth Census*. Washington, D.C.: GPO, 1913.

———. *U. S. Census of the Population: 1920*. Vol. 3, Composition and Characteristics, Fourteenth Census. Washington, D.C.: GPO, 1922.

———. *U. S. Census of the Population: 1930*, Vol. 3, Part 1, *Fifteenth Census*. Washington, D.C.: GPO, 1932.

———. *U. S. Census of the Population: 1940*, Vol. 2, *Sixteenth Census: 1940*, Vol. 2, *Characteristics of the Population*, Washington, D.C.: U.S. GPO, 1943.

———. *U. S. Census of the Population: 1970*. Vol. 1, Part 6, Section 1. Washington, D.C.: GPO, 1973.

———. *U. S. Census of Population: 1980*. Characteristics of the Population, Vol. 1, Chapter A, Part 6. U.S. Washington, D.C., GPO, 1982.

U. S. Commission on Civil Rights (1971). *Ethnic Isolation of Mexican Americans in the Public Schools of the Southwest*. Report No. 1, Mexican American Education Study. Washington, D.C.: U. S. GPO.

———. (1971). *Equal Educational Opportunities for the Spanish-Speaking Child: Bilingual and Bicultural Educational Programs*. Washington, D.C.: U. S. Department of Health, Education and Welfare. ERIC No. ED073866.

———. (1972). *The Excluded Student: Educational Practices Affecting Mexican Americans in the Southwest*. Report No. 3 Mexican American Education Study. Washington, D.C.: U. S. GPO.

————. (1974). *Mexican American Education Study, Report 6: Toward Quality Education for Mexican Americans*. Washington, D.C.: GPO.

U. S. Congress, House, 63d Cong., ed. sess,. 1914. "Report: Commission on National Aid to Vocational Education." In Lazerson and Grubb (1974). *American Education and Vocationalism: A Documentary History, 1870–1970*. New York: Teachers College Press.

U. S. Department of Commerce, Bureau of the Census, 1980. *Census of the Population Characteristics* (July 1982). California. PC 80-1-B6, Table 16, 6-30.

U. S. Statutes at Large, 1968. 81: 816 (January 2, 1968); 880 (b).

Valverde, Leonard (1976). *Segregation, Desegregation, and Resegregation of the Spanish-Surname Student in the United States*. Washington, D.C.: National Institute of Education, Department of Health, Education and Welfare. Eric No. ED131963.

Year-Round Education for the Third Century of America (A report of the 8th national seminar on year-round education, sponsored by the California State Department of Education, Wilson Riles, Superintendent of Public Instruction, Long Beach, Cal. (1976, January 25-28). Eric No. ED135084.

Young, C. C. (1930). *Mexicans in California: Governor Young's Fact-Finding Committee*. San Francisco: Department of Industrial Relations.

LOCAL SOURCES

[Joe Banks] (1976, January 22). *Migrant Education in Year-Round Schools of the [Brownfield] Unified School District*. Unpublished manuscript. Brownfield, California.

Borg, Jane (1977). *A Sampler of Early [Brownfield] Schools*. [Santa Rita]: P & M Business Service.

Brownfield Historical Association (n.d.). *A Historic Tour of the Brownfield Schools*. Brownfield, California.

Brownfieldite (newspaper). Brownfield, California.

Brownfield School District. *Racial/Ethnic Survey, 1967–1979*. Brownfield, California.

Brownfield Unified School District. *School Board Election Documents*, Brownfield, California, 1965.

Brownfield Unified School District. Board minutes. 1965–1979.

————. *Racial and Ethnic Balance, Policy Range: 6260–6269*, May 2, 1972. Brownfield, California.

County Office of Education [Santa Rita]. *Active Enrollments, 1944–1965*.

Kock, Margaret (1978). *Going to School in [Santa Rita] County; A History of [Santa Rita] County Schools.* Santa Rita County Office of Education.

Las Noticias (bilingual newspaper). Brownfield, California.

Orchard: Brownfield High School Yearbook, 1940–1960. Brownfield, California.

Rowland, Leon (1947). *Annuals of [Santa Rita] County.* Privately printed.

Santa Rita Guard (newspaper). Santa Rita, California.

Santa Rita Recorders Office (1914). Santa Rita, California.

COURT CASES

Brown v. Board of Education, 347 U. S. 483 (1954).

Green v. County School Board of New Kent County [Virginia], 391 U. S. 430 (1968).

Independent School District v. Salvatierra, 33 S. W. 2d 790 (Tex. Civ. App. San Antonio, 1930), cert. denied, 284 U. S. 580 (1931).

Keys v. School District No. 1, Denver, [Colorado], 413 U. S. 189 (1973).

Lau v. Nichols, 414 U. S. 563, 94 S. Ct. 786 (1974).

Mendez v. Westminster School District, 64, F. Supp. 544 (S. D. Cal. 1946), 161 F.2D 744.

Milliken v. Bradley [Michigan], 418 U. S. 717 (1974).

Swann v. Charlotte-Mecklenburg Board of Education, [North Carolina], 402 U. S. 1 (1971).

Index

Ability classes, 5, 71, 74, 76, 126, 127, 175*n10*

AB-1329. *See* California, bilingual education mandate

Acculturation, 18

Acuña, Rodolfo, 36, 37

African Americans, 42, 44*tab*, 57, 162–163*n54*; in California, 60; and IQ testing, 24, 25; and school reform, 1, 9, 124, 128; school enrollment, 126; and segregated education, 12, 120, 122–123

Agricultural development, 37, 38

Alger, Horatio, 83

Alvarez v. Lemon Grove (1931), 2, 128

American Association of School Administrators, 89

American GI Forum, 104

American Indians, 15; IQ testing, 25–26

Americanization, 11, 12, 13, 14, 17–19, 43, 107

Anglo middle-class culture, 5

Apple, Michael, 7

Arizona, 22, 36; IQ testing; Mexican American school enrollment, 125–126; and Mexican immigration (1910–1930), 38; urban Mexican American population, 29

Asians, 15, 41–42, 44*tab*, 130, 162–163*n54*, 176*n16*. *See also* Japanese Americans

Assimilation, 5, 11, 17, 18, 68, 83, 107

Association of Mexican-American Educators, 167*n46*

Atherton (Calif.): and school consolidation, 51–53; and school desegregation, 10, 119, 131–132, 135, 136, 137–139, 141–142, 171*n130*, 180*n42*; Mexican American enrollment in, 141–142

Atherton Improvement Association, 51

Atlanta (Ga.), 93

Aztlan (journal), 165*n2*

Azusa (Calif.), 15

Bell, Howard, 30–31

Bernal, Joe, 75

Bilingual aides, 73, 109

Bilingual-bicultural schools, 3, 5, 9, 60, 77–78, 80, 84, 87, 104, 105–107, 128, 129, 171*n30 (see also under* Brownfield)

Bilingual Education Act (1968), 105–106

Bilingual Master Plan (Brownfield), 110–117, 150–151

Binet, Alfred, 23–24

Bishop, Hazel Peck, 18

Black Power movement, 57

Bogardus, Emory S., 39, 42

Boston (Mass.), 130